D0035810

12 00

Defeating
the Powers of Darkness

"I wish every Christian would read **The Satanic Revival** and take its burning message to heart. Mark Bubeck writes from the trenches, not from the ivory tower; and what he says is biblical and practical. If churches don't get back to the battle, our country is done for. Without warfare praying and confrontation with the enemy, there can be no revival; and without revival, there is no hope for the nation. The situation is desperate—but the Lord is able!"

Warren W. Wiersbe
Author and Conference Speaker

"A pioneer in the field of spiritual warfare, Mark Bubeck speaks on this subject with the authority and insight of prolonged study and first-hand experience . . . While opinions will differ regarding certain of the issues he discusses, his perspective on today's desperate situation and his prescription for tomorrow's possible revival make this book a challenging summons to engage in prayerful battle against the powers of darkness."

Vernon Grounds
President Emeritus, Denver Seminary

"Mark doesn't write with just head-knowledge, but with years of experience of being on the cutting edge of the cause of Christ."

David Mains
The Chapel of the Air

"Mark Bubeck has the biblical knowledge, spiritual depth, personal experience, counseling exposure and cultural awareness that enable him to write this vital book. He is calling us to look at our lives and our times through the eyes of the Bible and to recognize our desperate need of God's mercy, renewal and grace."

Victor Matthews
Professor Emeritus of Systematic Theology
Grand Rapids Baptist Seminary

"This is the book we have been waiting for to confront satanism head-on. It will shock you, challenge you, and humble you. It not only exposes evil, it will drive you to your knees asking for a revival sent by God to defeat the satanic revival. It is *must* reading for every Christian who yearns for the Kingdom of God."

Dr. Ed Murphy
Vice President, O.C. International
Author, *Spiritual Warfare* Audio Series

"A prophet-like exposé of spiritual promiscuity and a passionate plea for Spirit-born repentance and revival."

Gordon R. Lewis, Ph.D.
Professor of Systematic Theology
and Christian Philosophy
Denver Seminary

"Whenever Mark Bubeck writes, Satan has serious problems as saints are enabled to advance. **The Satanic Revival** replaces ignorance with information, fear with boldness and immaturity with a workable plan of action."

Ron Susek
Evangelist
Continential Christian Crusades

"The church has an urgent need to respond to the aggressive satanic activity in our nation with the weapon of prayer. Dr. Bubeck issues an urgent summons to this new level of prayer and gives guidance in learning to pray this way. Required reading!"

Timothy M. Warner, Ed.D.
Professor of Missions
Trinity Evangelical Divinity School

"Dr. Mark Bubeck's latest book, **The Satanic Revival**, has to be one of the most-needed expositions of truth in print today . . . a 'must read.' "

John Wesley White
Associate Evangelist
Billy Graham Evangelistic Association

THE
SATANIC
REVIVAL

MARK I. BUBECK

Here's Life Publishers

First Printing, March 1991

Published by
HERE'S LIFE PUBLISHERS, INC.
P. O. Box 1576
San Bernardino, CA 92402

© 1991, Mark I. Bubeck
All rights reserved
Printed in the United States of America

Library of Congress Cataloging-in-Publication Data
Bubeck, Mark I.
    The satanic revival / Mark I. Bubeck.
      p.   cm.
    ISBN 0-89840-314-6
    1. Revivals. I. Title.
BV3790.B7658   1991
269 – dc 20   90-21926
                   CIP

Unless indicated otherwise, Scripture quotations are from *The Holy Bible: New International Version,* © 1973, 1978, 1984 by the International Bible Society, published by Zondervan Bible Publishers, Grand Rapids, Michigan.

Scripture quotations designated NASB are from *The New American Standard Bible,* © The Lockman Foundation 1960, 1962, 1963, 1968, 1971, 1972, 1975, 1977.

Scripture quotations designated KJV are from the *King James Version.*

Scripture quotations designated AV are from *The Amplified Bible,* © 1965 by Zondervan Publishing House, Grand Rapids, Michigan.

Cover photography by Visual Impact
Cover design by David Marty Design

For More Information, Write:
L.I.F.E. – P.O. Box A399, Sydney South 2000, Australia
Campus Crusade for Christ of Canada – Box 300, Vancouver, B.C., V6C 2X3, Canada
Campus Crusade for Christ – Pearl Assurance House, 4 Temple Row, Birmingham, B2 5HG, England
Lay Institute for Evangelism – P.O. Box 8786, Auckland 3, New Zealand
Campus Crusade for Christ – P.O. Box 240, Raffles City Post Office, Singapore 9117
Great Commission Movement of Nigeria – P.O. Box 500, Jos, Plateau State Nigeria, West Africa
Campus Crusade for Christ International – Arrowhead Springs, San Bernardino, CA 92414, U.S.A.

*To the
Siouxland Prayer Focus Intercessors
who have met at 6:30 A.M. every Tuesday
for more than five years
in a cry to God for
revolutionary revival.*

Acknowledgments

My deepest appreciation goes to Dr. John McFarlane for his hours of toil in putting the first manuscript drafts on his computer. It was a true labor of love. Though retired from his medical practice, his dedication to serve others has only increased.

My gratitude also extends to Sara Sue Larson who volunteered countless hours to ready the manuscript text according to the publisher's prescribed specifications. Most of all, without the loving devotion of my wife, Anita, my immediate family, and the prayerful encouragement of the Central Baptist Church body, the writing of this book would not have happened. I express gratitude to God for such enablers.

CONTENTS

REVIVAL PRAYER PATTERNS

These seven prayers are available in booklet form, and may be ordered for quantity distribution from the author:

Dr. Mark I. Bubeck
1551 Indian Hills Dr., Suite 200
Sioux City, IA 51104

"A Special Window of Time"

By David Mains
The Chapel of the Air

This is not just a time like any other time. It's a special window of time during which we either will see revival or see our country move closer to a day of judgment.

The reason for that conviction is that a widespread call to prayer for revival has been sounded. Response has been most encouraging, and the movement is gaining momentum. All around the country people are meeting in small prayer groups asking God to do a new work in His church. Many ministers are praying together weekly in gatherings that cross racial and denominational lines. At revival retreats for clergy, confession of sin is common. Tears are shed as God's leaders are asking Him for another time of awakening to come in full.

Are you involved in a revival prayer group? That's an important question. It's no longer enough to be a spectator, only observing what's going on. It's mandatory that everyone possible participate in the prayer movement on a regular basis. The momentum must build. It would be tragic if it peaked prematurely and then began to fall off.

Praying for revival is a difficult job to do by oneself. The objective is large, and the enemy is clever. Get involved in praying with someone else.

One of the highlights of my week is when the small revival prayer group of which I'm a part gets together. We pray for a Holy Flame to touch down in congregations all through the states and provinces. A movement of the Spirit is already obvious in many other parts of the world. We pray, "Lord, let it happen here as well."

I remember similar prayer times with Mark Bubeck early in my ministry. I recall how he used to wrestle with the Lord as he prayed. I learned a great deal just listening and praying with him. I'm thrilled that Mark has added his thoughts to the growing list of revival materials we now have available. He has much to share. Mark walks with the Lord. He longs for a major work of the Spirit in our day. He doesn't write with just head knowledge, but with years of experience on the cutting edge of the cause of Christ. His words manifest great power because they are filled with the Holy Spirit.

In my study of revival, I have found that it's usually a matter of three to six years between when the call to prayer goes out and the intense work of the Spirit comes in full. Usually along the way there are early indications that mark the progress of what's happening such as tears, confession of sins, churches experiencing a large number of conversions, etc. We're already seeing such signs, but what's happened to date is infinitesimal compared to what revival will look like when it hits with full force.

My word to you is to not let anything divert you from becoming a part of the prayer movement as quickly as possible. Don't wait another week. NOW is the time. Allow the pages of this book to increase your passion for that great gift of the Lord that He desires to give to His church, that gift called Spiritual Awakening.

◇ INTRODUCTION ◇

"A Strong Encounter With Satan"

Our culture has moved from curiosity about Satan into what seems to be a full-orbed obsession that is shocking the church of Jesus Christ. The only hope I see for confronting and stopping this frightening satanic revival is a revolutionary spiritual revival of righteousness and truth.

As a younger pastor, I often found myself crying out to God for revival during extended sessions of prayer. In the midst of one such prayer session an unusual, strong spiritual awareness suddenly overwhelmed me. I don't know how else to describe it. Although I did not hear a voice, there was a powerful communication to my spirit: *Before a revival like the one for which you are praying can come, there will have to be a strong encounter with Satan.*

The intensity of this awareness stunned me. I prayed, "Lord, I don't know anything about that subject, and I don't know anyone who does—but I am ready to learn."

God took me at my word. I started to read through my New Testament, marking every passage and text that spoke of the battle between light and darkness. Fresh insights came to me. The New Testament emphasis on the subject of spiritual warfare alarmed me.

I studied and read widely, devouring all the materials I could. Opportunities for ministry to those afflicted by Satan began to open up to me. I was a novice, but God taught me rapidly of His victory over darkness. Twenty some years later, my greatest concern still remains focused on the need for revolutionary revival—and I believe you will see how the need has accelerated until today we do, in fact, face "a strong encounter with Satan."

The Christian world must become aroused. God has allowed Satan to throw down the gauntlet to the church, but He has also provided the church with the spiritual resources to overcome the challenger. Isaiah 59:19 is our message of hope:

> So shall they fear the name of the LORD from the
> west, and his glory from the rising of the sun. When the
> enemy shall come in like a flood, the Spirit of the LORD
> shall lift up a standard against him (Authorized Version).

God is able to intervene. He holds the evil within His sovereignty. His might is infinitely greater than all the power Satan can amass.

Although this book exposes some frightening dimensions of the present revival of evil, that is not its major message.

Rather, believers are called to renew their confidence in the almightiness of their God. Believers are called to participate in a God-authored spiritual revival strong enough to abate the flood of evil. Believers are called to recognize the power of doctrinal prayer and use it in a practical way. Believers, united with God, are called to rise up and use their victory.

MARK I. BUBECK

◇ PART I ◇

Recognizing the
Powers of Darkness

◇ 1 ◇

THE POWERS
OF DARKNESS

About five years ago the phone's ring jarred me out of a deep sleep. My clock registered 1:10 A.M. as a frightened young woman rapidly poured out her story. "Dr. Bubeck, I'm scared. I think they're going to kill me. Someone told me that you understand these things and would help me. Will you?"

Since writing my books on spiritual warfare, I had become accustomed to desperate calls from emotionally and spiritually troubled people. I assumed this was another of that type, but as she told her story, strange new things came to my ears. A chilling sensation—fearful and foreboding—swept over me.

"I'm mixed up with a motorcycle gang of satanists," she continued. "I fell in love with the number-two guy in the gang and I've just kept getting deeper and deeper into this business. Now I'm afraid and I want out. Will you help me?"

Her pleading voice aroused my compassion, but I was a bit skeptical. It all sounded a little over-dramatic. Still, I assured her I'd do all I could to help, and after making an appointment for the next day, I prayed for her and tried to go back to sleep. It was a troubled attempt.

When the young woman arrived for her appointment, her fear was obviously genuine. Looking out the window of my office, she stated she was sure she'd been followed. She did not see anyone in the parking lot, so she settled down to talk. It was an incredible story about witchcraft and satanic ritual sacrifices of animals. Eating the raw meat of the animals was part of the ritual. Prostitution, drug sales, production of pornographic videos—all were controlled and administered by the gang. The purpose of the satanic ritual was to access the power and protection of Satan for their lucrative "businesses." Although I'd read of such satanic activities before, this was my first close encounter. I'm afraid I handled it poorly.

"I want out!" the young woman cried through her tears. "The gang is planning a human sacrifice to Satan and that scares me to death. I asked my boyfriend about leaving. At first he tried to talk me out of it, but he promised to talk to the gang leader about letting me go. He's supposed to give me the word when I meet him this afternoon."

My previous experience had not prepared me to deal with her need. I questioned the safety of her seeing her gang-member friend, but she assured me he really loved her and she could trust him.

Inadequate Preparation

The conversation turned to spiritual things and I was able to help her renew her profession of faith in Jesus Christ. She had first believed in Him in Sunday school as a little girl, and her joy in a renewed relationship seemed genuine. Gradually her troubled countenance disappeared, and she seemed peaceful and radiant as she left my office. She gave me her apartment telephone number, and we made an appointment for further discussion in my office the next day.

I never heard from this young woman again. I repeatedly called the number she had left. I tried for several days to reach her, and then the recorded voice of an operator announced that the number was no longer in service.

I was very troubled after that experience. I should have been more protective of her. My inadequate preparation to deal with someone caught in the web of satanism well may have cost her her life. She even may have become the gang's discussed human sacrifice. Accounts from former satanists make such a possibility more than plausible. The Lord has since calmed my troubled conscience with the remembrance of her radiant countenance following her prayer of renewal, but her story still haunts me.

I see this young woman's cry for help, and my inadequate response, as a parable of warning for concerned parents and church and community leaders living in this troubled hour. Her story was one further confirmation to me that a frightening satanic revival is under way in our nation and around the globe, and its tentacles of deceit and evil are spreading rapidly through powerful, devious channels.

Another Woman's Experience

I have in my possession an eighteen-page chronicle written by another young woman, in her early twenties. She was in a Satan-worshiping family the first nineteen years of her life. Her flashback memories of experiences from age 3 until her departure from the cult were so gruesome and vile that her counselor wondered if they were credible. He determined that she might be manifesting multiple personality disorder (MPD), which required the best medical expertise available.

Only recently, therapists have discovered that MPD is often the result of a patient's traumatic experience with satanic/ritualistic abuse. Dr. James G. Friesen, an expert in the field of multiple personality disorder, has written a groundbreaking book titled *Uncovering the Mystery of MPD* (Here's Life Publishers, June 1991). He reveals:

> Studies indicate that approximately 25 percent of those with MPD in North America have been subjected to SRA [satanic/ritualistic abuse], and SRA is why they developed MPD in the first place. It is the best way children have of dealing with the trauma.
>
> We are not talking about spanking children too hard,

or about the use of excessive forms of punishment. We are talking about children reporting that they were drugged, terrorized, and subjected to horrifying abuse, and that they witnessed the murder of animals and of other children during ceremonies of Satan worship.

My young friend's therapist arranged for her to be evaluated by the chairman of the department of psychiatry at a major university. This psychiatrist uses sodium amytal, sometimes called "truth serum," in evaluating an MPD patient's truthfulness and also as a means of assisting the integration of the multiple personalities being manifested.

After working at length with the young woman, the psychiatrist affirmed that, in his judgment, the horrible details she recalled in flashbacks to her childhood were indeed factual. This gracious woman has given me permission to share some of her personal memories as we look at signs of the satanic revival sweeping our culture.

Signs of Satanic Revival

1. Sexual immorality, including pornography and the free expression of sensuality.

Human sexuality is one of God's most sacred gifts to the human race. Not only is the gift of sex the means God has chosen for human procreation, but within marriage it also expresses some of God's best gifts to mankind—loving intimacy, oneness and the giving of ourselves to each other.

God chose this intimacy as the ideal, human-level illustration of the oneness between Christ and His church (see Ephesians 5:22,23). Could this be one reason Satan distorts sexuality—to soil that biblical illustration of oneness?

Satanic Sexual Acts

The written remembrances of my young friend document that the vilest sexual perversions are a regular part of witchcraft and satanic worship. I'll spare you the more

graphic details, but some references are necessary to establish the relationship between the sexual license of our times
and Satan's strategy.

The woman chronicles a hideous scene, one that took
place when she was age 4, of satanist men trying to force her
and a 6-year-old boy to engage in sexual acts so that the men
could "film us." Pathetically, she remembers, "We couldn't
understand what the men wanted us to do, and they got mad
. . . and one of them touched me sexually."

She also records how, when she was 8, a group of cultist
men who were "ready for some fun" forced her to engage in
sexual acts with an animal, and "the men then raped me,
which was very painful."

She describes numerous experiences of ritualistic rape
while the "worshipers" chanted ceremonial words of petition
and honor to Satan. Group sexual orgies were often a part of
her most hideous descriptions of human sacrifice and the
eating of "raw [human] organs from the bowl." Of this scene
she writes, "All the people seemed to be laughing and having
a lot of fun."

Her experiences are not unlike the testimonies of others
who have survived such ritual terror. All the counselors
whom I've talked with who have dealt with victims of
satanic/ritualistic abuse relate similar stories. More and
more therapists are realizing there is a vast, almost incredible network of Satan worshipers engaged in such practices. Often these are Mr. and Mrs. Joe America during the
day. Victims relate how hard-core devotees come from the
ranks of doctors, lawyers, accountants, politicians, police officers, teachers, day-care workers, and pastors (yes, even pastors, who sometimes lend the use of their church basements
for nighttime ritual sacrifices), as well as blue collar workers,
homemakers and otherwise respectable citizens.

At night these devotees engage in satanic/ritualistic
practices that range from oral chants and incantations to the
ritualistic torture and consumption of animal and human

flesh. These practices, which at one time we all probably considered rare, are now so widespread that most city police departments now have special task forces to deal with the problem in their communities.

As we were preparing this chapter, one of the editors mentioned *The Satanic Revival* to a schoolteacher friend in a middle-sized southern California city. The schoolteacher reported a recent incident which had made her think seriously about this growing trend.

"One evening I stayed at the school late, and was walking to my car in the dark," the teacher recalled. "In the parking lot, I was startled by a police officer who asked me several questions to verify that I was a teacher in the school.

"Then he told me, 'Please don't walk in this parking lot alone after dark—get someone to accompany you.' He went on to describe several frightening occurrences which had taken place there—suspicious strangers hanging around, the discovery of mutilated carcasses of animals, and what could have been an attempted kidnapping.

"He told me that the local police had noticed an alarming increase in activities fitting the pattern of satanic ritualism and, based on what they were learning from other departments, it was not unlikely that these people might now be looking for lone individuals to kidnap for ritualistic torture-murders."

An Extensive Study

Drs. Michael K. Haynes and Paul W. Carlin have written a syllabus which they use in their study seminars on satanism and occult awareness. This 450-page syllabus contains voluminous summaries of news stories, case studies, counselors' experiences and law-enforcement reports, including several case studies reported by child-abuse counselor LaVerne R. Campbell.

One of Campbell's studies tells of a 3-year-old girl "marked in a ritualistic marriage ceremony to Satan by being cut with a gold razor on her forehead, with a priest (in this case, her father) kissing it and thereby marking her for his sexual use until such time as she was to be sacrificed to Satan."

Another case cites a group of children ages 2 to 7 who were subjected to rituals that "included animal mutilations, drinking of blood mixed with urine and wine, witnessing children sexually violated by both sticks and males. They tell of balloons (perhaps condoms) being inserted into the little girls and expanded with helium to allow easy penetration by adult males, thereby leaving no scarring."

A third study is of a woman with three children. "She was evidently drugged with something placed in her tea on many ritualistic nights. Her husband and 14-year-old son, along with relatives and members of the coven, often used her (while she was sedated) for sexual purposes. The children give testimony to the most bizarre sexual activity with human sacrifice and related paraphernalia hidden in a series of tunnels connecting three houses."[1]

The research by Haynes and Carlin verifies what I have learned first-hand in my personal counseling as well as what other therapists and pastors tell me. Beyond a doubt, sexual abuse, sexual orgies and the most perverted sexual practices, often leading to further violence, are considered a key element in the ritualistic practice of satanism.

Today's "Sexual Revolution"

How might this relate to the "less horrifying" sexual revolution of our Western world? I believe it tells us that the perverseness of our times, which includes rampant distribution of pornography and many kinds of "free expression" of sensuality, is more than an expression of human sexual freedom. It is more than merely man's fallen nature expressing itself in immoral activity. It is even more than an evolving product of the world system and the attitudes ingrained by our mass media and entertainment industry.

I believe we're seeing a carefully orchestrated conspiracy at work, too sinister and subtle to be entirely of human origin. This conspiracy flows directly out of the realm of evil supernaturalism, and our only hope for any change necessitates divine, supernatural intervention. Only God's power, manifested in the hearts of a caring, concerned citizenry, can stop this onslaught of evil.

2. Crime, preoccupation with violence and death, and abortion.

As I write, today's newspaper carries three headline stories of terrorist violence, including the brutal killing of two families. One of the stories relates the capture of a 19-year-old murder suspect from Hilltown, Pennsylvania. He is accused of stabbing and slashing to death a 42-year-old widow and her 16- and 14-year-old sons while they slept. Satanist activity by the suspect is thought to be at least a partial cause for his violence.

Stories like these have become a regular part of our daily news. From international madmen such as Saddam Hussein to the street punk with an assault rifle to the solid citizen who shakes his fist, honks and pulls over for a brawl after getting "cut off" on the highway, such constant accounts of violence have dulled our sensitivities. To protect ourselves, we react with ambivalence. The horror of recurring brutality surpasses our capacity to comprehend, and worthy mental and emotional reactions are suppressed. Since we cannot handle it adequately, we block it away with repressive safeguards.

We must not miss this vital insight: Violence in all its expressions carries Satan's fingerprints, for "he was a murderer from the beginning" (John 8:44). Drug-related murders, abortion, suicidal deaths, and every other kind of violence all closely identify with the powers of darkness that work overtime to create havoc among peace-loving peoples.

Nowhere is violence more deliberate or maniacal than in

satanic rituals. My young informant records the "sacrifice" killing of a victim during a satanic worship ritual. She believes she was 3 or 4 at the time, and remembers "the one in charge" arguing with the unsuspecting victim when he suddenly "takes a knife and stabs her in the stomach. When she fell to the ground and began to moan, he cut her neck and walked over to the rest of the people." She relates another memory of the equally brutal killing of her 6-year-old friend "Billy" in ritualistic sacrifice.

This victim of exposure to satanism chronicles an event she herself took part in at about age 10. The cult members invaded the home of a man who had sought to leave the cult. He was sleeping when they went in. They "gagged him and tied his hands behind his back. Then we loaded him into the van and took him to the clearing in the woods. He looked scared, but he didn't really fight much at all." The cultists "seemed to have a lot of fun kicking the man."

She then confesses in horror how, as a 10-year-old girl, she was herself swept up by the satanic outrage. "The man was lying face down on the ground, moaning. I had been kicking him, too, and I had fun doing it. I decided I wanted to be the one who got to finish him off, so I got a rock from the fire ring and hit him hard on the back of his head. It kind of went 'thud' and I heard a crack. Somebody cut his fingers off and roasted them in the fire. We ate them to celebrate."

Her confessions left me in stunned disbelief. Yet, the evidence keeps mounting that what this girl reveals is common among those deeply involved in satanic worship.

Satanism and Abortions

Our nation is locked into a debate over so-called "pro-choice" versus "pro-life." At this writing, we Americans "legally" have aborted more than 24 million unborn babies. Is it possible that the cultural acceptance of abortion as a means of birth control is another sign of the satanic revival?

It is interesting to note that in satanic/ritualistic worship, abortion is often part of the ceremony.

The victim sharing her story with me relates two different accounts of satanic cult abortions performed on her. The first was when she was only 12. She relates the gruesome account of her aborted fetus being sacrificed in ritual worship that included cannibalism.

When she was 16, another baby, conceived in a satanic ritual, was aborted in his seventh or eighth month of development. The cult brought the baby to birth three days before Easter, and kept him alive until the night before.

Again I will spare you the more grisly details. (It may be difficult to believe that what I'm relating are the "mild" parts of the story. Even these details weigh heavy on my heart, but I feel I must share them so you will know what is happening.)

"My baby's little body was tied to a little cross," my friend writes. "I was tied to a bigger cross which was short enough for me to stand on the ground. My feet were tied together. There was a small bonfire. I don't remember much of what happened that night except that my boy's little body was burned."

Ritual sacrifices involving aborted fetuses and newborn babies are regular practices of many satanic cults. Some young women tell of being "breeders," conceiving and carrying the child of a father, uncle, older brother, or fellow cult member for the sole purpose of a future sacrifice.

These accounts are traumatic to hear. But when it comes right down to it, what ultimate difference is there between a satanic/ritualistic abortion and the tearing apart of an unborn child in an abortionist's office? Have we not subtly conditioned ourselves to reject the one and accept the other, when indeed either practice is the taking of an innocent life?

A Satanic Scheme

The Scriptures tell us that the toleration of such things

does not go unnoticed by God. We read of King Manasseh, who seemed to be a part of such evil:

> He had filled Jerusalem with innocent blood, and the LORD was not willing to forgive (2 Kings 24:4).

Isaiah also warned of how much the shedding of "innocent blood" endangers a culture answerable to a holy God:

> When you spread out your hands in prayer, I will hide my eyes from you; even if you offer many prayers, I will not listen. Your hands are full of blood; wash and make yourselves clean (Isaiah 1:15,16).

There is so much more to the abortion scandal of our country, and the world, than merely "a woman's right of choice" or a viable means of population control. I believe our acceptance of this holocaust is one subtle dimension of the accelerating worldwide satanic revival. Yes, it is taking place in the dark pits of hard-core satanic worship, but it is also taking place in the more "civil," "legal" offices of our duly sanctioned abortion clinics.

As I look at how our nation has tolerated, even advocated, the killing of our innocent unborn, I am convinced that our hardness of heart is the direct result of Satan's overall scheme to subvert the goodness of God in our land. The situation will not be resolved by marches, protests or shouting matches, nor by the physical blocking of abortion clinics, nor even by a judicial reversal of *Roe vs. Wade*. Only divine intervention, resulting in widespread spiritual revival, can effectively reverse our downward course.

3. Growing involvement in the occult.

Spiritism in its multiplicity of forms is everywhere. Interest, experimentation and involvement in the occult seems epidemic. It has permeated all levels of our culture.

Children. Occult themes abound in the toy departments of our stores. Ouija boards and games like "Dungeons & Dragons" lay the groundwork for serious spiritistic experimentation. Spooks, monsters and grotesque "other-world" characters become the treasured toys and comic-book heroes of children. Videos, morning cartoons, Halloween costumes, and even some widely accepted school reading textbooks help saturate our children with occult influence.

On the surface, these may all appear to be harmless fantasy—just part of growing up, much as "Jack and the Beanstalk" and "Goldilocks and the Three Bears" were part of our own childhood. Yet I believe the almost-constant presence of these influences in our children's culture prepares their minds to be comfortable with the imagery of evil as they grow older.

Youth. Teenagers have an even more bold involvement, for their adventurous spirit and investigative curiosity allow them to go much more deeply into the occult.

Some of today's rock music is downright blatant in its message of death and darkness. In *How to Prepare for the Coming Persecution,* Dr. Larry Poland excerpts lyrics from two "black metal" groups whom many of our youth adore:

> Killer, intruder, homicidal man,
> If you see me coming, run as fast as you can.
> A bloodthirsty demon who's stalking the street,
> I hack up my victims like pieces of meat.[2]

> I drink the vomit of the priests,
> make love to the dying whore. . . .
> I am decreed by Lord Satan's fine evil
> to destroy what all mortals love most.
> Satan, my master incarnate,
> hail praise to my unholy host.[3]

I hold in my hand an interoffice memo from the Iowa Department of Human Services. Its subject: "Satanic and Cult Activities." This nine-page document seeks to educate the Human Services people to the increasing problems of satanism and cultic practices troubling midwestern rural Iowa. It summarizes the findings of Steve Daniels, a probation and parole officer for the state of Wisconsin, who has made a special study of the problem and shares the watch signs and recognition clues endemic to the growing number of teenage youth who are experimenting in satanic rituals and occult activities. Among the clues are:

1. Alienation from family and Christianity.

2. A drastic drop in grades and a lack of school involvement.

3. Evidence of increasing rebellion against society and authority.

4. Cut or tattoo marks on the body. The little or middle fingernail of the left hand, painted black, indicates a dedication to evil.

5. Heavy involvement with fantasy or role-playing games.

6. Compulsive interest in "heavy metal" or "black metal" music.

7. Increasing involvement with alcohol and illegal drugs.

8. Growing interest in the occult and the use of occult/satanic symbols drawn on hands or arms and on books and other possessions.

9. Possession of occult books and magazines, black candles, ceremonial knives, a chalice, altars, robes, animal or human bones and other ritual paraphernalia.

10. Heavy interest in "horror" videos, TV programs, movies and books.

11. A lack of humor. Smiles are rare.

12. Seeming pleasure regarding the suffering of animals or people.

13. A fascination with death or dying.

14. Sudden behavior changes (depression, fear, outbursts of anger); nightmares and screaming in one's sleep.

15. Sudden use of obscenities or vulgar language to express anger or displeasure.

The problem is becoming so pervasive among America's youth that nearly all high and junior high schools in the nation are now seeing signs of satanic seduction of our youth. Small organized groups of satanist experimenters make their presence known by their dress and satanic symbols. True, many youth do not go beyond the point of dabbling. But in many other cases the dabbling has grown addictive, leading to actual devil worship, violence, rapes, and even documented cases of torture-murders among classmates.

Adults. In no way is the satanic revival just a "youth problem." Adult business people manufacture and market children's toys and games that promote occult themes. Adult authors write voluminous amounts of books that flood the marketplace, promoting satanism and other occultic interests. Adult producers, actors and sponsors generate music, movies and videos that provide theatrical allure of satanic themes. Adult practitioners of witchcraft lead thousands of covens throughout the United States that ritually abuse children, youth and women. And just over our border . . .

America and Mexico were shocked in April of 1989 when police in Matamoros, Mexico, unearthed a mass grave containing dismembered parts of twelve bodies. It was reported that a satanic drug-smuggling cult had made human sacrifices to Satan to gain his protection. One of the victims was an all-American 21-year-old pre-med student from the University of Texas, who had been kidnapped from a border town during a break from his studies.

Churches. Satanism is also invading our Christian churches. To my horror, my informant revealed that the two leaders of the satanic cult she exposes were the pastor and associate pastor of an evangelical church. Their double life was a deliberate attempt to gain Satan's favor and to dishonor evangelical churches. The "pastor" of the church was a graduate of one of our leading evangelical seminaries.

Though they are no longer in that pastoral role, one of them is still involved in a "Christian" ministry.

The bold advance of satanism knows no limits. There is growing evidence that the satanic movement has plotted to infiltrate and undermine our nation's effective ministries and churches. I have learned that in many communities satanists are posing as dedicated Christians and either volunteering as lay leaders or hiring on as salaried staff members. Their purpose: to create dissension, discredit the pastoral staff, and in some instances even seduce the leaders into sexual immorality in order to debilitate their ministries.

The New Age Movement

Perhaps the most far-reaching evidence of this occultic, spiritistic revival is the New Age movement. This "New Age" title has a rather inclusive gender—it covers a wide spectrum of different groups and movements that often do not have identifiable connections with each other. Sometimes their tactics are subtle, but their desired goals and general purposes are similar.

The purpose of mentioning the New Age Movement in the context of the spiritistic, occultic trends of our time is that many Christian leaders see it as satanically orchestrated. Some of them see New Ageism as the incipient beginnings of the religious, philosophical, political and economic globalism over which the antichrist will one day rule. This unifying New Age agenda seems to be part of a sophisticated scheme of things that goes back into antiquity.

Tal Brooke's book, *When the World Will Be as One,* is a must for the reader who desires to understand the supernatural superintending of the New Age movement. Brooke had two decades of intense involvement in exploring the occult before his conversion to Christ. This has given him first-hand insight. He sees a supernatural superintendent at work; Satan is his name. Brooke expresses the amazing acceleration of this movement in these graphic words:

It is the late 1980s and things are exploding in all directions. Esoteric spiritual paths that I had explored for years, placing me in a distinct minority, have become by now almost the consensus view of America. The plan is unfolding with the force of a charging freight train.[4]

That's what we face as we view the need. Celebrities like actress Shirley MacLaine have given the movement fanfare and popular appeal, but it is much deeper than tinsel and lights. New Ageism promotes a dark, sinister element that elevates man to god status. Death is denied; good and evil are declared illusions. A blind optimism emerges based upon a false, unbridled hope for the world and humanity. This excited hope fuels the movement. In our day of so much despair and darkness, the New Age holds much appeal. The younger, more educated leaders of the world are being drawn by the thousands into this false hope.

The Lure and the Threat

What a challenge we face! It is increasingly clear that satanic seduction has infiltrated our culture in ways both insidious and subtle. In its more blatant forms, the satanic revival threatens the very lives of our citizens and our children. In its more subtle forms, it seems to be luring us into a complacent acceptance of both pseudo-religions and outright anti-God lifestyles. In *all* its forms, the satanic revival is not something to be regarded lightly, for it threatens the very fabric and soul of our families, our communities, our nation. We must therefore open our eyes to what is taking place among us and resolve to confront it boldly, with a confidence that comes only from being in tune with the one who defeated Satan at the cross.

Can we stem the tide? Turn things around? Get back on the path toward being a righteous, God-honoring people? Yes! That is what this book is about. Together, we *can* defeat the powers of darkness.

Levels of Organization in the Satanic Cult

There are different ways of categorizing involvement in the satanic cult movement. Drs. Michael Haynes and Paul Carlin list *three levels*: (1) the Sophisticated Level; (2) the Serious Level; and (3) the Self-Styled Level. Their scholarly approach is worth careful review by those who are interested in pursuing the subject from the Christian perspective.[5]

The law enforcement agencies, however, are more interested in what they call the Law Enforcement Cult-Crime Model. They usually identify four levels of satanic cult activity: (1) traditional satanists; (2) organized satanists; (3) self-styled satanists; and (4) dabblers.

Traditional Satanists

This is the highest level of Satan worshipers, those deeply committed to their cause. They maintain a strict vow of secrecy. The penalty for breaking the pact of silence is death. Influential people in society often are a part of this group. Political leaders, military professionals, medical doctors, educators and wealthy business people provide unlimited intellectual and financial resources. This group also has transgenerational family ties to satanism. Some investigators believe this level maintains an international underground of planned strategy to seed evil into the culture of the entire world. A regular practice of human sacrifices to Satan is carried on to keep his favor on their efforts. Promotion of people at other levels is a direct result of the efforts of these traditional satanists.

Organized Satanists

People at this second highest level of satanic activity follow the teachings and leadership of Anton LaVey, sometimes called "the Black Pope." LaVey, a former police photographer and circus performer, founded the Church of Satan in San Francisco, California, in 1966. This group also threatens severe punishment for breaking vows of secrecy. A high priest leads these organized satanists and they follow the satanic calendar religiously. They practice frequent sexual abuse of children and minors. Witchcraft activity and the conjuring of demons often intimidate the participants and they greatly fear leaving the cult.

Organized satanic covens often are led by influential people who double as community leaders.

Self-Styled Satanists

This level often causes severe problems for law enforcement people. Serial murderers and habitual criminals use their satanic beliefs to justify their bizarre violence. People in this group often exhibit antisocial behavior patterns, drug addiction, prostitution and pornography addiction. Many times they are "loners" who avoid the group settings. Law enforcement officials believe that many sociopaths and psychopaths have been a part of organized satanism in the past and have suffered the mental disaster of the evil belief system.

Dabblers

The dabbler level of satanic involvement becomes the recruitment center for the higher levels. A broad youth subculture of dabblers reaches into high schools, junior highs and even elementary grades. Youngsters often are drawn in by heavy metal rock music, horror movies or occultic literature, all with their sensual, power-centered, satanic themes. Youth interest in the occult focus on symbols of Satan, body tattoos, pentagrams and inverted crosses. Satan-related graffiti, bizarre dress styles and some animal mutilations appear at this level. Criminal activity, suicidal and murderous acts sometimes transpire as a part of this culture. Seances, levitation and Ouija board experiments, and the use of other occultic tools are practiced by young people with their peers. Because of the immaturity of these dabblers, serious emotional, social and family breakdown usually occurs. In many respects, this level bears evidence to the success of the higher levels as they sell their message and get the broader culture involved.

2

Are We Doomed to Repeat History?

On a trip to Africa not long ago, I met a high govern-ment official who had read my books and wanted my counsel regarding spiritual warfare. As my visit with this Christian leader ended, she made a statement that startled me—and still troubles me as I share it with you today.

"Dr. Bubeck," she said, "I do not know of a single government in Africa that does not attribute its power to Satan. Most of them engage in a regular practice of sacrifices to the devil—even human sacrifices—to be able to stay in power."

More recently, my colleagues and I have joined together on several mornings to read aloud the dramatic story of Israel's history during the time her kings ruled. This nation had once thrived in splendor during the reigns of King David and King Solomon, but then it fell victim to division, chaos and defeat. As we read the Old Testament account, it became clear to us that God preserved Israel's story in the Holy Scriptures for a reason: so that men and women in centuries to come might learn from it and avoid the harsh consequen-ces Israel suffered.

While reading of Israel's downfall, my mind went back to what that African official had told me. I also thought of other nations—especially the United States of America—and asked myself, *Have we learned the lesson of ancient Israel? Or are we doomed to repeat its history?*

I believe that story of Israel's fall contains some amazing parallels, and some urgent warnings, to our own nation and culture.

A Weakening of the People

Many of the kings of Israel failed and were removed from leadership because they "did not turn away from the sins of Jereboam, son of Nebat, which he had caused Israel to commit." This phrase or a similar equivalent appears more than thirty-five times, mostly in 2 Kings. The eventual national disintegration of Israel came because of the weakening brought upon the people through their practice of Jereboam's sins. The Assyrian conquest and the eventual deportation of most of the people in 732 B.C. was ascribed to this same tragedy of following in the "sins of Jereboam."

What were those sins?

The Scriptures carefully catalog them for us, and from them we can learn some important lessons.

Jereboam was a competent, powerful leader. In 1 Kings 11:28, he is called a "mighty man of valour" (KJV) and a man of "standing" (NIV). His ambitions, however, led him to unscrupulous actions. His self-interests and his reach for power motivated him to rebel against King Solomon, and when Solomon ordered his execution, Jereboam fled for his life to Egypt.

Israel's later rebellion against the harsh tactics of Solomon's son Rehoboam brought Jereboam back to power and honor. He was chosen to rule over the northern ten tribes of Israel. Fearful that the trips his subjects made to Jerusalem to worship would eventually entice them away from his control, this new king sowed the seeds that eventually destroyed his nation.

The Sins of Jereboam

The sins of Jereboam, listed in 1 Kings 12, can essentially be lumped together in five categories:

1. He introduced idolatry by forming two golden calves and setting them up as objects of worship in the cities of Bethel and Dan. "Here are your gods, O Israel, who brought you up out of Egypt," he proclaimed (verse 28).

2. He built shrines in certain "high places" for the purpose of carrying out spiritistic worship practices common to the heathen nations they had supplanted (verse 31).

3. He appointed religious leaders, who had no Levitic heritage, as "priests." They were probably chosen for political reward or for certain "spiritistic gifts" they seemed to have (verse 31).

4. He instituted religious festivals and spiritual celebration times that had no tie-in with God's appointed historic feasts (verse 31).

5. He personally sacrificed animals to his false gods and encouraged his people to do the same (verses 32,33).

Follow the Leader

When a nation's leaders or key influencers tolerate evil, the people of that nation generally follow suit. If the entertainment media, for example, constantly proclaim that sexual activity outside of marriage is fine "as long as no one gets hurt," its audience gradually begins believing and acting accordingly. When university professors declare to every new class that "all is relative . . . there are no absolute truths, no absolute rights and wrongs," then whole generations are churned out, without a moral compass, into society. If spiritual leaders assure a searching populace that "it doesn't matter what you believe, as long as you're sincere," we have a growing populace that is sincerely confused. If elected representatives get away with selling their integrity to corrupt savings and loan executives, then the citizenry senses it's okay to skirt morality and honesty—as long as the price is right.

The Bible records that as Jereboam led, Israel followed. Her acceptance of satanic influence as part of everyday life weakened the moral fabric of the nation, leading to eventual captivity by Assyria. Second Kings 17 summarizes the reasons for this national tragedy (you'll note that the reasons follow the pattern of Jereboam's sins):

1. They worshipped idols and false gods (verse 7).

2. They did "secret things" at their shrines that were similar to "the practices of the nations the Lord had driven out before them" (verses 8,9).

3. They followed their false religious leaders to worship in their high places at "sacred stones" and "Asherah poles" (verses 10,11a).

4. They had frequent religious celebrations that involved "wicked things" practiced by the previously judged heathen nations (verse 11b).

5. They entered into worship practices that probably involved animal sacrifices to false gods (verse 12), and in "stiff-necked" obstinence they refused all of God's ways (verses 14,15).

The account shows where this spiritistic false worship eventually led. The people "bowed down to all the starry hosts," looking to the stars for guidance and good fortune. They worshiped Baal instead of the God of Abraham, Isaac and Jacob. They engaged in human sacrifice to their false deities. They got into all kinds of sorcery, witchcraft, prostitution, and other things detestable to God and harmful to the well-being of humanity (verses 16-19).

For these sins, the once-resplendent nation of Israel perished. The Scriptures use rather forceful language to describe God's part in their doom. Such phrases as "he thrust them from his presence" and "he tore Israel away from the house of David," describe God's exceeding displeasure (verses 20-23) with the choices this nation had made.

Have God's Standards Changed?

Are God's standards any different today? Some of us seem to live as though God has come to His senses over the years, realized He was too harsh, and admitted that these types of sins are "really all right, as long as you're sincere."

The truth is, God's standards have not changed—ours have. We have tolerated, even defended, the subtle forces of evil in our land. This has dissipated our spiritual sensitivity and desensitized us to Satan's growing influence. As a result, we are completely unprepared for the overt satanic terrorism now sweeping through our communities.

The pastor of a leading evangelical church in Iowa asked me to come and teach his people about spiritual warfare during a weekend Bible conference. On other occasions, my talks on this topic aroused noticeable interest and concern among my audiences, as evidenced by their eager questions and interaction afterward. But on this occasion in Iowa, although I taught with my usual level of gusto, the people showed no evidence of interest or concern. They listened and thanked me for my ministry, but my words seemed to fly right past them.

It wasn't until the pastor pulled me aside that I began to understand what had happened. "Please pray for my people," he confided. "Many of them have become dull to the ways of the world. Many of them see nothing wrong in periodic gambling vacations to Las Vegas, or with purchasing lottery tickets on a regular basis, or with 'social drinking' or going to R-rated movies."

These were not the words of some legalistic, puritanical religionist. This pastor was genuinely heartbroken at how the ways of the world had dulled the spiritual sensitivity of God's people. It was little wonder that my warnings of Satan's growing boldness was now passing over their heads for, like the proverbial frog in the kettle, they had accepted and tolerated Satan's cool-to-lukewarm subtle ways so easily that now his boiling, overt ways were of little concern.

Is it then any wonder that satanism marches through our culture like an unchallenged army of evil? The only troops who can do anything about it seem too dull to care.

More Unlearned Lessons

In the next chapter we will consider *why* satanic influences lead to the demise of a nation. Before we do, however, we should take a quick look at Judah, the southern kingdom of the divided nation of Israel. Judah survived about 150 years longer than the ten tribes of the northern kingdom. Eventually, Judah too became an extinct nation as Nebuchadnezzar "carried them away" between 609-586 B.C.

Judah had considerable advantage over Israel. The Temple at Jerusalem and the Levitic scrolls of Holy Scripture had remained in their hands. The national leaders followed the Davidic blood line, though that did not keep them from sinning.

Despite the advantages, the sins of Judah were very similar in kind and degree to those of Israel. The one redeeming factor that kept the nation of Judah in existence longer than Israel appears to have been revival awakenings. Periodic spiritual awakenings happened under kings like Asa, Joash and Hezekiah.

Judah also had several other "good kings" who "did what was right in the eyes of the Lord" (2 Kings 14:3). These statements are followed by pertinent qualifying observations: "The high places, however, were not removed; the people continued to offer sacrifices and burn incense there" (2 Kings 14:4; 15:4,35).

The wicked potential of the human heart is not

eliminated simply because you have a correct place to worship, priests who are approved, a viable spiritual tradition, or even preserved copies of the Word of God in your hands. The history of Judah was replete with most of the same sinful practices catalogued against Israel. Even under Solomon's son Rehoboam, Judah was into such things as . . .

> sacred stones and Asherah poles on every high hill and under every spreading tree. There were even male shrine prostitutes in the land; the people engaged in all the detestable practices of the nations the LORD had driven out before the Israelites (1 Kings 14:23,24).

King Ahaz took heathen practices so far that he . . .

> even sacrificed his son in the fire, following the detestable ways of the nations the LORD had driven out before the Israelites (2 Kings 16:3).

Ahaz corrupted the Temple in his vile schemes of sin. If it had not been for the revival that came to Judah under the reign of Ahaz's son Hezekiah, the demise of that nation probably would have come much sooner.

Sin is cumulative in its destructive disaster. The longer it goes on, the deeper go its roots of damage. Thus it is not too surprising that Manasseh, Hezekiah's son, became the most wicked of all Judah's kings.

Manasseh reigned for fifty-five years in wickedness:

> He did evil in the eyes of the LORD, following the detestable practices of the nations the LORD had driven out before the Israelites. He built the high places his father Hezekiah had destroyed; he also erected altars to Baal and made an Asherah pole, as Ahab king of Israel had done. He bowed down to all the starry hosts and worshiped them. He built altars in the temple of the LORD, of which the LORD had said, "In Jerusalem I will put my Name." In both courts of the temple of the LORD, he built altars to all the starry hosts. He sacrificed his own son in the fire, practiced sorcery and divination, and consulted mediums and spiritists (2 Kings 21:2-6).

Manasseh's sins captured the loyalty of the people. Though they had God's Word in their possession, we read:

> But the people did not listen. Manasseh led them astray, so that they did more evil than the nations the LORD had destroyed before the Israelites (2 Kings 21:9).

A Short Reprieve

Yet God's mercy was great. Under Manasseh's grandson Josiah, another revival awakening came to Judah. A discovered copy of the Word of God was read in Josiah's presence. His response to the Word brought some of the most beautiful expressions of repentance recorded in the Bible (see 2 Kings 22:11-23). Josiah thoroughly cleaned house, and a few more years were granted to a badly bruised nation. Still, the recovery was short-lived; in about twenty years, a total collapse came. In the warnings of the prophet Amos, God's cart was overloaded with the wickedness of the nation: "Now then, I will crush you as a cart crushes when loaded with grain" (Amos 2:13).

Despite the marvelous repentance and reform launched by Josiah, the Scripture records this tragic refrain:

> Nevertheless, the LORD did not turn away from the heat of his fierce anger, which burned against Judah because of all that Manasseh had done to provoke him to anger. So the LORD said, "I will remove Judah also from my presence as I removed Israel, and I will reject Jerusalem, the city I chose, and this temple, about which I said, 'There shall my Name be'" (2 Kings 23:26,27).

Is God Removing His Hand of Blessing?

As I observe Satan's tentacles of influence pervading multiple levels of American society, and his ways being accepted and sometimes even endorsed in our entertainment, news media, judicial system, school systems and halls of government, I wonder: *Does Israel's story parallel our present course? Might God remove His hand of blessing from our great nation,* which historically has held to the precepts of God's design but now tolerates obscenity in the name of free speech, infant genocide in the name of free choice, sexual perversion and pornography in the name of free expression, and satanic terrorism in the name of freedom of religion?

Those who know me will tell you I am a positive person—an optimist. I see the glass half-full rather than half-empty. Yet the Scriptures tell us that God will not be mocked, and I must take Him seriously when He says:

> This will happen when the Lord Jesus is revealed from heaven in blazing fire with his powerful angels. He will punish those who do not know God and do not obey the gospel of our Lord Jesus. They will be punished with everlasting destruction and shut out from the presence of the Lord and from the majesty of his power (2 Thessalonians 1:7b-9, NIV).

Yes, I do believe Israel's story is a glimpse into our own future—unless we change course quickly. Where Satan reigns unchecked, disaster inevitably follows. Unless we learn this lesson of history, we are doomed to repeat it.

A Prayer for Our Time in History

Loving Heavenly Father, thank You for the overflowing evidence of Your mercy and grace displayed through the ages. Thank You for Your sovereign justice and power that enables You to bring sinful nations and cultures to account. I worship You in the wonder of Your holy majesty and loving mercy. I open my heart to You that You might light Your fire of concern within me to grasp the need of my land. I make myself available for Your Holy Spirit to use me to participate in the rescue of my broken nation. I pray Your Holy Spirit will arouse Your holy church to the challenge of our day. In the mighty name of our Lord Jesus Christ, I ask that You begin to effect a revolutionary national revival. Amen.

3

Why
Nations Fall

It happened in a small midwestern town, in a local elementary school. The bell was about to signal the return to class. In the girls' restroom, five intelligent, popular sixth-grade girls, with arms linked in a circle of oneness, gazed intently into the large mirror above the sinks and chanted in unison: "Bloody Mary, appear to us! Bloody Mary, appear to us!"

Their incantation droned on, building in intensity.

"Bloody Mary, appear to us!"

Suddenly, a ghost-like apparition materialized in the mirror directly above their reflected faces. It was a hideous face, with a sneering, sinister smile. The girls ran screaming from the restroom, their hearts pounding.

As they hurried to their next class they began to giggle nervously, now somewhat exhilarated over their flirtation with the supernatural.

The following Sunday, one of the girls told the story to her Sunday school teacher. The teacher was alarmed by the young girl's nonchalant attitude as she related the "fun thing" that had happened. She kept the girl talking, and gradually the full story came out.

The five girls had been conducting regular "seances" and enjoying extended sessions with a Ouija board. A couple of them had checked out a book on witchcraft and sorcery from the public library, and they were experimenting with putting curses on people they didn't like. All five were excited over the new powers they seemed to be discovering, and the apparition in the mirror was their latest triumph.

As the Sunday school teacher shared this story with me, I could scarcely believe what I was hearing. How could this type of evil enter a child's world? What has happened when, even in Smalltown, U.S.A., young girls who should be riding bikes and discovering boys are instead playing dangerous games with the supernatural?

To find the answer, we must pull back from our closeup view of such incidents and observe our national culture as a whole. No, we have not as yet embraced satanism as an official national religion, but we have somehow created a climate in which satanic influences seem free to prey on the minds of our people.

The Vicious Cycle

In the United States of America, in this last decade of the 20th century, our children are fed an almost constant diet of other-world cartoons and videos, whose heroes and villains extol satanic and New Age values.

Much of our young people's rock music and music videos contain explicit satanic and satanic/sexual lyrics and imagery. Modern horror movies and slasher films are no longer content with monsters or killers-on-the-loose; today's antagonists are often demons direct from hell.

High schools and colleges, where organized Christian activities are often banned in the name of "separation of church and state," frequently sponsor assemblies and classes on "alternative lifestyles," New Ageism and witchcraft.

All during our children's growing-up years, the timeless values of God are either mocked or ignored. The theory of evolution is taught as fact; creationism is scoffed at as being ancient superstitions of closed-minded fanatics. If Jesus Christ is acknowledged at all, it is merely as a man of history who lived and died, period. Those who are "with the times" belong to the New Age; those who believe in the Bible belong to the Stone Age.

These values are reinforced twenty-four hours a day in the entertainment, news and music media, sometimes subtly, sometimes blatantly, until they become an ingrained part of young-adult thought.

And then we have children, and begin teaching them our new, "enlightened" values. We elect each other to government posts, where we write and enforce new laws ensuring the proliferation of our enlightened values. We run news stations and newspapers, where we select and slant stories that present our enlightened values as mainstream thinking. We produce an endless array of TV shows and movies that depict all traditional-value advocates as either backwoods idiots or corrupt fanatics.

And then our children have children, and the cycle starts all over again. Our hearts grow colder and harder. What little spiritual discernment we did have disintegrates further . . . and the powers of darkness gain greater foothold in the individuals who constitute and govern our nation.

God's Sovereignty Over Nations

As we consider the future of our country, it is important that we first acknowledge the ultimate sovereignty of God over nations. This principle is one of the timeless absolutes of Scripture:

> Surely the nations are like a drop in a bucket;
> they are regarded as dust on the scales;
> he weighs the islands as though they were
> fine dust . . .
> Before him all the nations are as nothing . . .
> He brings princes to naught

and reduces the rulers of this world to nothing . . .
he blows on them and they wither,
and a whirlwind sweeps them away like chaff
(Isaiah 40:15,17a,23,24b).

The Scriptures assure us that God is slow to anger. In fact, Israel's history shows Him to be much more patient and forgiving than His people deserve. He knows and wants what is best for us. Yet when a nation hardens its heart and thumbs its nose at the Lord God as though He were merely an outmoded commodity, God acts swiftly and suddenly.

The Book of Daniel records arrogant King Belshazzar of Babylon carrying his rebellious rejection of the God of Israel into a final drunken party. In their revelry, they drank to their heathen gods from the sacred gold goblets taken "from the temple of God in Jerusalem." Suddenly, the finger of a human hand began to inscribe a divine message on the plastered wall—and the orgy of indulgence fell into silent shock. The finger wrote:

God has numbered the days of your reign and
    brought it to an end . . .
You have been weighed on the scales and found
    wanting . . .
Your kingdom is divided and given to the Medes
    and Persians . . .

That very night Belshazzar, king of the Babylonians,
was slain, and Darius the Mede took over the kingdom, at
the age of sixty-two (Daniel 5:26-28,30,31).

God may not always write His message on the wall, but He does write it in His Word.

Why Nations Fall

In the previous chapter we looked at the collapse of Israel and Judah. The Word of God declares that His sovereign hand worked in their demise. Why does such disaster come to nations and cultures?

As we study the fall of Israel and Judah, three major stages seem to stand out. Each is worth thoughtful reflection, because each carries a message for us today.

1. The culture becomes demonized.

The basic reason for and first stage of Israel and Judah's collapse has a terrible note of tragedy about it. I refer to what I call *the demonization of a culture.*

I'm convinced that no people can commit the sins Israel and Judah committed without their culture first being permeated with demonization. Idol worship and the sacrifice of animals to false gods had dreadful consequences in Israel and Judah. Their spiritistic experimentation in "high places" invited Satan to rule. Humans, both children and adults, were sacrificed to false gods, and the broad practice of sorcery, witchcraft, and ritual prostitution opened the doors further for demonic powers to control the participants and ultimately the entire culture.

Unfortunately, similar conditions are seen in today's world. Dr. and Mrs. Larry Tiedje have been serving God in Nigeria and Liberia, Africa, for the past twelve years. Dr. Tiedje, a dentist, has a unique vision and burden for world evangelization. Forced to take his family and leave civil-war-torn Liberia for their safety, Dr. Tiedje described the conditions there as being of "satanic turmoil."

Now the Tiedjes have been given a temporary assignment working with foreign nationals in a major university in the United States. After settling into their new American community, Dr. Tiedje recently sent a letter to his supporters, from which I quote:

> Life in our [new] city: Someone recently asked me how we liked living in our city. I told them I felt we were living in a sewer. Vulgarity and pornography seem to be the standard of the day. In our city, three abortions are performed for every birth. A recent issue of the local paper contained advertisements for the following support groups:

lesbians, newly gay women, bisexual men, and bisexual women. Drug abuse and occultism abound. Pray for our family as we [serve] this needy community and the internationals living in the midst of this wickedness.

He's talking about a sophisticated, learned United States community, culturally advanced in the eyes of the secular world. The abhorrent conditions illustrate the chaos that develops in any culture when the powers of darkness begin to dominate. The demonization of the culture makes it unfriendly, uncomfortable, and dangerous for people who want to practice biblical morality.

Demonization Through the Individual

When my first book, *The Adversary,* was published in 1975, its call to aggressive spiritual warfare was not widely received by the Christian public. Its major message was "The Christian Versus Demon Activity," but that involvement seemed distant to most believers. The intervening years, however, have effected a change of thinking among devoted Christians. Demonization is now recognized as a major problem by an ever-increasing number of evangelical leaders as the satanic revival engulfs multitudes of hurting people.

I frequently receive visits and phone calls from pastors seeking my advice on satanic problems they encounter in their church ministries. In recent days, three different pastors have sought me out for counsel, and all three apologized for attitudes they had held toward me since reading my book. When *The Adversary* first was published, they felt my observations and teaching were bent toward extremism. Recent counseling experiences, however, had changed their attitudes. One of the pastors told how he had become completely unnerved when obvious demonic powers threw a counselee onto the floor of his study and the individual jerked convulsively. "When [the counselee] was writhing on the floor, I fairly ran to get your neglected book off my shelf," confessed the pastor. Pastors cannot minister in a demonized culture without being confronted by demonized people.

In my years of counseling demonically oppressed individuals, I've discovered two major sin areas that seem to invite the problem. One is *dabbling in occultism;* the other involves the broad spectrum of *sexual sin.*

In God's Old Testament law, both of these sins were punishable by death. I believe one reason for such drastic punishment was that once demonization took place, under the Old Testament religious system, there was no known way to deal with it. It was not that these two sins were greater against God than many other sins, but that occult activity and gross sexual sins dangerously open a person's life to demonic control. Once wicked spirits had demonized a person, their claim was fixed. Little hope for release existed in the Jewish faith.

One of the wonders of the ministry of our Lord Jesus Christ is that demons are subject to Him. The Jewish people of Jesus' day and their religious leaders saw that when demonic invasion of human lives was confronted by the authority and power of the Lord Jesus Christ, the invasion was defeated and the demons were forced to leave permanently. That was something dramatically new to Judaism, and it was a great marvel (see Mark 1:21-25).

The Generational Aspect

A further tragedy of individual demonization must be addressed. The Word of God hints that when demonic powers get their hooks into a person's life, a problem of a transfer to succeeding generations is created. Demons that control a human person exercise that control only as long as that person lives. When he dies, the demonic powers live on. Since they don't die with the person, they seek to carry on, and the most direct claim for their next work seems to be the deceased person's children, grandchildren, nieces and nephews. Thus demonization becomes a generational problem.

Biblical students of spiritual warfare see this conse-
quence indicated in this Scripture:

> You shall not bow down to them or worship them; for
> I, the LORD your God, am a jealous God, punishing the
> children for the sin of the fathers to the third and fourth
> generation of those who hate me (Exodus 20:5).

This warning is associated with the worship of false
gods, which characterized both Judah and Israel in the years
preceding their destruction.

The redeeming blood of Christ is revealed in 1 Peter
1:18-22 as being sufficient to free us from all that has been
handed down from our forefathers. Salvation through the
shed blood of our Lord Jesus Christ cancels all legal claim of
demonic powers upon a believer's life. However, if a person
has opened his life to demonic control, those powers will
harass even a born-again believer. This is observable with
people who have been deeply into the occult. It is extremely
important for such people to know the doctrinal ground of
God's provided victory over darkness. Believers must know
and continually apply that victory in the Lord Jesus Christ
on an aggressive basis. Resisting the devil steadfastly in the
faith effects the enemy's defeat and the believer's freedom.

As I wrote this paragraph, I received a call from a counselor in a distant city. He sought guidance in helping a young
man get free from his entanglements with satanic ritual
abuse. The young man has been a believer for two years, but
he still faces a great battle. His joy and his considerable degree of freedom from demonic rule bear ample testimony to
the power of our Lord Jesus Christ. Yet at times he is almost
overwhelmed by assaults of evil powers which still torment
his mind, his will, his emotions and even his body. They flood
his thoughts with their claims on the satanic involvement of
his family lineage, declaring to him that he belongs to them
and can never be free.

Such lies and torments are common to a new believer who seeks to exit a satanic cult, especially when several generations of the person's family have been involved.

This family lineage problem has far-ranging cultural implications. The more extensive the personal involvement becomes, the more the larger community represented by that individual will manifest demonic chaos. Demonization can become the plague of a whole culture.

Indications of Cultural Demonization

I believe both Israel and Judah provide evidence of cultural demonization. As the people engaged in these sins, they gave Satan's kingdom claim upon them, and the demonization permeated the culture. Brief interludes of repentance and revival awakening, which did occur in Judah, were short-lived. In such spiritual awakenings, Satan was forced to sublimate his vile program for a time, but his hooks were so deeply imbedded in the culture that his efforts would soon be evident again — and his kingdom rule would quickly reassert itself.

The demonization of an individual is Satan's rule lived out in a human life; the demonization of a culture is Satan's rule spreading to the entire society.

The Demonization of America

I'm convinced that our own nation is rapidly undergoing demonization. Virtually everything that gave ground to Satan in Israel and Judah is now happening in our culture. Innocent blood is being shed as millions of unborn babies are being aborted. Spiritistic religious practices are epidemic among our children, youth and adults. New Agers do their "channeling" which is nothing but mediumistic spirit communication.

Meditators seek to get in touch with their "higher selves," or they seek a "spirit guide" who will help them make wise decisions. They don't realize they are being demonized in that very process. Their "spirit guide" is a demon.

Gross sexual sins are heralded as "sexual preference." Some denominations are ordaining practicing homosexuals to guide their flocks. Animal and even human sacrifices are not only made to "false gods," but many blinded souls also are openly performing such rituals to worship Satan directly.

At least in Judah and Israel, they thought they were worshiping gods of stone or gold. Today, people sacrifice to Satan and know it. I know of no time in history when such direct worship of Satan was practiced on as large a scale as is now evident in our nation.

Characteristics of a Demonized Culture

What are the characteristics of demonization? Noah's day depicts such a culture. The Scripture speaks of "how great man's wickedness on the earth had become, and that every inclination of the thoughts of his heart was only evil all the time" (Genesis 6:5). Lot, too, lived in the midst of a demonized culture. Peter describes Lot's experience of living in Sodom as one where Lot . . .

> was distressed by the filthy lives of lawless men (for that righteous man, living among them day after day, was tormented in his righteous soul by the lawless deeds he saw and heard) (2 Peter 2:7b,8).

Sodom and Gomorrah obviously were demonized cultures.

The apostle Paul gives us sharp insight into a demonized culture as he describes the conditions of humanity that bring forth God's wrath. He states that people's "foolish hearts were darkened," indicating the rule of the kingdom of darkness over them. They were locked into occultic worship as they "exchanged the glory of the immortal God for images made to look like mortal man, and birds and animals and reptiles" (see Romans 1:21-23).

When such conditions prevail, God removes His protective restraint. Repeatedly we read "God gave them over . . . " (Romans 1:24,26,28). This giving over certainly included more than the perverted human practice of the sexual sins described. As mankind engages in such sins, demonic powers take over; they then can rule because God removes His restraining grace. The resulting chaos is described vividly:

> God . . . gave them over to a depraved mind, to do what ought not to be done. They have become filled with every kind of wickedness, evil, greed and depravity. They are full of envy, murder, strife, deceit and malice. They are gossips, slanderers, God-haters, insolent, arrogant and boastful; they invent ways of doing evil; they disobey their parents; they are senseless, faithless, heartless, ruthless. Although they know God's righteous decree that those who do such things deserve death, they not only continue to do these very things but also approve of those who practice them (Romans 1:28-32).

According to those who have worked with demonized people, the terms used above often are taken by the wicked spirits as names because they describe the nature of those demons' work. This also describes the final stages of a demonized culture.

A Powerful Difference

This is the kind of condition we face now in our society. It's a desperate hour. Our culture is being demonized before our very eyes, and nothing can confront or change this accelerating problem but a God-authored, revolutionary revival.

It is important that God's people know why nations fall. The satanic revival presently under way demands a spiritual response from God's people that is strong enough to meet the challenge. Only the power of the gospel, unleashed through a concentrated season of prayer and repentance, is mighty enough to dismantle a satanic revival. Believers must know that and act upon it.

In Israel and Judah's time, there was no gospel message to confront and defeat the satanic rule the people had brought on themselves. That's the difference between then and today. We have such a message. The death, burial, resurrection, ascension and glorification of the Lord Jesus Christ has released sufficient grace to meet the challenge. The Holy Spirit has come. He is able and ready to convict any individual or an entire culture of sin, righteousness and judgment to come. We believers must rise to use our weapons of warfare. God has equipped us with all we need to win this great battle. Survival demands revival.

2. Gross sin brings on natural weakening.

The second stage of a nation's fall has to do with the natural weakening that gross sin interjects into any culture. Greed, lawlessness, drugs, immorality, sexual dissipation, drunkenness and violent anarchy always serve to undermine the character and resolve of a people.

We see this in the fall of both Israel and Judah. As each nation came to its end, short reigns of its kings, who were beset by intrigue and betrayal by trusted associates, were common. In Israel, Zechariah had reigned six months when one of his associates, Shallum, conspired against him and assassinated him. Shallum reigned one month before he was assassinated. Pekahiah had reigned two years when conspiracy overtook him. King Menahem ruled when Pul, king of Assyria, first invaded Israel. Menahem bought time by giving Pul thirty-seven tons of silver as tribute. Hoshea is called Shalmaneser's "vassal" who paid tribute to this Assyrian king. Later the Assyrian king discovered Hoshea to be a "traitor" and Israel's doom was sealed. Sin had taken its toll—the Assyrians terminated the nation.

The same weakening conditions prevailed as Judah faded away. Jehoahaz reigned only three months before Pharaoh Neco deposed him, carried him off to Egypt, and set Jehoiakim up in his place. Jehoiakim had to pay large amounts of silver and gold to Pharaoh Neco to retain his position as ruler of his nation. His safety was short-lived, however: Nebuchadnezzar of Babylon invaded. The nation's weakness and lack of resolve is illustrated by the raids and invasions of such armies as the Moabites and Ammonites. Jehoiachin came to power, ruled three months, and was carried away in disgrace to Babylon, along with his nation's treasures. King Zedekiah was able to rule as a vassal of the Babylonians for eleven years. He tried to marshal Judah's power in order to rebel against Babylon, but it was to no avail. Babylon surrounded the city and broke through the wall, and Zedekiah's demoralized troops "fled at night through the gate" (2 Kings 25:4).

There was no strength left in the nation. Sin had drained it all away. The Word says of Judah's tragic demise: "In the end he [Jehovah] thrust them from his presence" (2 Kings 24:20).

Sins of Israel and Judah's kind weaken a culture, sap the national resolve, and make a nation easy prey to earthly enemies. Even if God did not bring such nations to judgment, sin's power alone would so weaken them that they would soon fade.

The Weakening Sins

The Holy Spirit catalogs for us a list of the weakening cultural sins that will precede the final collapse of civilization as we know it. Reference to "the last days" tells us it's just about over for the demonized culture Paul describes:

> But mark this: There will be terrible times in the last days. People will be lovers of themselves, lovers of money, boastful, proud, abusive, disobedient to their parents, ungrateful, unholy, without love, unforgiving, slanderous, without self-control, brutal, not lovers of the good, treacherous, rash, conceited, lovers of pleasure rather than lovers of God—having a form of godliness but denying its power. Have nothing to do with them.

> They are the kind who worm their way into homes
> and gain control over weak-willed women, who are loaded
> down with sins and are swayed by all kinds of evil desires,
> always learning but never able to acknowledge the truth
> (2 Timothy 3:1-7).

We need to pause here long enough to see how terribly weakening and destructive these sins are to the resolve of any culture. Note that these verses describe a demonized culture. The Greek word *kalepos* used here translates to "terrible times" or "violent men," and is the same word Matthew uses to describe the torment of the two demonized Gadarenes in Matthew 8:28. These are the only times that word is used in the New Testament.

"Lovers of themselves" describes an anarchy of "me-ism." "I'm number one. No one else matters if I get mine." This is the direct opposite of a strong culture where loving God and loving others holds the culture together.

"Lovers of money." Colossians 3:5 urges believers to "put to death . . . greed, which is idolatry." This is the opposite of finding it "more blessed to give than to receive" (Acts 20:35).

"Boastful." The Greek word means to puff oneself up in speech. This is the vocalization of pride, the direct opposite of "the meekness and gentleness of Christ" (2 Corinthians 10:1).

"Proud." Pride, the opposite of humility, is an arrogant display of excessive self-esteem and often expresses overbearing scorn for inferiors.

"Abusive" describes the mistreatment of others by words or actions, taking advantage of an inexperienced or weaker person for selfish gratification, often through verbal, physical or sexual abuse. It connotes taking pleasure in inflicting hurt on others.

"Disobedient to parents." This is the opposite of obedience. Obedience is "better than sacrifice." Samuel warned Saul that "rebellion is as the sin of witchcraft, and stubbornness is as iniquity and idolatry" (1 Samuel 15:22,23, KJV). Defying God's constituted authority by refusing or neglecting to obey those who have authority over us destroys the very foundations of society.

"Ungrateful" signifies the display of a thankless, thoughtless attitude toward the favor others have shown. It conveys a "you owe it to me" attitude.

"Unholy." Unholiness shows deliberate disregard for what is holy. Sacred moments are mocked by cursing, blasphemy or outrageous behavior.

"Without love." Kindness and love toward others are rejected. Hate, violence and brutal words or actions are inferred.

"Unforgiving." Vengeful, bitter anger and spite flow out from the unforgiving heart, defiling everything it touches (Hebrews 12:15).

"Slanderous" is the opposite of commending and complimenting. It means to utter false charges or deliberately misrepresent facts in order to damage another person's reputation. People who resort to such tactics create chaos.

"Without self-control." Such a person is driven by desires or emotions, regardless of the consequences to himself or others. One's appetites rule the moment: "If it feels good, do it." It's the opposite of self-discipline.

"Brutal." Brutality describes a ruthless, unfeeling disregard and/or cruelty toward others. Dr. Vance Havner often said, "I used to say that civilization is going to the dogs, but I quit saying it out of respect for the canine kingdom." People can be more brutal than animals. Cities terrorized by street gangs know this truth only too well.

"Not lovers of good." This phrase describes those who love evil and who do wicked, sinful things.

"Treacherous." Treachery describes that which looks trustworthy and good suddenly giving way beneath you. It means to betray a trust or to violate an allegiance.

"**Rash**" is the opposite of wise, cautious and considerate. It describes hasty actions that take no thought of the consequences to others.

"**Conceited**" describes an excessively high opinion of one's importance which implies contempt for others. Others are regarded as being far inferior.

"**Lovers of pleasure rather than lovers of God**" is another way of describing those who have made personal pleasure their god. Pleasureful feelings occupy first place in their thoughts and actions. Our nation's preoccupation with sex, alcohol and the eternal high indicates that we value pleasure above personal morality.

"**Having a form of godliness but denying its power.**" Religious form replaces the genuine, inner reality of a personal faith in God. Religious expressions of such people give no evidence of a regenerated life which has been transformed by a saving faith in the Lord Jesus Christ.

When any culture begins to manifest these symptoms in the lifestyle of its people, the seeds of weakening have been sown and are taking root. The more sinful a culture becomes, the less endurance it has.

3. God's determination is sovereign.

The third stage of a nation's fall has to do with God's sovereign judgment. This is the ultimate, deciding factor. Regarding Israel and Judah, the omnipotent God of eternity looked at their rebellion and determined to bring those nations to their finish.

Though secular historians, philosophical intellectuals and earthly rulers may not recognize this fact, it remains an absolute: The God of history and eternity knows no challenge. Nations are in His hands.

Of the rulers and nations that rebel against God, the psalmist declares:

The one enthroned in heaven laughs;
the LORD scoffs at them.
Then he rebukes them in his anger
and terrifies them in his wrath, saying,
"I have installed my King
on Zion, my holy hill" (Psalm 2:4-6).

Manasseh ruled fifty-five years in terrible wickedness, and despite a revival under Josiah, Manasseh's grandson, this sovereign note of God's control sobers us:

Nevertheless, the LORD did not turn away from the heat of his fierce anger, which burned against Judah because of all that Manasseh had done to provoke him to anger (2 Kings 23:26).

God declares His decision concerning two of the greatest nations of history:

I will remove Judah also from my presence as *I removed Israel* (verse 27a, emphasis added).

Because of the established pattern of an omnipotent God's dealings with nations, I believe our own nation is in great peril. This factor alone ought to motivate believers in our country to prayer, repentance and movement toward revolutionary revival. Our window of opportunity is rapidly closing—but praise God, it is still open. People who are ready to use God's provided weapons can confront the satanic revival with a God-authored, God-empowered spiritual revival.

In the following chapters we'll see how we can make it happen.

PART II

Confronting the Powers of Darkness

◇ 4 ◇

Confronting Demonic Activity

> Restore us again, O God our Savior, and put away your displeasure toward us. Will you be angry with us forever? Will you prolong your anger through all generations? Will you not revive us again, that your people may rejoice in you? Show us your unfailing love, O LORD, and grant us your salvation (Psalm 85:4-7).

When cultures and nations become demonized, what can God's people do? What can confront such unleashed demonic control and send it into retreat? What is the Christian's answer to the resurgence of satanism in our world?

In His earthly life, the Lord Jesus Christ confronted demonic activity by the person and power of the Holy Spirit. Three Gospel writers record the sad details of the Pharisees' saying, "It is only by Beelzebub, the prince of demons, that this fellow drives out demons" (Matthew 12:24).

Jesus' Method

The Lord Jesus Christ immediately addressed the absurdity of their accusation with powerful logic. In the process the Savior reveals how He drives out demons.

> Jesus knew their thoughts and said to them, "Every kingdom divided against itself will be ruined, and every city or household divided against itself will not stand. If

Satan drives out Satan, he is divided against himself. How then can his kingdom stand? And if I drive out demons by Beelzebub, by whom do you people drive them out? So then, they will be your judges. But if I drive out demons *by the Spirit of God,* then the kingdom of God has come upon you" (Matthew 12:25-28, emphasis added).

Luke's account of this same event speaks of the Holy Spirit as "the finger of God" (Luke 11:20). The Gospel accounts indicate further how a demonized culture can be freed from such terrible bondage:

How can anyone enter a strong man's house and carry off his possessions unless he first ties up the strong man? Then he can rob his house (Matthew 12:29).

Luke's account makes it even more forceful:

When a strong man, fully armed, guards his own house, his possessions are safe. But when someone stronger attacks and overpowers him, he takes away the armor in which the man trusted and divides up the spoils (Luke 11:21,22).

These texts establish the fact that demons are defeated and sent away by the mighty work of the Holy Spirit. He is the "someone stronger" who is able to overpower the strong kingdom of darkness. The Holy Spirit is the one able to strip away all of Satan's defenses and rob Satan's house of those he holds in bondage.

A Necessary Balance

My counseling experience with demonized persons has frequently demonstrated the importance of the Holy Spirit's ministry in bringing the troubled person to freedom. The apostle James instructs believers to "resist the devil, and he will flee from you" (James 4:7*b*). That's a strong imperative for every believer to practice, but we must never forget that it is immediately preceded and followed by equally strong demands:

> Submit yourselves, then, to God . . . Come near to
> God and he will come near to you. Wash your hands, you
> sinners, and purify your hearts, you double-minded.
> Grieve, mourn and wail. Change your laughter to mourn-
> ing and your joy to gloom. Humble yourselves before the
> Lord, and he will lift you up (James 4:7a,8-10).

James uses nine words to call believers to aggressively resist the devil, but forty-two words to call us to repent and allow the Holy Spirit to clean up our lives. In simple mathematics, it is nearly five times more urgent for us to yield to God than to resist the devil.

That's a good reminder of the importance of keeping our perspective in spiritual warfare. Allowing the Holy Spirit control of one's whole being is the prerequisite to effectively resisting the devil.

Most counselors of demonized persons find this admonition from James a very necessary balance. Freedom from demonic control demands that all areas of sinful rebellion be confessed and cleansed away by the blood of Christ. Yielding to the Holy Spirit's sanctifying and filling is an important ingredient in that redemptive process. When this happens, the believer's freedom is near at hand.

A composite of difficult counseling experiences testify to the importance of that truth. Freedom from the rule of darkness doesn't come until believers honestly and deeply deal with the sin problems that originally gave Satan ground. Important to that dealing is the submissive invitation for the Holy Spirit to bring wholeness through the finished work of Christ into the person's being. When that happens, resisting the darkness is tremendously effective.

Breaking the Control

Prayer confrontation that follows such dealing with sin and submission to God is usually dramatic and the results are precious to the troubled person. I often pray like this:

In the name of the Lord Jesus Christ and by the power of His blood, I invite the Holy Spirit to search out any rule of darkness in any area of Tom's person and being. Search the conscious, subconscious and unconscious level of Tom's mind, will, emotions and body and totally control him with the Holy Spirit's fullness. In the name of the Lord Jesus Christ, we demand that all demonic powers relinquish their control to the Holy Spirit and that they immediately go where the Lord Jesus Christ sends them.

When sin is being dealt with and submission to God is happening, the tormenting darkness is broken by resistance. The churning battle ends. Release comes and floods of inner peace from the Holy Spirit supplant the ugly rule of evil.

The Holy Spirit's mighty work in an *individual*'s life illustrates what must happen to reverse the effects of Satan's rule over a *culture*. When human sin and wickedness give Satan powerful control over a whole culture, weak remedies will never be sufficient. Satan's powerful force for evil is not easily dislodged. Such deep entrenchment requires "someone stronger" to confront this "strong man" in all areas of his rule.

Power Encounter Studies

We have heard and read in recent years about "power encounter evangelism," "power encounter deliverance" and "power encounter church growth." Most of this writing comes from the mission fields where the populace fully recognizes evil spirits and evil powers. They understand that evil spirit beings can blind people, keeping them from believing the gospel, and that they can afflict people with their oppression. Dr. Timothy Warner in his 1988 Church Growth lectures at Fuller Theological Seminary defined "power encounter" with these well chosen words:

> Power encounter is the demonstration by God's servants of God's "incomparably great power for us who believe" (Ephesians 1:18), based on the work of Christ on the cross (Colossians 2:15) and the ministry of the Holy

Spirit (Acts 1:8), in confrontation with and victory over the work of Satan and demons (Luke 10:19) in their attacks on God's children, or their control of unbelievers resulting in the glory of God, and in the salvation of the lost and/or the upbuilding of believers.[1]

C. Peter Wagner, a former missionary, presently teaches in the Fuller Seminary School of World Missions as professor of church growth. He has written extensively about power encounter ministry and has studied particularly how this approach affects world evangelization and church growth. Most of the statements in Wagner's articles and books are cautious and exploratory. The July 1989 *Evangelical Missions Quarterly* carries an eleven-page article by Dr. Wagner entitled, "Territorial Spirits and World Missions." He documents his article with numerous power encounter approaches being used in world mission fields. He points out that this vital concept is relatively new and that there is not yet an evangelical consensus on it.

Dr. Timothy M. Warner, another missionary leader who writes and speaks about power encounter, presently directs the School of World Missions and Evangelism at Trinity Evangelical Divinity School in Deerfield, Illinois. His ministry was in Sierra Leone, West Africa. He laments an all-too-common situation, familiar to most missionaries:

> I look back on my own missionary experience in a tribal village in West Africa with a combination of regret and incredulity that I attempted ministry there with almost no understanding of either the biblical teaching on demons nor of the reality of the demonic world to the people with whom I lived and worked.
>
> While I have spoken on the issue in the years since my days in Africa and have continued to study the subject, it was only this year [1986] that I ventured to teach a whole course on the subject. The response from the missionaries in the classes has been overwhelmingly positive. Many have expressed thoughts like, "If only I had had this course before I went to the field!"[2]

Other evangelical scholars are also teaching and writing on this subject. Dr. C. Fred Dickason, chairman of the theological department of Moody Bible Institute, teaches extensively in the field of spiritual warfare and has written *Demon Possession and the Christian.* Dr. Ed Murphy of Overseas Crusades, formerly a professor in missions at Biola University, has taped a series on spiritual warfare which has a balanced, biblical thoroughness. Dr. Gordon Lewis of Denver Seminary, Dr. Gerald E. McGraw of Toccoa Falls Bible College, Dr. Neil Anderson of Talbot Seminary and Biola University, and Dr. Victor Mathews of Grand Rapids, Michigan, are other notable evangelical scholars doing creative study and work in the field. There are numerous others, I am sure. My point is, our Lord seems to be raising up careful evangelical scholarship to provide guidance in this field. Such an important area deserves the best historical and biblical perspective available from trained scholars.

A Muslim Power Encounter Experience

Ruth Veldcamp has served as a missionary with the Christian Reformed Church in East Central Nigeria, Africa, for more than twenty years. After periodically observing her work, Dean Hochstetler of the Mennonite Church calls her "the world's most effective missionary to Muslims." The success of her ministry to Muslims is directly related to a power encounter approach to evangelism.

In the early years of her missionary work, Ruth did not see large numbers of Muslims turning to Christ. A few were won but most of them were young and fearful of declaring their faith in the Muslim community. Troubled by the slow progress, Ruth began to see that Muslims in large numbers would never come to Christ until the religious leaders themselves, the "Mallim," led the way. They have studied the Koran and are looked to as authorities in spiritual matters.

In her years of working with the Muslims, Ruth became convinced that Islam is essentially animistic and spiritistic;

the Mallim "have inevitably dealt in some way with occult powers." Many of them practice witchcraft and sorcery as an integral part of the Muslim religious system. She realized these leaders were so bound to their sorcery and religious loyalties that to reach them would require confronting them with a mighty display of the power of God. They would not be reached by logic or argument.

As she prayed about it, the Lord took her to Exodus 17 where Moses, Aaron and Hur interceded on the hilltop while Joshua and the Israelites fought the Amalekites in the valley. When Moses prayed, the battle went in Israel's favor. When he grew weary and ceased to intercede, the battle went the other way. Only with the help of Aaron and Hur was Moses able to continue the intercession and assure the victory.

Ruth states, "I thought maybe that's the secret. I wrote home to all the people supporting me and asked for prayer warriors who were willing to pray every day for Satan to be bound, and that churches would come up in Muslim communities, stay in Muslim communities and be a witness for Christ there."

One hundred people signed up right away to pray daily. The number has grown now to more than 250. She sends monthly updates, including the names of those she feels are key to the desired breakthrough. When she first asked for the prayer support, remarkable things began to happen.

How did God answer those prayers for power confrontation to pull down strongholds of darkness ruling the Mallim?

Ruth says, "He did it in the one way that will get through to Muslim sorcerers. God brought them direct dreams and visions. The very first one I had contact with was Stazu [real name changed]. He had a series of four dreams or visions. In one of them a verse of the Koran lit up and came out at him which said that all men were meant to be one community. The verse further said that if it had not been for the *Word of God*, they would have been judged because they differed. Stazu knew by the Holy Spirit's conviction that the *Word of God* is one of the titles given to Jesus in the Koran."

In another vision, Stazu saw a Muslim bowing in his daily prayer ritual. A powerful voice thundered to Stazu, "This man is still under condemnation." You can't get much more explicit than that.

Ruth adds, "Every Mallim who has become a Christian has had a vision. The common theme of each vision is that salvation comes only through Jesus Christ."

This illustrates God's power encounter with the deceptions of evil supernaturalism. Spiritual warfare praying brought the desired breakthrough.

Ruth's account of Stazu's conversion is graphic. "This man was a sorcerer. As a Mallim, Stazu had done the sorcery and the cursing that turned three people completely insane. They threw off all their clothes; they didn't know what was going on around them; and they were walking naked through the towns in a pitiful state. After he became a Christian, Stazu became convicted that he should do something to reverse their condition. His first reaction was to go and undo it as he would have done as a sorcerer. I had a sense that would cause more trouble than he realized. I said to him, 'You can undo it quite all right but in a different way than you would have done it before.' "

Ruth had learned, through her study of spiritual warfare, that the power of our Lord Jesus Christ and His finished work can cancel Satan's curses and sorcery.

"Well, in the end, Stazu did go to the place where the sorcery 'stuff' was that he'd used in the cursing ritual. He prayed over it in the name of the Lord Jesus Christ and destroyed the stuff. The very night he did that, all three of those 'mad' people came back to their normal senses. Can you imagine the impact that had on a Muslim, animistic society in those African towns?"

Another Muslim Breakthrough by Power Encounter

Gerald E. Otis has served with the Christian and Missionary Alliance in the Philippines since 1967. He tells of Ahmad, 85 percent illiterate, who was a new believer in a Muslim fishing village in the southern Philippines. A number of the people in the village challenged him, "If you can cast out the devil from this woman, we will truly believe and embrace immediately the faith in Jesus Christ."[3]

He accepted the challenge and the time was set for the confrontation. Ahmad spent much time waiting upon the Lord and trusting Him for wisdom and for the Holy Spirit's presence and power. On the appointed day, Ahmad, without hesitation, in the name of the Lord Jesus Christ, confronted the powers controlling the woman. Here is what happened:

> Words flowed from her lips indicating the battle to come. "You are nobody to me, I can eat you alive," a voice from within the woman said. "The only one I'm afraid of is the Holy One within you," the voice continued.

With every eye focused on Ahmad, he commanded the demon to depart in the name of Jesus Christ the Savior.

The demon again spoke, "Yes, I will go away."

After a time of jerking and struggling, which rendered her seemingly lifeless, the woman awoke fully sober and sane, totally free from the chains of Satan.[4]

The following day, those who had issued the challenge came to Ahmad's house, confessed their sins, repented, and received the Lord Jesus Christ as their Savior and Lord. This one encounter continues to extend the work of Christ into the Muslim world in that part of the Philippines.

Challenges to Abou's Jesus

Loren Entz, a church-planting missionary with the Africa Inter-Mennonite Mission (AIMM) in Oradara, Burkino Faso, relates the story of a Muslim sorcerer, Abou. After listening to a cassette-taped testimony of an ex-Muslim leader who had experienced salvation in Jesus Christ, Abou felt God's powerful call for him to follow "the Jesus road." He destroyed all of his magical devices, and after five days of agonizing, he found peace with the Lord Jesus Christ. This was followed by a month of illness that Abou calls his "cleansing experience." He saw it as a time to repent and get rid of all the evil he had done. During that month, AIMM missionaries sat with him, prayed, and read the Bible to him.

As Abou got well, he greatly desired to share his new faith. The missionaries taught him, gave him visual tools to use and encouraged him to witness. This led to an open challenge from the occult fetishers of Abou's village to prove if the power of Abou's Jesus was greater than theirs. They poisoned Abou's food, but Abou prayed over it, ate and suffered no ill effects. Entz records the next part of the test:

> Then the elders took him to their sacred grounds late that night. Abou was placed beside a huge gaping hole. The six elders sat on the other side of the hole. Fire escaped from the hole. A special whistling brought poisonous bees from the pit to do their evil work against Abou, but again with no success. Abou could not be stopped or injured.

> They had one test left, a test which no one else had ever escaped. The old men whistled a second time and a huge snake about 18 inches in diameter emerged. It came toward Abou. It tried to push him into the pit as countless others before him had been pushed in and disappeared. But the snake could only brush his leg. The snake itself fell into the pit. There was no doubt whose power was greater. God's power working through Abou was superior to that of the fetishes through the village elders. The rest of the night Abou preached Jesus to them until daybreak, when he returned to Oradara.[5]

A second encounter occurred between Abou and a group of sorceresses who claimed their powers to be greater than the fetish powers of the men. Victory over the women in that encounter also led to a night of preaching the Lord Jesus Christ. Fatimata, the leader of the sorceresses, was miraculously converted. As the chief person of influence in the village, her conversion brought many to saving faith.

The next challenge came from Makoura, considered to be the most powerful person in that whole region of Africa. Her source of power was a special evil spirit which had enabled her to kill hundreds of people through her curses. She did not want Abou's Jesus to succeed in her realm.

The AIMM missionaries prayed much with Abou before he went to accept her challenge. He gathered a cassette tape player, tapes, Bible pictures and a change of clothes, borrowed a bicycle, and headed toward the appointed meeting with Makoura. Entz records what happened:

> Suddenly, with an explosive noise, the bicycle burst into flames. Abou miraculously escaped unharmed with the Christian teaching materials but everything else burned. Even sand wouldn't put out the fire immediately, so Abou continued on foot to his destination.
>
> On [his] arrival, Makoura exclaimed, "What are you doing here? You are supposed to be dead."
>
> Abou answered, "You invited me, and I've come with the power of Jesus." Abou was invited to share this source of power with Makoura. He spent the night in the house of the evil spirit which was no longer able to live there. It had not been victorious in the power encounter with Abou's Jesus.[6]

Makoura was miraculously converted, and Loren Entz asks us to pray for Abou and his continuing power encounter ministry to those in occult bondage in Burkino Faso.

Such accounts from the mission field verify to us that believers do face an enemy who is capable of powerful activity against the truth of the gospel. Yet when faithfully applied, the power of our Lord Jesus Christ always triumphs.

Lessons From Power Encounter

These accounts, from various geographic locations, related by different denominational leaders, say something to those of us who desire revival. The laboratory of human experience confirms the truth of God's Word. In an account from closer to home, author and counselor James G. Friesen relates:

> The door was closed. That was not particularly unusual, but as I knocked on the door and was invited in, a strange feeling came over me. A few students sat around a small metal typing table. Their hands rested lightly on its top, and their little fingers overlapped to form an unbroken ring of human contact. "What's going on?" I asked.
>
> The reply: "A seance."
>
> I did not know how seances were carried out, so I just went over to the other side of the room and quietly watched as the students continued. In subdued voices they were asking questions of a spirit. The table would tip to one side for yes, to the other side for no.
>
> To spell out a word, it would tip once for *A*, twice for *B*, and so on to twenty-six times for *Z*. The table was spelling out a sentence when I came in. The participants, fascinated and totally involved, hardly noticed my entry. I was not surprised at what I saw. Without any direct human help, the table tipped from side to side—and the students were in contact with the spirit world. It was right there. I could not help but believe what I was seeing.
>
> After about twenty minutes I realized this was more to these students than a novel way to spend the afternoon. They excitedly sensed a mixture of belief and disbelief at what they were discovering. They were in contact with a spirit who had spelled out its name as "Hoz," and who claimed to have been a court magician from the middle ages. Spinning out its story in answer to the students' questions, the spirit drew them deeper and deeper into the mysteries of Hoz's life and death. The seance was about a half hour old when I had entered the room . . .
>
> I had been taught about the Bible throughout my childhood. My mother would read to me for hours from a Bible story book, and I had been a Christian for quite a few years. I knew practically verbatim the accounts of Jesus casting out evil spirits in the New Testament and I had

heard stories from missionaries in third world countries, telling how they had, in the name of Jesus, cast out evil spirits. It occurred to me that I had such an entity in front of me. I found myself with a chance to discover if using the name of Jesus would expel an evil spirit.

Thinking things through, however, I ran into a dilemma. If I spoke the words out loud, "In the name of Jesus I command you to leave," the students could take their hands away from the table, or somebody could hold the table down to prevent any tipping. I might not know if the name of Jesus could be used effectively if I said it out loud. So I decided to just *think* the command.

I directed my gaze toward the table and thought the instruction: "Hoz, in the name of Jesus I command you to leave!" The students had no idea that I had just cast Hoz out. The table was in the middle of spelling out a word, and at the very second I finished my thought-command, it stopped. The students kept their hands as they were, and tried to figure out why the contact had been broken, but could come up with nothing. The table would not move, *period*. They backed off from it, and glanced back and forth at each other, shocked and puzzled.

I told them what I had done. They expressed irritation with me and tried to start the seance again, but they could not conjure up Hoz or any other spirit. That was the end of the seance, and the power of Jesus' name had been demonstrated to me.[7]

Believers who maintain a right relationship with their Lord Jesus Christ need have no fear in any encounter with Satanic forces. Unusual things may happen when we confront the powers of darkness in prayer or in other ways, but this abiding assurance remains:

> In all these things we are more than conquerors
> through him who loved us. For I am convinced that
> neither death nor life, neither angels nor demons, neither
> the present nor the future, nor any powers, neither height
> nor depth, nor anything else in all creation, will be able to
> separate us from the love of God that is in Christ Jesus our
> Lord (Romans 8:37-39).

Setting the Stage for Revival

You welcomed the message with joy given by the
Holy Spirit. And so you became a model to all believers in
Macedonia and Achaia. The Lord's message rang out from
you not only in Macedonia and Achaia—your faith in God
has become known everywhere (1 Thessalonians 1:6*b*-8*a*).

Surprising, dramatic history was made on Christmas
1989 in Romania. Two weeks later *Newsweek* magazine made
observations and quoted some of the people who lived it:

All over Romania, people let out a collective sigh of
relief and bitterness when the visible proof of Ceausescu's
downfall and death was broadcast last Tuesday, a day after
his execution on Christmas night.

"The antichrist is dead," murmured a man who
watched the broadcast in Bucharest, the capital.

"He died too easily," complained a soldier in the city of
Timisoara, where the popular uprising against Ceausescu's
hated dictatorship began.

"I would have kept him in a cage in a public square,"
said a Bucharest hotel manager, "so that people could spit
on him and pelt him with stones."[1]

The secular news media covered the dictator's last days
from the political and military perspective, but they missed
the real story. The bitterness mentioned in *Newsweek* was
not the predominant characteristic. The spiritual struggle

between light and darkness was. Without that dimension the account is tragically incomplete.

It has been my honor to develop a personal friendship with the Reverend Josef Tson, who for the past eight years has served as president of the Romania Missionary Society, headquartered in Wheaton, Illinois. He had been the pastor of the Second Baptist Church in Oradea, Romania, where he served with renown and significant spiritual impact. His successes so threatened the communist authorities that they exiled him under threat of imprisonment if he remained in his pastorate. Immediately following the death of Ceausescu, Josef Tson returned to his beloved homeland. Soon after he arrived, he sent me a video briefing of the overthrow. I am indebted to him and his firsthand accounts from the spiritual perspective for much of what I am able to share here.

The breaking of the bonds of Ceausescu's communist rule in Romania becomes a parable illustrating how believers may rise up to break the revival of satanism that is sweeping through our culture. It merits attentive study so we may understand the part believers had in overthrowing a tyrant. Ceausescu's rule of cruel terror was similar to Satan's rule in human lives.[2]

Romania's Overthrow of Communism

Communism was an experiment conducted in a laboratory large enough to include nearly 40 percent of humanity. It was an experiment in a new type of government, a new type of society, a new type of economy and a new type of attitude toward religion. It was designed to produce heaven on earth without God, but in the words of Tson, "Whenever you try something without God, you go with Satan. Satan always lands in hell. The end of the experiment proved to be hell on earth."

As the communist regimes of Eastern Europe toppled like dominoes, Romanians across the world groaned and questioned: "Why are we the last ones? Why no movement in

Romania? Why are the Romanians so cowardly? Why don't they show courage like the other nations?"

Tson confides, "We started to feel embarrassed and ashamed that we were Romanians." It is not pleasant to realize your country might remain an island of repression and suffering because of inaction among its people.

Tson explains the reasons behind the delay with words of insight: "Nobody knew at that time how evil was the evil in Romania! In Romania the communist dictator developed a system of secret police so evil, so satanic, so merciless, so cruel that nobody could conceive it. No one knew . . . until the population exploded. It was then that people learned of how mercilessly the secret police were willing to slaughter anyone and everyone. The cruelties, the carnage and the crimes of these tyrants showed why the Romanians didn't move before."

Much about Ceausescu's ruling tactics hints of "satanic evil": his brutal repression of the Christian faith, his desire to build self-exalting monuments of achievement and his cruel repression of all dissent. Few will fail to see the evidence of satanically inspired persecution, repression and hate that the church had to endure in Romania.

Not a Revolution—a Miracle

Joseph Tson describes the overthrow as a "beautiful uprising." Secular people called it a revolution but believers described it differently. Doina Cornea, a retired teacher and a famous personality in Romania, pointed this out on national television. She protested the uprising being called revolution. "Don't call it revolution!" she said. "Call it God's miracle in Romania, because it was all God's doing!"

It started on December 15, 1989, in the city of Timisoara around the house of the Reverend Liziw Toderic, a Reformed Church pastor. The police wanted to evict him from his house and his pastorate because of his bold stand for Jesus Christ. About two hundred of his parishioners came to

defend him and to prevent the eviction. They boldly surrounded his residence and intimidated the authorities to the
point where they retreated to gain reinforcements.

On Saturday more people came, many from different
churches. They were protesting the intrusion of the communist government into the ministry of the local church.
Saturday evening, a young man from the First Baptist
Church of Timisoara brought candles and handed them out
to the hundreds of people now surrounding the house. He lit
the first candle, and the people all lit theirs from those previously lighted. A blaze of lighted candles flickered in the
night. That moment seemed to trigger the uprising.

As the people sang hymns and held their lighted candles,
the secret police opened fire, wounding or killing many of
those courageous Christians. The young man who brought
the candles was shot in the leg, an injury so severe that his
leg had to be amputated. When his pastor visited him in the
hospital the young man said, "I lost a leg, but I lit the first
light."

For three or four days these Christian people kept going
to the pastor's home even though they were being gunned
down periodically with automatic weapons. As the people
faced the brutal carnage, they kept shouting, "Freedom!
Freedom! We don't mind that we die!"

At that point Romanian people began to realize that
freedom was more precious than living. Dying was preferred
to slavery. The Romanian police state was doomed. Nobody
could stop the will of a spiritually aroused, freedom-loving
people.

Various pastors were invited to those public places
where huge crowds of protestors began to assemble. These
gatherings became worship and praise meetings toward God.
Crowds of 100,000 people knelt on the pavement in reverent
worship, while repeating the Lord's prayer together.
Reverently they listened as the pastors led in the corporate
expressions of prayer, praise and petition.

In Timisoara, a girl from the Pentecostal church appeared on a balcony where a large gathering of people had assembled. She recited a beautiful poem:

> We are not creatures made by chance;
> we are not monkeys;
> we are God's creatures.
> God exists!

After each stanza those two words, "God exists," were repeated. The words were picked up by the multitude and became the slogan of the uprising. The cry, "God exists! God is with us!" was heard everywhere in Romania.

A well known Romanian hymn became the song of the uprising:

> We live at the end of the age;
> An age of darkness, hate and war;
> But soon Jesus comes back to us;
> Jesus comes back to us.

A God-Centered Uprising

Everything about the uprising was God-centered. Most of the Romanian people, when interviewed about the revolution, declared, "God did it!" They saw God's hand everywhere. In fact, the Romanian weather is usually bitterly cold in December, but during the week of the uprising the temperatures were unusually warm, in the 60- to 70-degree range. The people were able to stay day and night in the streets. They quickly pointed out that even in the weather, God was with them, supporting their outcry against tyranny.

In the capitol of Bucharest, the young people were in the forefront of the uprising. University students as well as other, younger, people went out to meet the secret police who faced them with machine guns and automatic rifles. The young people shouted, "You with weapons, we with flowers! You with weapons, we with flowers! No violence, no violence!"

Despite the youth and immaturity of the crowds, no shop windows were broken and no riotous looting or other activities characteristic of mob violence and uprising occurred. During the entire time the masses gathered, a respect for property and people prevailed. Pastors, Christian believers and young people were in the forefront of it all, and solemnity and a reverential worship of God stood out as the prevailing strength.

An Earlier Trip to Romania

Why was the Romanian uprising like that? What explains the God-centered dignity maintained despite the secret police and government-supported violence that killed as many as 10,000 people in Timisoara and Bucharest? Living in such a repressive, brutal police state usually produces a seething caldron of hate and bitterness in the hearts of the people. Why didn't a vindictive, violent revolution erupt in Romania? My personal experiences during a trip to Romania three years earlier helped me to understand . . .

The palms of my hands were moist and my mouth was dry. I recognized the symptoms of deep anxiety. We prayed, "Loving Heavenly Father, we are coming to Romania to encourage our brothers and sisters in Christ and to encourage ourselves by the vibrancy of their faith. We yield ourselves fully unto Thee. We pray that the medicines we are bringing may be allowed into the country. May the Christian books we are bringing be overlooked by the border inspectors. We know that Jesus Christ who made blind eyes see is also capable of making seeing eyes blind when it is His will and purpose to do so. May your guardian angels attend us and intervene in our entrance into Romania . . ."

As one of the four men in our group continued to pray, I sensed the return of a peaceful calm. If we were, as we believed, on a divine mission with a sovereign plan, the Lord would bring it all together. The plans for this trip had been initiated two years before, during the annual missionary conference of our church. Pastor Josef Tson was the Bible Hour speaker. His church in Romania was the largest Baptist church in continental Europe. During the conference, God had graciously spoken to us concerning the believers of the "suffering church." We American Christians saw with keener insight the pressures of living in the hostile environment of a government committed to the promotion of atheism.

Pastor Tson was impressed by the deep spiritual faith of a number of Christian medical doctors within our body, and a plan began to form in his mind.

The members of the Second Baptist Church of Oradea had chosen Dr. Nick Gheorghita as their pastoral leader when Pastor Tson was exiled. Dr. Nick was both a preaching layman and a Romanian medical specialist in endocrinology. Because of the demands of the thriving ministry at Second Baptist Church, another layman with a degree in clinical psychology, Dr. Paul Negrut, had been added to the pastoral leadership. Tson felt that a church-related visit from Western Christian medical people would both encourage these laymen leaders and strengthen their position in the eyes of the Romanian government.

The three men who had joined me in this ministry venture were my son-in-law Hans Finzel, a missionary in Austria with the Conservative Baptist Foreign Missionary Society; Dr. Charles Hamm, a family practice physician from Kingsley, Iowa, the missions committee chairman of our church, and on his first overseas missionary journey; and Dr. Michael Chandra, a cardiologist with impressive credentials, who was excited at the opportunity to witness for Christ and to learn of the practice of cardiology in Romania. Dr. Hamm and Dr. Chandra each brought a large piece of luggage filled with a variety of medicines. Word had come to us that certain medical drugs were in short supply in Romania and the believers were in need. I had felt impressed to bring twenty-five copies each of my two books on spiritual warfare. I had scattered the books in different places in my luggage hoping that at least some would escape detection. I planned to present them as gifts to fellow pastors in Romania.

The returning calm was welcome as we suddenly were at the border crossing. A long line of cars had come to a halt. Armed soldiers and large steel cross-beams barred our path. We would go no further without proper clearance from Romanian officials. With passports in hand, the four of us stood by the car waiting for instructions. No one seemed in a hurry to give us any. Our tension mounted as the time passed. Then I heard a familiar noise. My eyes followed the sound into the rafters holding the steel roof over the inspection area. There, a resting dove cooed out the sounds of its comforting presence, and I immediately sensed a symbolic message. The Holy Spirit had descended as a dove upon the Lord Jesus Christ. I felt reassured. God was with us.

Before we left Vienna, Hans had telephoned Dr. Paul to tell him of our expected time of arrival, and Dr. Paul asked, "Do you have the medicine for the hospital?"

Hans assured him that we had a generous supply.

"Good! I'll try to meet you at the border and help you through customs," Paul responded.

We felt reassured, knowing that a friend was going to meet us. We wondered, though, about his reference to "medicine for the *hospital.*" What exactly did he mean?

An official finally came to the car and asked for our passports. Taking them, he left us waiting to be told what to do next. Other people were spreading their luggage open before the inspectors. Like most Americans, we impatiently wanted to get on with the process. After what seemed a much longer time than it actually was, things began to happen.

The Hidden Books

Several officials moved our way, some in uniform and some in civilian clothes. They greeted us warmly, and we became aware that they, the official committee from the

Oradea Hospital, had been waiting at the border for us. The chairman of protocol introduced himself, the hospital director, and the hospital director of nursing. They assured us that as soon as we cleared customs, they would escort us to our hotel. Excusing themselves, they went back into the building, leaving us with the inspector who would examine our car and its contents.

The inspector was dressed in a military uniform. His stern appearance, piercing eyes, and businesslike manner told us he would look us over thoroughly. Each of us was instructed to lift his luggage from the car, open it and stand by it until it was inspected. Carefully, the inspector looked through the emptied car, probing here and there, thumping the sides, testing the door panels and inspecting under the hood. The police state looks everywhere. As this went on, all I could think about was my books. Because of their titles, *The Adversary* and *Overcoming the Adversary,* they did not seem to be the type of books that would get through if discovered. Thoughts were going through my mind: *How will I explain the presence of so many of these books? Will their discovery ruin what seems to be a cordial welcome from the officials and the hospital medical committee?*

My thoughts were suddenly interrupted by the inspector's move toward my things. After asking me to identify my pieces of luggage, he began to probe through the clothing. A lump formed in my throat. I saw his hands go into my suitcase at the very spot where ten of my books had been placed. They were wrapped in groups of five, and I knew he would see or feel them. As he pushed the clothing aside, I stared in amazement at the spot. The books weren't there! I didn't see them and neither did the inspector. He motioned for me to close my luggage and he moved on to Dr. Hamm. Eagerly I complied. Placing my luggage back in the car, I wondered, *Did I put the books someplace else?*

The inspector finished Dr. Hamm's inspection, and I was surprised to see him give clearance. I knew that one of Dr. Hamm's carry-on bags was jammed full of the medicines for the Christian believers. Why had the inspector not mentioned the medicine? Though I wondered about these events, I was not to grasp their full impact until later.

Hidden Medicine

My curiosity was further aroused as I watched the inspector examine Dr. Chandra's luggage. A large suitcase was opened. It was full of the latest cardiac medicines and drugs supplied by various U.S. pharmaceutical companies. Seeing the drugs, the inspector was obviously alerted. He took several of the samples and disappeared into the adjoining building. He soon reappeared with the smiling hospital officials. To our happy surprise, Dr. Paul was with them. Arrangements were made for Dr. Chandra to present the medicines immediately as a gift to the hospital. We were not permitted to carry them to the hospital. Dr. Chandra was allowed to keep in his possession two of the latest cardiology books which he planned to present as a gift to the cardiologists of Romania. A formal presentation was planned for the next day at the hospital in Oradea.

As we followed the car of the welcoming committee into Oradea, we had opportunity to debrief on the details of our entrance. With excitement, Dr. Hamm shared how the inspector had overlooked completely his opened travel bag with the large supply of medicines. Though it was on the ground beside the table holding his other luggage, God had protected it from discovery. Perhaps an unseen angel had stepped in front of it, concealing it from the probing eyes of the inspector. The believers would have their medicines.

With equal excitement, I shared my experience of the undiscovered books. We rejoiced together. We had just witnessed the mystery of God's sovereign, miracle ways. When we later arrived in our hotel room, I eagerly opened my luggage. Sure enough, the books were right there all the time. In ways known only to God, He had shielded their presence from physical view. As I later presented them to different pastors, some asked, "How did these ever come through the border without confiscation?" What a joy to tell them that the Lord had miraculously prevented the books' discovery.

After arranging for the official hospital visit the next day, the four of us enjoyed a delicious meal at the hotel with Dr. Paul as our host. We relaxed in happy fellowship. Dr. Paul was young, in his early thirties, and his handsome, confident appearance made him impressive. His keen alertness, sense of humor and spiritual warmth drew us to him. God had lifted this outstanding champion from among his peers to lead His church in such a time as this. Satan's program is destined to fail with such men of God in leadership.

Four Miracles

Later, in a more private setting, Dr. Paul shared with us the four miracles he had witnessed in our entrance into Romania. They were firsts as far as he knew: (1) A group recognized as Christians from the West were received as official guests by the government authorities; (2) Dr. Chandra as a Christian physician was officially invited to address the medical doctors on any subject in the field of cardiology; (3) we were received without needing to agree to any daily rate exchange fee required of all westerners; and (4) the official welcoming committee included not only the hospital medical people and the communist protocol chairman but also one of the pastors of the Second Baptist Church of Oradea.

Dr. Paul went on to say, "This could never happen in Romania, but it did. God is still sovereign!"

Being a Christian in a communist country demands carrying a cross with many painful barbs. We spent the evening of our arrival in the home of Dr. and Mrs. Paul Negrut who obviously loved their country and the people of Romania with a great loyalty. People came and went in a constant procession. The love and warmth of Jesus Christ drew them like bees to flowers. Such popularity did not go unnoticed by the communist authorities. Christian leaders like Dr. Paul and

Dr. Nick were held in constant suspicion. The church itself was viewed as a threat to the communist system.

The Igniting Sparks of a Church Under Communism

Despite the hardships the believers faced by living in a communist state, the church remained vibrant and strong. We saw revolutionary revival in process. Some of the healthiest Christianity in the world of our day existed in communist-ruled Romania. When Billy Graham was permitted to preach there in 1985, a glimpse of spiritual revival in Romania was seen. He had been invited by the leaders of the "Department of Cults" to visit Romania, and meetings were arranged in various churches and centers throughout the country. These meetings were not given publicity or advance notice, but crowds exceeding ten to thirty thousand people would appear wherever Dr. Graham spoke. Knowledge of the meetings spread through an invisible network of believers.

When we were there, we witnessed a spiritual fire that could not be quenched burning in Romania. The Lord Jesus Christ had lifted up a people hungry for Him and His Word. The thirst for "living water" continued to increase despite the obstacles. Jesus Christ was building His church in Romania. We observed a spiritual uprising standing in the wings ready to make a grand entrance, and no one was able to stop it. Only God's sovereign plan and His providential timing could know the moment of outbreak.

Since we made that trip to Romania, so much has happened there. I have had opportunity to reflect upon the biblical factors we saw displayed that started the spiritual fires burning. The principles we witnessed at work are not unknown in the history of the church. The same principles have fueled the fires of every spiritual awakening that has ever graced the church. Those principles can and do break Satan's bondage in any age. We'll look at them in the next chapter.

◇ 6 ◇

Breaking
the Bonds

Some of the sparks of spiritual revival we observed in Romania in 1986 were ignited in no small way by Dr. Nick and the Second Baptist Church of Oradea. He said his people were fervently praying. "I am believing God for the renewal the church is experiencing here to erupt in a great spiritual revival. I believe it will jump the wall that separates East and West and will spread throughout Europe and the world."

Dr. Nick's vision seems in the process of fulfillment. God has previously used suffering churches to initiate revivals. An oppressed church in New Testament times exploded and "turned the world upside down" (Acts 17:6, KJV). In these closing days of history, perhaps God in His grace will do it again.

Ingredients That Break Bondage

Though the ingredients that bring spiritual power and contribute to revival are not new, Satan attempts to keep them clouded. We saw them operating among the Romanian believers, and the force of the impact will not soon be forgotten. Those ingredients include fervent prayer, joyful worship, refinement of persecution, courageous faith, a hunger for God's Word and a strong bond of fellowship.

I communed with the Lord about my preaching to the believers in Romania, and I felt the Holy Spirit's leading to make prayer the subject of my first message. As things turned out, I was somewhat embarrassed—the teacher became the student.

The first service we attended was at 6 P.M. on a Friday night. We arrived shortly before that to find a small, humble church building. Nestled there in the midst of the surrounding newly constructed apartment buildings, it appeared insignificant. We saw only a few cars in the small, dirt-covered parking area. Conditioned to the American scene, we wondered where the people were. To our thinking, few cars meant few people.

Dr. Nick interrupted our thoughts with, "Look at them come! Look at them come! Isn't that a great sight?"

Suddenly, our American-conditioned minds understood. Instead of cars entering a parking lot, people were walking, converging from every direction upon that house of worship. Small groups and large groups poured in from everywhere—with happy, smiling faces—expecting spiritual food.

We were ushered into the pastor's study where we gladly joined deacons and leaders of the church in a circle of clasped hands, and several lifted up prayers for the service. The language barrier didn't hinder the power or fervency of our prayers at all. Leaving the office, we were led through crowded aisles. The people who were standing there pressed together to make room for us. A chorus of "Pachay, pachay" (Peace, peace) hummed in our ears. Many reached out to touch us or to grasp our hands, and we felt their sincere love. A breath of spiritual ecstasy swept over us. As we moved to the platform, our inner excitement grew.

The people were singing a familiar hymn, "To God Be the Glory," and we followed Dr. Nick's example and reverently knelt before our Lord in silent prayer. In a few moments, we stood to our feet and began to sing with the people. We sang in English—they sang in Romanian.

I looked out over the sea of joyous faces. They had no hymn books—each was singing from memory. Their radiance told of their love for Christ. The scene was invigorating, almost overwhelming. I had never witnessed such a service.

1. Frequent, Fervent Prayer

> The prayer of a righteous man is powerful and effective (James 5:16*b*).
>
> If my people, who are called by my name, will humble themselves and pray and seek my face and turn from their wicked ways, then will I hear from heaven and will forgive their sin and will heal their land (2 Chronicles 7:14).
>
> After they prayed, the place where they were meeting was shaken. And they were all filled with the Holy Spirit and spoke the word of God boldly (Acts 4:31).

After the hymn ended, the pastor called the church to prayer. Many of the people went to their knees, and a quiet hush enveloped the body. The pastor asked for men in a given area to lead in prayer. Without a moment's hesitation, a man began to pray with great fervency. Though I could not understand his words, my eyes filled with tears as he prayed. Dr. Chandra later remarked, "When these people began to pray, it was like the thunder of heaven." Ushers extended a microphone toward the praying person's voice, enabling everyone to hear. Interjections of "Ah-meen! Ah-meen!" rippled through the congregation adding a melodious touch to the prayer. As quickly as one prayer ended, another began. Though we could not understand their language, we heard their cry. These people knew how to pray, and they loved to pray.

The pastor shifted the prayer participation to another area of the church where the women were seated. The response from the women was equally instantaneous and electric. They prayed as fervently and effectively as the men.

After several had prayed, the giant choir that filled the entire balcony sang, "God, the All Merciful!" The spiritual impact of their music was deeply moving. As soon as the choir ended, the church was at prayer again. By this time there was no longer room to kneel in the packed aisles, so the congregation stood as the same pattern of prayer flooded forth from the young people.

Three times during the two-and-a-half-hour service these prayer interludes were interjected into the worship. At least forty minutes of the service time was devoted to this participating, fervent intercession.

I have focused much of my ministry on prayer, but by the time I was introduced to speak on my chosen topic I felt like a novice. Yet as the interpreter delivered my thoughts to the people, I sensed unusual freedom and power to preach. The prayers of the people had unlocked my lips. I now knew that our miraculous procession through the border check point had had a much deeper prayer base than just the prayers we had offered as we rode in our car. Prayer is the life's breath of the Romanian believers, and the flow of corporate prayer from these committed believers testifies of their vital, individual, private prayer life. Satan's program cannot stand before a praying people of such obvious, sincere fervency. Prayer breaks the bondage of darkness.

2. Joyful, Genuine Worship

Worship is sometimes defined as "ascribing worth-ship." In biblical worship, God is the audience and the worshipers offer their adoration to Him. Love flows from each believer's heart toward the heavenly Father and the Lord Jesus Christ by the enabling of the Holy Spirit. True worship requires sincerity from hearts that are clean before God.

Anne Ortlund, in her helpful little book *Up With Worship,* writes:

> Not often do churchgoers find themselves in the Presence. But when they do—all is changed. They may destroy their idols, as in Genesis 35:2. They may, as a group, promise to obey all of God's Word, as in Exodus

24:7. They may have a great musical time, as in 2 Chronicles 5:11-14. They may be moved to weeping, as in Nehemiah 8:9. They may just have a wonderful "ball" enjoying God! In Nehemiah 8:6 they said, "Amen," lifted their hands toward heaven, and then bowed and worshipped with their faces toward the ground. In any case, they are moved to move! Repent—weep—rejoice—*something*. When God is present in power, if the people don't respond, the very stones will.[1]

She has captured something of the ingredients of the joyful worship we observed in Romania: full of spontaneity and participation; hymns sung from memory; upturned faces focused in worship toward God and expressing joy; music reaching out with a forceful message of biblical truth, yet communicating spiritual warmth; and rapt attention to Scripture reading. Quiet expressions of "Ameen, Ameen," heard as God's Word was read, carried the natural beauty of the sound of water tumbling down a mountain stream.

"I couldn't understand their language, but I surely understood their worship," Dr. Hamm remarked after that Friday night service.

To these believers, God is everything. They have no hope but Him. He remains the focus of their joy and the recipient of their praise. There is an obvious longing for His presence. Suffering had lifted their worship to a high and holy level.

Such in-depth worship was a vital key to the strength of the believers in the Romanian uprising.

3. The Refinement of Persecution

When our Lord Jesus Christ addressed Himself to the church at Laodicea, He counseled those "wretched, pitiful, poor, blind, and naked" believers as to how their disgraceful condition could be healed—they needed to buy from him "gold refined in the fire . . . white clothes to wear . . . and salve to put on your eyes, so you can see" (Revelation 3:18).

"Gold refined in the fire . . . " What a descriptive statement of divinely superintended suffering and persecution.

Bruce Shelley writes in *Church History in Plain Language* that one of the reasons the gospel spread in such an extraordinary way during its early years was that persecution publicized the Christian faith.

> Martyrdoms were often witnessed by thousands in the [Roman] amphitheater. The term *martyrs* originally meant witness and that is precisely what many Christians were at the moment of death.
>
> The Roman public was hard and cruel, but it was not altogether without compassion; and there is no doubt that the attitude of the martyrs, and particularly the young women who suffered along with the men, made a deep impression. In instance after instance what we find is cool courage in the face of torment, courtesy toward enemies, and a joyful acceptance of suffering as the way appointed by the Lord to lead to his heavenly kingdom. There are a number of cases of conversion of pagans in the very moment of witnessing the condemnation and death of Christians.[2]

It's possible that Christian believers in Romania have suffered more under communism than in any other country. Many have read of the pain and tortures suffered by Richard Wurmbrand and other believers in the early days of the communist takeover in that country. One would be naive to say that such persecution has not hurt the advance of the church. Yet, the benefits of persecution are evident, just as Shelley wrote about the early church.

One of them is the refinement our Lord Jesus Christ spoke of in His message to the church at Laodicea. Persecution burns away the sinful, worldly dross that limits our usefulness to the Lord. A lack of separation between Christians and the world, expressing itself in questionable practices, is not tolerated in the lives of believers who are going through persecution.

At our reception at the hospital in Oradea, after we had been served the meal, a young man posing as a medical technician (but whom Dr. Nick said was really a part of the secret police) tried to fill our glasses with vodka. I was glad I had already filled my glass with mineral water, because in such a situation you don't know what to do lest you offend your hosts. Dr. Nick and Dr. Paul, though, resolutely refused the vodka, even though their glasses were empty. They wanted these officials to know that, as Romanian believers in Christ, they did not drink strong drink.

Dr. Nick and Dr. Paul later chuckled over the uncertainty with which we "tee-totaling" American Christians handled the situation. After assuring us that we handled it well under the circumstances, they told us why it was so defined for them. In their church, drinking alcoholic beverages of any kind is cause for immediate dismissal from membership. To many American Christians, such censure for a questionable practice would seem too legalistic. In Romania, though, it has no such designation. Rather, it is an expression of the healthy refinement that persecution produces. Any questionable practice ceases to be a point of debate — it has to go. Believers long to be free of anything that might quench or grieve the Holy Spirit.

The "gold refined in the fire" has given them spiritual power and effective witness which is seen particularly in their resolute devotion to their faith while showing kindness toward their persecutors. We saw this displayed in the way Dr. Nick and Dr. Paul related to the government chairman of protocol, who was known to be a part of the Romanian secret police. He knew, and those two godly pastors knew, the grief and persecution he had helped inflict on them. Yet, with winsome kindness, they were gracious at all times toward him. He was well aware that Dr. Paul had personally arranged the gift of medicine to the hospital, and that Dr. Nick had worked to bring the expensive medical equipment to the hospital at no cost to the Romanian people. The return of love for persecution baffled that communist as it has persecutors of Christians for centuries.

4. Courageous, Confident Faith

> And now, compelled by the Spirit, I am going to Jerusalem, not knowing what will happen to me there. I only know that in every city the Holy Spirit warns me that prison and hardships are facing me (Acts 20:22,23).

Words like these spoken by Paul in the face of brutal persecution show courageous, confident faith that moves everyone it touches.

Because of Josef Tson's bold witness and open challenge to the communist system, he had been arrested. Threats, long interrogations and painful beatings were dealt out to this dedicated pastor. Eventually, he was ordered to leave Romania or go to prison.

When Josef Tson was given that ultimatum, though he had already laid his life down for his Lord Jesus Christ and was ready to face prison if necessary, the confusion and pressure were enormous. Josef sought out Dr. Nick for advice.

Josef respected his good friend's wisdom. In essence Dr. Nick said, "Josef, if you stay here, at best you would continue to have a congregation of 2,500 people to preach to every Sunday. If you go to the West and broadcast back into Romania, you will have a congregation of millions."

That counsel liberated Josef to see God's plan. He courageously accepted his exile, and God rewarded him. For eight years he beamed a broadcast into Romania over Radio Free Europe. Millions of people listened every Sunday afternoon to the Bible preaching ministry of Josef Tson.

Little did Dr. Nick realize what far-reaching results Josef's going would have in his own life. A Christian physician with a respected medical practice, he was also a weekend preacher, but he was sure this would be the limit of his duty to Christ for the rest of his years.

Losing Josef Tson was a severe blow to the church at Oradea, but eventually they sought God's leading regarding their next pastor and then extended a call to Dr. Nick. He was a gifted expositor of God's Word, and his wise, fervent preaching had made him a favorite supply for the church. At first, Dr. Nick turned down the call. In the process of time, though, and through the persuasion of the church leaders, God showed Dr. Nick he should accept.

The people of the church were overjoyed, and God's blessing was quickly seen in weekly conversions to Christ and increasing growth.

Dr. Nick could appear only on Sundays, though—since he was a medical doctor, he must remain a medical doctor. The communist authorities would not allow him to be a Baptist pastor. They did everything in their power to keep that from happening. It soon became obvious that the church needed him full time, but the authorities simply refused him permission to move to Oradea.

The pressure mounted. Any traveler was required to carry an "internal passport" at all times, or he was subject to arrest, imprisonment and heavy fines. In the government's power play to keep Dr. Nick from Oradea, they confiscated his internal passport. Not only could he not move to Oradea, but now even traveling there to preach and pastor the church was illegal. He could be arrested and imprisoned at any time.

The church was broken-hearted. Would they never be able to have Dr. Nick as their pastor? They prayed and wept the week that news came.

Dr. Nick, too, was struggling over what to do. Should he give the whole vision up and return to his former pattern of medical practice and weekend ministry? The prospect of imprisonment, severe fines and possible torture was not easy to face. Sunday drew near, and the tension mounted. Dr. Nick felt it was a lost cause. Then the Lord used his wife to help release him from the intimidation.

"Nick," she said, "God has called you to pastor the Second Baptist Church of Oradea. You have accepted that call. You are their pastor. Those people are counting on you. You cannot let them down, even if it means jail."

Sunday morning arrived. Aggressive young Paul Negrut and the rest of the deacons had worked hard trying to get permission for Dr. Nick to come, but to no avail. They would have to make do with one of them preaching. The burden was heavy upon Paul—and then the phone rang. It was Mrs. Ghiorghita. "Paul," she said, "you meet the train. God has arranged a speaker for you. 'Silas' is coming."

Paul left for the train station wondering who this "Silas" might be. Deep in his heart he hoped it might be his beloved pastor. Would this "Silas" risk imprisonment to serve his God as the biblical Silas had done so many years ago? Would Dr. Nick come without his passport? Dr. Nick did indeed come, and tears accompanied their embrace as he and Paul met at the train station. They both knew full well the price this step might exact.

At the church, the people, not knowing of Dr. Nick's coming, had gathered in extra numbers—crisis brought them together. They began singing the hymns under a cloud of sadness. While they were singing, Dr. Nick started pressing through the crowded aisles toward the platform—and suddenly everything changed. A holy hush fell on the people. Most of them started to cry. "Ah-meen! Ah-meen!" echoed throughout the church. Their pastor had come! He loved them enough to face prison.

Even more dramatic, Dr. Nick conducted a funeral that Sunday afternoon for an important government man. The man's wife was a member of the church. Many communist officials attended the funeral, and they knew that Dr. Nick did not have his internal passport. As he spoke, Dr. Nick contrasted, in a dynamic message, what Jesus Christ and Karl Marx could do for a dead man. Such fearless faith ignites the confidence of the persecuted and confounds persecutors.

Those officials didn't know what to do—but they did not arrest him.

Eventually, Dr. Nick was permitted to move to Oradea and now serves there as one of the world's most gifted pastors. If revival comes to our world, his bold faith and his courageous people will have been a part of the fire that started it.

If revolutionary revival is to come to us, the same faith and courage must become motivating fires in our hearts as well.

5. The Hunger for God's Word (see Hebrews 4:7-13)

One of the important keys to any revival awakening that will break Satan's bonds is *biblical balance*. Revivals by their very nature tend to promote extremism, and that can lead people off on a tangent that distorts biblical balance. J. Edwin Orr's lifetime study of evangelical revival awakenings has convinced him of the danger of extremism. He warns that nearly every past revival or spiritual awakening cooled when a tangent extremism was introduced. Sometimes it was an "organization extreme," sometimes a "nationalism extreme," or a "glossalolic (tongues speaking) extreme," or a "signs and wonders extreme," etc.

I like the way the Holy Spirit evaluated the post-Pentecost revival that ebbed and flowed for many years in New Testament times. Acts 2:42 summarizes the early church revival with this formula:

> They devoted themselves to the apostles' teaching and to the fellowship, to the breaking of bread and to prayer.

This biblical balance carries a four-fold emphasis: (1) study of the Word ("the apostles' teaching"); (2) body life ("fellowship"); (3) worship ("the breaking of bread"); and (4) prayer.

It's important to note the first emphasis for good balance: "the apostles' teaching." Through the apostles God gave the New Covenant revelation to His people. The apostles taught the Old Testament Scriptures, recalled the teachings of the Lord Jesus Christ, and recorded the Holy-Spirit-authored new revelation in various writings and epistles. For those first-century believers, the apostles' teaching was equivalent to what we treasure now as our New Testament. They heard the Word of God—they devoted themselves to "the apostles' teaching."

When it's dark, really dark; when the situation is desperate; when you need hope and there is none visible; when people are hurting and the enemy seems in full control; there is only one source for real hope and comfort. It is the Word of God.

Perhaps that explains why there is such an appetite for the Word of God in Romania. Conversely, it also explains why the atheists, the communists and the satanist movements do everything they can to stamp out the Scriptures.

When we attended the Monday night youth meeting at the church in Oradea, we noticed that very few of the young people had Bibles. Prior to the uprising, it was hard to get a Bible in Romania. Despite the constant desire of the churches for more Bibles, the government kept a tight restraint on the number that could be published. Some Bibles were smuggled into Romania, but it was dangerous, often led to arrests, and at best was a limited answer. It could never meet the need of hurting people—yet some of them found ways to get God's Word. One way was that people would lend their Bibles to other believers who would copy whole books by ancient typewriter, or more commonly, by hand.

One of the apprentice pastors was teaching the young people a Bible lesson from Nehemiah that Monday night. We could not understand his lecture, but it was obvious to us that his teaching methods were not up-to-date. He read from handwritten notes in a dry monotone. With no overhead projector or even a blackboard, he was giving a seemingly dull lecture. We watched for more than twenty minutes, and we were amazed! The four to five hundred young people in attendance were taking it all in, most of them writing notes at a furious pace, trying to retain every word they could of the book of Nehemiah.

They obviously hungered for God's Word.

The one hope for us in this dark time of satanic revival is that we will hear the Word of the Lord. Only the Word has the power to save us in this late hour.

6. The Bonding of Christian Fellowship
(see 1 Thessalonians 1:4-10)

An early church tradition says the first Gentile Christian martyr lost his life at Thessalonica. From what we know about the Thessalonian church, that is probably true. When Paul was there, Jewish rejecters formed a mob and led in riotous opposition to his preaching the gospel message. Under cover of darkness, Paul and Silas fled to Berea. The militant opposition from Thessalonica was so intense that they followed Paul and Silas and stirred up a riot in Berea, too.

That militancy created the climate in which the church of Thessalonica had to live and function. It was tough to be a Christian in that city and to be a part of that church.

An understanding of the persecution and suffering of the believers at Thessalonica will greatly deepen our appreciation of this New Testament epistle, especially when we see that one of the major messages of the book is the importance of Christian fellowship and closeness. Today we sometimes call it "body life" or church "koinonia." Kittel says the word "denotes 'participation,' 'fellowship,' especially with a close bond."[3]

Paul continually refers to this vital bonding of fellowship in the suffering Thessalonian church. It was so precious to him that he did not want to leave them and miss it. He speaks of this in some of his most deeply moving words:

> But, brothers, when we were torn away from you for a short time (in person, not in thought), out of our intense longing we made every effort to see you. For we wanted to come to you—certainly, I, Paul, did, again and again (1 Thessalonians 2:17,18a).

Paul found great comfort in the bonding of their fellowship, in the "body life" of that church.

Body Life as the "Day" Approaches

As I write these words, my mind's eye focuses on the throngs of happy people we saw gathering for prayer, worship and instruction in the churches of Romania. They came together because they needed to be together. We felt the bonding power in every gathering of the church. Such conditions produce revival warmth.

This body life was recognized by the communist authorities as deadly to their goal of stamping out the church. That's why they opposed church gatherings with such a vengeance and why they bulldozed church buildings. They didn't want the people to be together.

We marveled at the believers' courage, but Dr. Nick stated repeatedly, "The communists fear us much more than we fear them."

When the church is in spiritual health, its body life is one of the most potent ingredients it has going. The writer to the Hebrews speaks eloquently of the need for fellowship:

> Let us hold unswervingly to the hope we profess, for he who promised is faithful. And let us consider how we may spur one another on toward love and good deeds. Let us not give up meeting together, as some are in the habit of doing, but let us encourage one another—and all the more as you see the Day approaching (Hebrews 10:23-25).

On our final night in Romania, we went to Dr. Paul's home. There we saw extended body life in action. Different groups were meeting in every room. In one, Dr. Hamm and Dr. Chandra examined people who had come for medicine and they consulted over the difficult cases. In the kitchen a one-to-one discipling relationship was shared. In another room, those who had come for medical treatment visited with each other. Dr. Paul's wife conducted a small group Bible study in another room. Hans and I looked for a place to settle, but were "pushed" out by yet another group, so we went for a long walk. As we walked the streets of Oradea, we just talked and prayed and marveled together over the church. Despite the oppression and opposition, this church was alive and well on the Romanian portion of planet earth.

As it turned out, we were right. This church, and dozens of others like it, were at the forefront of the Romanian miracle of Christmas 1989. They had prayed and worshipped faithfully. They were ready when God chose to move to confront the powers of darkness in their land.

7

Where
To Begin

How does a believer who recognizes the need for a revolutionary revival get a handle on lifting himself, his city and his culture toward it? What can believers do to see a revival awakening today like those we've considered? Dare we expect another revival that will impact the whole culture and turn our nation around?

The offer of revival is still with us. God has not closed off His day of grace. The promise from the prophet Joel that Peter applied to the beginnings of the church age has not yet been canceled.

> In the last days, God says, I will pour out my Spirit on all people. Your sons and daughters will prophesy, your young men will see visions. . . . Even on my servants, both men and women, I will pour out my Spirit in those days, and they will prophesy (Acts 2:17,18).

I believe these verses hold a unique promise for our day.

Beginning the Rescue of a Culture

Our growing congregation desperately needed a larger building. The architect had drawn up beautiful plans for a new sanctuary, and everyone was excited and ready to go. We had one major problem—no money and little prospect of finding any. Our church body had just extended itself in a major effort to clear the mortgage on our existing building. I could not now ask them to enter another building fund drive.

What to do? We examined bonding programs, professional fund drives and denominational assistance. A major lending institution told us our track record was not good enough to warrant their loaning us the amount we needed. If they did make the loan, the interest level would have to be high because such a loan would be a major risk to them. The door seemed closed, but we prayed. We needed the building to keep the work moving, so we kept trying doors.

Our bank had never given a church loan and had turned us down earlier even for consideration. Sensing God's leading, I returned to our bank and asked the vice president if I could present our case to the loan committee. Her reply was less than positive, but she agreed to check it out. Much to my delight, the bank agreed.

I'll never forget that experience. How I prepared. I assembled a carefully worded prospectus. Financial reports and projections of growth were meticulously charted. The artist's concept of the new building was framed and in hand. Documents were ready to place in the hands of the loan committee, officers and board representatives. I practiced and practiced presenting my case. I prayed, and others prayed, that I would be granted wisdom. Aware of my youth and inexperience, just 30 years old and in my first full-time pastorate, I dressed conservatively for the occasion—I wanted to appear as mature and dignified as possible.

Finally, the hour came. I dried my wet, anxiety-betraying hands, entered the room, and for about forty minutes poured out our case and answered each of their questions with as much wisdom as I could. They would let me know their decision in a few days.

The waiting was not easy. Days passed and I wondered if that might mean bad news. Finally, the vice president phoned. "I have good news for you," she said. "Your church can have a loan for fifteen years at 6 percent interest." The amount approved was for more than we'd requested—just in case it might be needed!

"I guess you know," she continued, "this is very unusual for our bank. The presentation of your case with such responsible candor made the difference. Congratulations!"

I was deeply thankful. I found myself wrestling in a somewhat futile attempt to remain humble. What an exhilarating success for a young pastor!

This youthful experience has an important application as we seek a beginning place for the rescue of our culture. I had presented the needs of our church body to the people in the bank who could help us resolve our need. Careful preparation and my best efforts were vital to my approach.

As believers, we have the privilege of presenting the needs of those around us to the one who can help us resolve those needs. The very concept of finite, failing humans being able to address and influence the infinite, almighty Jehovah staggers the mind. Yet, that's what prayer is.

Prayer is serious business. There is a proper attitude, dignity, sobriety, reverence and carefulness that should be observed. It is the most important work we can do in this world. To have audience with Almighty God concerning things important to Him and to us puts every other human endeavor far down on the list.

In *Don't Just Stand There, Pray Something*, Ronald Dunn says, "Prayer is not a religious exercise—it is a human necessity."

He adds:

> Prayer means that I never have to say, "There's nothing I can do." I can always do something. . . . I discovered that prayer is the secret weapon of the kingdom of God. It is like a missile that can be fired toward any spot on earth, travel undetected at the speed of thought, and hit its target every time. . . . There's more. Satan has no defense against this weapon; he does not have an anti-prayer missile. . . . We do not pray by default—because

there's nothing else we can do. We pray because it is the best thing we can do.[1]

Intercessors Must Be Raised Up

To confront the satanic revival in our culture, we must begin our efforts by observing God-authored principles, those that He follows in claiming a city, a state or a nation for our Lord Jesus Christ. One principle is: *Preparation is made through serious intercessors.* God always works this way in the affairs of humanity.

The coming of the Holy Spirit on the day of Pentecost was preceded by serious intercession. Before that time, God had His 120 disciples shut away in prayer for ten days in the upper room. The prayers of the psalmist and the prophets reveal that Christ's birth also was preceded by much prayer. Simeon and Anna carried this intercession on through the time of His birth and His Temple dedication (Luke 2:21-38).

Nehemiah was God's sovereignly chosen instrument to bring renewal to Jerusalem, yet he didn't even start until after he presented his case to the heavenly Father. At least four months of careful, travailing prayer preceded those beginning steps that led to revolutionary revival (December-April, Nehemiah 1:1; 2:1).

This principle does not change. Revolutionary revival will not visit any culture without previous fervent intercession. Apart from travailing prayer, our nation can never expect the revival we need to save our culture from disaster. As we look at Nehemiah's story, I hope that message comes through.

We must note that the prayer needed does not flow from aimless, emotional wishes. It must show a prepared, purposeful, deliberate, God-honoring pattern. Nehemiah's prayers had that. There is a dignity, a majesty of greatness, about his praying. The earlier description I gave of my preparations to present my case to the bankers doesn't hold a candle to the dignity and care of Nehemiah's approach to the God of Israel. Let's note the characteristics of his praying.

Characteristics of Prayer That Will Save a Culture

1. Prayer that saves a culture will be both private and corporate. Nehemiah began by praying alone:

> When *I* heard these things, *I* sat down and wept. For some days *I* mourned and fasted and prayed before the God of heaven (Nehemiah 1:4, emphasis added).

We usually do our greatest praying alone, when God is our only audience. A genuine sincerity, a true measure of our burden, begins to emerge. There's no one to impress when we're alone.

> When you pray, go into your room, close the door and pray to your Father, who is unseen. Then your Father, who sees what is done in secret, will reward you (Matthew 6:6).

These words of our Lord Jesus Christ focus upon this private aspect of prayer, and He observed the same principle Himself:

> Very early in the morning, while it was still dark, Jesus got up, left the house and went off to a solitary place, where he prayed (Mark 1:35).

In my own experience, the Word of God has become practical as I've prayed it back to God. I've learned more about God and His ways through my private shut-away times with Him than I've learned from any other source. It's only out of my maturity of years and tested practice that I feel at liberty to bear such testimony. Private prayer has been the greatest delight of my whole Christian experience.

Private prayer provides opportunity for significant personal spiritual growth. It becomes a well-spring from which refreshing waters flow out of our lives to others and is of paramount importance to revival.

Corporate prayer is equally as important. Though we have little insight into how it developed in Nehemiah's time, it definitely was present. "Oh LORD, Let your ear be attentive . . . *to the prayer of your servants* who delight in revering your name" (Nehemiah 1:11, emphasis added). At some time during those months of Nehemiah's private prayer, he linked up with others who shared his "delight in revering" God's name. This corporate prayer indicates a time of sharing with others who had a similar burden for the rescue of Jerusalem.

For many years, I felt restricted when I prayed with others. When they were listening to what I was saying, it was hard for me to be open and honest before God. I much preferred just being alone with Him. Eventually, I sensed His rebuke for that preference. I saw, in the cry of the disciples, "Lord, teach *us* to pray," that corporate prayer is just as essential to God's plan as private prayer.

When believers meet to pray, the liberty comes and the hindering of spiritual progress is broken. Revival demands both private and corporate travail before God.

2. Prayer that saves a culture will flow out of the need.

> I questioned them about the Jewish remnant that survived the exile, and also about Jerusalem. They said to me, "Those who survived the exile and are back in the province are in great trouble and disgrace. The wall of Jerusalem is broken down, and its gates have been burned with fire" (Nehemiah 1:2*b*,3).

Nehemiah felt the need of his city. No doubt he expected a better report. Zerubbabel's returning remnant had done much to rebuild the temple. Ezra had re-established worship and had led in an earlier time of spiritual renewal. But now this—broken walls, burned-up gates, and his people experiencing "great trouble and disgrace." The awful need began to penetrate Nehemiah's security of a good job and a nice home. The need has to come close to us personally before we'll do much about saving a culture. We spoke of our demonized culture and its need in the earlier chapters, but we must keep fresh to the urgency each passing day.

A teenager said it well in this week's newspaper:

> I live in a well-to-do suburb in Denver. Within the last four years I have seen ten classmates die from drug overdose or suicide. Five classmates became pregnant. Dozens of my friends became addicted to cocaine. At least double that number are beer drunks. Several have told me that their parents get bombed or stoned every night. A few weeks ago, a junior high kid went on a shooting rampage and killed three people. Divorce and unemployment are so common that I am considered lucky by my peers because my parents are still married and working.[2]

This high schooler's description of the stress level felt by today's youth reveals our broken walls and burned-up gates and the great trouble and disgrace of our culture. Can we see the need?

I heard the news columnist, Cal Thomas, whom I consider to be one of America's most articulate, recently being interviewed by Dr. James Dobson on his radio broadcast. Thomas's Christian stance gives us a biblical perspective of the serious need of our day. He named the AIDS epidemic and the abortion proliferation as tragic evidences of man shaking his fist in the face of God. He cited a recent law, passed by the board of supervisors in San Francisco, called "the domestic partnership law." This law gives homosexual and heterosexual couples who are not married the right to live together and to receive the benefits from the state and city that are normally reserved for heterosexual married couples. Under this new law, insurance benefits, hospitalization coverage, and other benefits from government-supplied money for married couples will now go also to recognized homosexual partners and unmarried heterosexual couples. This is the first such ordinance in the United States, but other cities seem sure to follow. Similar national legislation may not be far behind.

The arrogance of man in flaunting his rebellion and sin before a holy God seems to know no bounds. Dr. Dobson read a copy of a 1989 proclamation that was issued from the office of the mayor of the city of Milwaukee. It says:

> WHEREAS, Milwaukee's gay/lesbian community has become a growing force in the cultural and political life of this city, and
>
> WHEREAS, Milwaukee's gay/lesbian community will come together during the period from June 16-27, 1989, to celebrate Milwaukee's gay/lesbian pride week, and
>
> WHEREAS, the theme of this year's gay/lesbian pride week is "Stonewall 20, a generation of pride,"
>
> NOW THEREFORE, I, John O. Norquist, mayor of the city of Milwaukee, do hereby proclaim the period from June 16-27, 1989, to be Milwaukee gay/lesbian pride week throughout the entire city of Milwaukee. We are proud of who you are.
>
> Signed—John O. Norquist, Mayor

Cal Thomas stated that if this mayor had tried to put out a proclamation for a day of "fasting, humiliation and prayer" as Abraham Lincoln did in 1863, he immediately would have been in court answering charges of violating church-state separation.

Broken walls, burned-up gates, people in great trouble and disgrace. That's what sin is doing. This is how it is. If it's to change, someone has to care. Someone has to see the need. We live in a culture of broken, broken walls. Many in Nehemiah's day saw the need only on a superficial level. Nehemiah's brother and the other men could see the need in a "wring your hands in despair" kind of mode. They could recite the problem in graphic details, but apparently the need did not touch them personally like it did Nehemiah. He saw it. He felt it. Broken walls, burned-up gates, and people in great trouble and disgrace moved him to prayer. The saving of a culture, even a demonized culture, is in the wind when that happens.

3. Prayer that saves a culture will focus upon the greatness of God.

> Then I said: O LORD, God of heaven, the great and awesome God, who keeps his covenant of love with those who love him and obey his commands, let your ear be attentive and your eyes open to hear the prayer your servant is praying before you (Nehemiah 1:5,6).

Nehemiah had a high view of God. During his four months of prayer for the saving of a city, I'm sure he must have lingered long and often at this point of worship. That's what prayer is meant to accomplish in each of our lives. Worship is our highest calling. Nehemiah worshiped the Lord. Worship is loving God. It's recognizing His majesty. It's seeing Him as Jehovah, the God of heaven. Worship is bowing before "the great and awesome God" and staying there long enough to glorify Him, to marvel over who He is and what He does.

In *Don't Just Stand There, Pray Something,* Ronald Dunn asks, "Why does God delight in answering prayer? Why does Jesus commit Himself to act when we ask?" Then he answers his own question:

> That the Father may be glorified in the Son (John 14:13). . . . Here is the supreme motive of all praying. . . . not that we get what we ask for, but that God is glorified in our getting it.[3]

People who have God's vision to save a culture, to see revival come, are not in a hurry. They have embarked upon a venture of entering into God's sovereign will and plan. They take time to tune in to God, to know God. An important part of revival praying is just loving God. The intercessor must see that this God to whom he prays is mighty enough and sovereign enough, with sufficient knowledge, wisdom, mercy, grace and power, to turn the most hopelessly rebellious to Himself. The Old Testament prophet Daniel states well why this is so important. As he depicts the arrogant rebellion of the anti-Christ against God, he adds this closing statement:

"But the people who know their God will firmly resist [the anti-Christ]" (Daniel 11:32b). Another translation states the meaning of the text even more graphically: "But the people who know their God will display strength and take action" (NASB).

This is a prerequisite for the intercessors who help save a culture or a nation. They must *know God*. The better we know the God of heaven, the great and awesome God, the greater will be our display of strength sufficient to take action. How important to take time to seek earnestly to know God and to allow Him to reveal Himself to us.

God's Natural Attributes

Doctrinal praying has become one of life's richest experiences for me. Doctrinal praying in worship is praising God for what we're learning about who He is and what His attributes tell us about His person. Doctrinal truth about God lifted from His Word is not something to be filed away for future reference. His name and His attributes are places for extended meditation and worshipful prayer. It's when we linger over these lofty truths in prayerful worship that they become part of us. Especially is this true in extended times of private prayer. God can begin to fill us with awe about Himself. That's what He did with Nehemiah. Permit me to briefly mention an outline of God's natural attributes for your time of prayer and meditation.

A. **God is omnipotent** (Job 42:2; Jeremiah 32:27).

B. **God is omniscient** (Psalm 139:1-6).

C. **God is omnipresent** (Isaiah 57:15a, KJV; Psalm 139:7-10).

D. **God is eternal** (Lamentations 5:19, NASB).

E. **God is immutable** (Psalm 102:25-27; Hebrews 3:8).

F. **God is transcendent and beyond man's comprehension** (Isaiah 55:8,9; Romans 11:33-36).

G. **God is absolutely sovereign** (Daniel 4:34b,35).

How great are God's natural attributes. His infinite, self-existent, self-sufficient person deserves our wonder and worship. We constantly need to stretch the outer limits of our capacities to appreciate the greatness of God revealed in His natural attributes.

God's Moral Attributes

God relates with His creation through His moral attributes; His nature is expressed in His moral attributes.

A. **God is holy, righteous and just** (Psalm 89:14; Isaiah 47:4; Deuteronomy 32:4).

B. **God is loving, merciful, patient and graciously good** (Jeremiah 31:3; Romans 5:8; 9:14-16; 2 Peter 3:9; Psalm 106:1; Romans 5:20,21; Ephesians 2:8,9).

C. **God is wise, truthful and faithful** (Isaiah 40:28; Daniel 2:20-23; Titus 1:2; Deuteronomy 7:9).

D. **God is a wrathful, jealous God** (Exodus 34:6,7a; Romans 1:18; John 3:36; Exodus 34:14).

Satan is always busy manipulating us to doubt God in some way, as he did Eve. He wants us to question God's goodness or wisdom, or some other attribute of His. God's character and attributes are never to be measured by our circumstances or by the things we see over a short span. If we know God by His attributes as they are divinely revealed in His Word, we will always know that He is loving, good, kind, etc. His very nature means that He could never be anything but what His attributes make Him—a great God.

Praying What We Learn Back to God

Written prayers have great value. The Bible has many of them for our learning process. I find it of great benefit to read the prayers that I have taken the thought and time to write out. I love to memorize as many of the prayers of Scripture as I can. It's a wonderful worship time to then pray them back to God out of my own heart.

Written prayers can be of vital help in learning how to pray, but they are not a substitute for expression of prayers in our own words. They are a means of learning, developing and growing in our prayer practice. Some of you may wish to write out your own prayers.

Jesus' disciples recognized their need for help in praying:

> One day Jesus was praying in a certain place. When he finished, one of his disciples said to him, "Lord, teach us to pray, just as John taught his disciples" (Luke 11:1).

Much praying that goes on in evangelical Christianity is superficial—even shallow. I hope that doesn't sound critical or judgmental. Rather, I trust it will motivate and stimulate you to prepare yourself more fully to approach God. The unlearned, innocent, meek cry of a newborn child of God means just as much to Him as any well-thought-out prayer. Yet, if after years of being a Christian, we approach God with only neophyte understanding, that must be very sad for our loving heavenly Father. God certainly expects more from our praying as we learn more of Him. *Lord, teach us to pray!*

The publisher grants permission for the prayers in this book to be copied for convenience in usage. Credit the source of each, but remember the prayers are not to be copied for selling. Revival prayers are available in booklet form. Instructions for ordering appear in the Table of Contents.

REVIVAL PRAYER PATTERN 1
FOCUS: TEACH ME TO KNOW YOU

Loving Heavenly Father, I come before You in this time of prayer to open my heart to You about the brokenness and need I see about me. I see great needs in my own heart, in my family, among my fellow believers and in my culture, community and world. Teach me to care, and to pray about those needs as Your servant Nehemiah learned to pray. I long to honor You as the "God of heaven, the great and awesome God," whose greatness is sufficient to meet the urgent needs of this day. I long to love and worship You, Heavenly Father, as You are worthy to be worshiped. I do love You; not as perfectly as I one day will, but I do love You and worship You now. Teach me to know You. Even as I worship You this moment, grant me new insights into Your greatness and sufficiency. As I speak to You, please speak to me.

Thank You, Heavenly Father, that You are omnipotent, almighty and sovereign. I praise You that it was no threat to Your sovereign omnipotence to create Satan and all of the angels who fell, even though You foreknew they would rebel against You. Thank You also, that it was no threat to Your sovereign omnipotence to create man in Your own likeness and image, even though You knew man would fail the test and would sin. I sense comfort and assurance from such a great and awesome God who could keep it all within His sovereign oversight and controlled limits. I rejoice that even the great needs of this day are no threat to Your omnipotent power and sovereign design.

I pray for a revolutionary revival to come from Your sovereign hand and I affirm that Your omnipotence is sufficiently strong to bring it to pass. I affirm that Your omnipotent power is sufficient to humble the most hostile arrogance of man in a moment of time. I affirm that Your omnipotence is able to bring to nothing the most careful strategy and plan of Satan and his kingdom.

By faith I hold Your omniscient knowledge and Your total awareness in perspective as I pray. Thank You that there is no wickedness or sin that escapes Your knowledge. Thank You that the cross and redemptive work of our Lord Jesus Christ was sufficient to enable You to forgive the wickedness of man. I praise You that in Your omniscience You were able to apply His atoning blood to cleanse away the guilt of all my sins; none were missed. I hold Your omniscient understanding over the tragic conditions of the wicked rebellion of our age and ask You to humble us and bring us to repentance before You.

I worship You in the wonder of Your omnipresence. With the psalmist I acknowledge: "Where can I go from your Spirit? Where can I flee from your presence? If I go up to the heavens, you are there. If I make my bed in the depths you are there." Thank You that You are present wherever the dawn rises. In all of the extremities of space and in all of Your creation, You are there. Thank You that You inhabit eternity itself.

I rejoice that Your presence is as much with us in our day as it was there in the revival awakenings of history. I ask You to unveil Your presence among us. I invite You to draw near to us that we might experience the brokenness and the awareness of our sinful need that Your presence brings. I affirm that revival comes as people become broadly aware of the near presence of our Holy God. I hold Your mercy and Your grace before You as providing sufficient ground for the fulfillment of the cry of my heart.

I exalt Your unchanging perfection in all that You are; that You are the same yesterday, today and forever. Thank You that Your promises are trustworthy. I believe that if Your people unite with You in the wonder of Your person and will seek Your face in humble prayer, You will hear. I affirm my desire to turn from all my wicked ways and I cry out to You to hear from heaven, to forgive our sins and to heal our land. In Your immutable, sovereign plan, I look to You to effect all that is necessary to bring us to revival.

I exalt Your justice, Heavenly Father. I rejoice that You will one day banish all evil forever from Your presence in Your perfect plan of holy wrath. I also rejoice to see Your justice and truth displayed in loving mercy at Calvary. I acknowledge that Your holy wrath was requited by the atoning sacrifice of the Lord Jesus Christ. Thank You for being willing to place upon Your own Son the judgment that we, who have received Your grace instead, deserved. The wonder of that escapes my full capacity to understand. Yet, I know that Your justice, shown in such mercy and grace, remains at the very core of my prayer for revival. I ask for Your justice to draw near to us. I acknowledge that our culture deserves what came to Sodom, and to the earth in Noah's day. I plead rather for the justice that came at Pentecost.

Thank You that many of those same people who cried out for Christ to be crucified, cried out at Pentecost in broken repentance, "What shall we do? What shall we do?" Do it again, oh God. Judge us not with wrath as You did Sodom, but judge us with terrible conviction of sin until repentance flows down before You in rivers of tears.

You are wise and truthful, and faithful to Your Word of truth. I marvel and wonder after Your patient endurance with us. I acknowledge that I ask of You a hard thing. Thank You that You remain transcendent above all of the chaos upon this earth. I rejoice that, in the infinite greatness of Your highness and loftiness, You abide in the divine stillness of Your perfection.

I hunger and thirst for Your righteousness. I know it will necessitate a revolutionary revival for such righteousness to touch our culture in large degree, but in Your greatness, You can bring it to pass. As I worship You in Your greatness, I claim the Word of Your promise: "For this is what the high and lofty one says—he who lives forever, whose name is holy: 'I live in a high and holy place, but also with him who is contrite and lowly in spirit, to revive the spirit of the lowly and to revive the heart of the contrite' " (Isaiah 57:15). I ask that You would bring the truth of that loving promise to reality in my life and my culture. I affirm that there is sufficient merit in the name and finished work of our Lord Jesus Christ to accomplish even more than I ask. It's in His name I pray. Amen.

8

In Touch
With God's Burden

Restore our fortunes, O LORD,
    like streams in the Negev.
Those who sow in tears
    will reap with songs of joy.
He who goes out weeping,
    carrying seed to sow,
will return with songs of joy,
    carrying sheaves with him (Psalm 126:4-6).

George, a hard-driving executive and a successful businessman, was tireless in his effort toward excellence and efficiency. Employees who did not share his zeal for hard work often received fierce tongue-lashings laced with "colorful" language. Though a professing Christian, George's faith had not brought the change of life God intended. A Christian friend happened into George's office one day and overheard one of his angry tirades. George was embarrassed by this exposure, but he dismissed it as a "bad day."

A Prelude of Brokenness

The friend recognized George's spiritual need. He had fought the same problem in his own life and the Lord had set him free. He shared his concern with me and we discussed how we could help George. We both were close to him, so we proposed a weekly early morning discipleship time for the three of us to share. Prayer, Bible study and Scripture memorization would be our format. George eagerly accepted. We said nothing to him about his anger. Several weeks passed. The spiritual hunger in all our hearts and the memorization of the Word followed by the times of prayer bore good fruit in each of our lives. Some of the psalms spoke deeply to George.

Considering Psalm 19 to memorize, we read through it, each reading a few verses. George finished it, reading aloud the last three verses:

> Who can discern his errors?
>   Forgive my hidden faults.
> Keep your servant also from willful sins;
>   may they not rule over me.
> Then will I be blameless,
>   innocent of great transgression.
> May the words of my mouth and the
>   meditation of my heart
> be pleasing in your sight,
> O LORD, my Rock and my Redeemer
>   (Psalm 19:12-14).

As he read, George experienced a deep brokenness, and he began to weep. Being a strong leader, he felt some embarrassment, but we were so moved by what God was doing that we shed tears with him. We started to pray, and all went well until George's turn came. His emotions were suddenly overwhelmed. Deep, broken sobs rolled up from the depths of his being. "I'm so sorry! I'm so sorry!" was all he could pray.

Reluctantly, we eventually had to end our prayer time. As we went our separate ways, each felt deep gratitude for the Lord's special presence with us.

George went to work, but God was not finished. George was reading one of Andrew Murray's books and he'd stay at his desk with that and with his Bible most of the day. His repentance was so deep that sometimes he'd leave the office and go to the private retreat of his car. There he felt free to let his emotions flow. Humbling tears and deep sobs of repentance accompanied the transformation God was effecting within him. This process of God's grace went on for several days. God was at work, preparing a chosen vessel for an anointed ministry.

A Transformed Leader

A beautiful transformation of George's life came out of his unique encounter with God. His devotion to the Lord's work moved into high gear. In his mid-fifties, he sold his business and retired. He became a wise spiritual leader in our local church, and he prayed for enlarged service for his Lord.

Through God's sovereign working, George received an appointment on a leading evangelical mission board with more than five hundred missionaries. He has served there many years, managing retirement monies for the missionaries, and he has traveled the world, counseling and ministering to missionaries concerning their personal and field financial needs.

As we've seen, prayer that confronts Satan's rule and rescues a culture keeps in touch with God in His greatness. However, our concept of God's greatness must come from a well deeper than that of any intellectual awareness of truth. It must arise from the depths of God's own burden for His creation. It must affect our deepest feelings until we move in unity with God's will into actions that change things.

We must share in the deep burden of God's feelings. The spiritual rebuilding of burned-up gates and broken walls requires a people who can weep over the ruins. When God prepares to use someone greatly, He must first bring him to a place of personal brokenness, as He did George.

Prayer That Saves a Culture Expresses God's Burden

Nehemiah experienced a similar brokenness before the Lord. As God prepared him for the rescue of a broken culture, He let Nehemiah feel His own burden.

> When I heard these things, I sat down and wept. For some days I mourned and fasted and prayed before the God of heaven. Then I said: " . . . let your ear be attentive and your eyes open to hear the prayer your servant is praying before you day and night for your servants" (Nehemiah 1:4,6a).

The burden of the Lord produces a unique insight to feel and understand the longing love of God's heart for broken people. When we've seen the Lord Jesus, we've seen the heavenly Father too. Jesus assured us of that. The Lord Jesus Christ was emotionally affected by the blindness and brokenness of the culture of His earthly sojourn. See His broken heart as He made His triumphal entry into Jerusalem:

> As he approached Jerusalem and saw the city, he wept over it and said, "If you, even you, had only known on this day what would bring you peace—but now it is hidden from your eyes" (Luke 19:41,42).

The broken walls and hurting people of our demonized culture surely merit the tears of our Lord flowing from His burdened people.

1. Nehemiah wept. "I sat down and wept." His sorrow expressed more than compassionate, human tears. He felt the burden of his Lord. He shed the tears of God.

There are plenty of examples of superficial emotionalism around today but not many tears of God. This broken, hurting world of satanically wounded people needs such tears. God's Spirit enables intercessors to feel His burden. God earlier used Babylon to discipline His people, but He had taken no pleasure in the hurt of those He loved. At least three times in Ezekiel, God states:

> As surely as I live, declares the Sovereign LORD, I
> take no pleasure in the death of the wicked, but rather
> that they turn from their ways and live. Turn! Turn from
> your evil ways! Why will you die, O house of Israel?
> (Ezekiel 33:11; see also 18:23,32).

God weeps when He must deal with man's rebellion and rejection. God's people sharing in the emotional burden of the heart of our loving Lord is necessary to revival praying.

2. Nehemiah mourned. "For some days I mourned." He felt God's burden even more deeply. As set forth in the New Testament, this kind of mourning ties in closely to the work of the Holy Spirit.

> In the same way, the Spirit helps us in our weakness.
> We do not know what we ought to pray, but the Spirit him-
> self *intercedes for us* with groans that words cannot ex-
> press. And he who searches our hearts knows the mind of
> the Spirit, because the Spirit intercedes for the saints in
> accordance with God's will (Romans 8:26,27, emphasis
> added).

The Greek word for "groans" has a close affinity to the Hebrew word Nehemiah used for "mourn." For days Nehemiah felt the mourning, the groaning of God for the hurt of His people.

Today, most of us run from groans and mourning. If they come from a human condition and hang on "for some days," we may need our pastor or counselor, or we may even need to seek psychological help. But when the mourning is of the Lord, there is nothing wrong with letting it go on "for some days." Revival praying needs people who are willing to share God's groans for our broken world. The Holy Spirit will share His groaning burden with us if revolutionary revival is to be brought about.

3. Nehemiah fasted. "For some days I . . . fasted and prayed before the God of heaven." There was nothing limited about what God was doing in Nehemiah's heart. Fasting is a secret, private expression of longing for God to intervene.

More than he wanted the comfort of food, Nehemiah hungered for God to save His people.

A word of care needs to be interjected here. People who are thinking of fasting need to study the biblical approach to it. Proper medical consideration needs to be given as well. God's people must not harm their health through some unwise practice of this Christian discipline.[1]

On the other hand, it does have New Testament endorsement. Our Lord Jesus Christ honored the discipline, and the apostle Paul practiced it. (See Matthew 9:15; Acts 9:9; 13:2,3; 14:23; 2 Corinthians 11:27.) The broken walls as evidenced by the satanic revival in our culture warrant prayer and fasting.

4. Nehemiah prayed day and night. "Your servant is praying before you day and night for your servants." We know what it is to go without sleep to study, to pay our bills, to work, to enjoy a concert, to socialize or to file our tax return. Nehemiah went without sleep to pray. The burden of the Lord touched his tears, his feelings, his desire for food and even his desire for sleep.

When prayer takes on the deeper dimensions of God's burden, one can expect some sleepless nights. Sleep is temporarily replaced by the need to pray. Our responsibility is to yield to Him, to make ourselves available. We may even need to confess our coldness and lack of interest in these deeper levels of prayer.

Prayer That Saves a Culture Expresses Repentance of Sin

I confess the sins we Israelites, including myself and my father's house, have committed against you. We have acted very wickedly toward you. We have not obeyed the commands, decrees and laws you gave your servant Moses (Nehemiah 1:6b,7).

Not only must we weep over the rubble before we can do much to rebuild broken spiritual walls, but we must also do something about removing it. In the rubble of the broken walls of Jerusalem, there were some salvageable, usable materials. That's true of most rubble, even that of our sinful failures. Much of it just has to be removed. The hurtful damage of sin must be taken away. Yet, lessons are learned and insights are gained; humility and brokenness emerge, and God uses what He can of it to rebuild spiritual walls.

That is repentance: getting rid of useless matter so God can start to rebuild with what is left.

1. The repentance was personal. "I confess the sins we Israelites, including myself . . . committed against you." Most of us can see the failures around us, but it's quite another matter to acknowledge the wrongs within ourselves. Spiritual pride keeps them hidden. We experience true repentance when we are broken enough to weep over our own sins.

> Search me, O God, and know my heart;
>   test me and know my anxious thoughts.
> See if there is any offensive way in me,
>   and lead me in the way everlasting
>   (Psalm 139:23,24).

Revival is intensely personal. That's why its beginnings bring us such brokenness over our own sins. Carnality is rife among believers in evangelical churches, and cleansing cannot come until we acknowledge our need in repentance as Nehemiah did.

If we want revolutionary revival to come, we must clean up our act. Personal repentance must become important to us. That's the place to start.

> Surely I was sinful at birth,
>   sinful from the time my mother conceived me.
> Surely you desire truth in the inner parts;
>   you teach me wisdom in the inmost place
>   (Psalm 51:5,6).

2. The repentance had family dimensions. "I confess the sins . . . my father's house [has] committed against you." Next to ourselves we are most responsible for our families. Family sins are rampant in our culture. Neglect of family devotions, a lack of caring for one another, and wrong family entertainment are among the things that could be named. Incestuous sexual abuse has reached alarming levels and, along with physical and verbal abuse, does deadly harm within a family.

What does one do with such sin? If we harbor resentment or hatred toward those family members who violate us, we only add to the already burning fire of destruction. How can we avert the continuing damage of family sin?

I don't want to oversimplify the problem, but in the final analysis we must do what Nehemiah did. We must repent of our family's sins. Such repentance does not excuse the perpetrator for his wickedness; only his own personal repentance and acceptance of the Lord Jesus Christ as Savior and Lord can ever erase his guilt. Yet, great good can come when a violated person prays as Nehemiah did: "I confess the sins my family member committed against You."[2]

Many find liberating relief by pouring out such repentance for the hurtful wrongs family members have done to them. God is honored in the open honesty of such confession. That kind of praying by even one family member also can bring hope for more of the family to participate in the repentance. God's sovereign hand will begin to move in that family when just one person begins to deal with the family's sin.

3. The repentance was cultural. "I confess the sins we Israelites. . . have committed against you. We have acted very wickedly toward you. We have not obeyed the commands, decrees and laws you gave your servant Moses."

We have called the wickedness of our society a satanic revival that has led to a demonized culture. Where do we begin to deal with this? I commend those believers who work hard at the legal and political levels to turn the tide. Such effort has to be. It's part of our being "light" and "salt." Yet, I'm convinced we'll never really correct our cultural wickedness by marches, or by legal or political efforts. The most urgent ingredient in cultural change is what Nehemiah entered into, what I call "intercessory repentance."

The sins of our culture are a terrible affront against a holy God, and someone must begin to express repentance for them. God has already told us how He deals with cultural sins like ours when there is no repentance. He lets the sin become its own judgment.

Ask yourself these questions:

- Who will express sorrow to God for the wickedness of the rampant drug and alcohol addiction if I don't?
- Who will confess the murderous, violent tearing apart of little unborn babies in legal abortion procedures if I don't?
- Who will repent of the pornography, the vile cursing, the sexual promiscuity, the divorce scandal and all the rest of it if I don't?
- Who will repent of the ritual sacrifices and increasing openness of Satan worship if I don't?

Repentance begins with believers who care, and it is related to the weeping and groaning mentioned earlier.

If there remains only silence in our land for our cultural wickedness, we cannot expect anything but "God giving us up" to deeper and deeper levels of destructive sin. Repentance on the broad spectrum doesn't come first—deep repentance by a few believers does. Believers lay hold of God's grace and mercy in repentant intercession for their culture.

Nehemiah did that, and he included himself and his family in identifying with his culture's sins. When revival finally came to the city, the tears and repentance flowed freely from all the people. In Nehemiah 8:9, we learn that the planned celebration turned to a time of great sorrow. God was working deeply among his people, and His work would not be denied. In chapter 9, the repentance from the people rolls out like it did previously from Nehemiah.

> Those of Israelite descent had separated themselves from all foreigners. They stood in their places and confessed their sins and the wickedness of their fathers. They stood where they were and read from the Book of the Law of the LORD their God for a fourth of the day, and spent another fourth in confession and worshiping the LORD their God (Nehemiah 9:2,3).

As people draw near to God and He to them, there always follows a longing to be clean.

◇ 9 ◇

In Touch
With God's Promise

Remember the instruction you gave your servant Moses, saying, "If you are unfaithful, I will scatter you among the nations, but if you return to me and obey my commands, then even if your exiled people are at the farthest horizon, I will gather them from there and bring them to the place I have chosen as a dwelling for my Name."

They are your servants and your people, whom you redeemed by your great strength and your mighty hand (Nehemiah 1:8-10).

This prayer reveals that Nehemiah had searched the Scriptures during his four-month pilgrimage. He synthesizes truth from numerous parts of the Old Testament Pentateuch, the psalms and the writings of the prophets. Some feel his words of prayer reveal his studies in Deuteronomy 30, Psalms 106 and 107, and perhaps some of the prophetic writings of both Isaiah and Jeremiah.

Effective prayer is always in close harmony with everything God reveals in His Word about His will and plan. Nehemiah's prayer was within that harmony.

Prayer That Saves a Culture Appropriates God's Promises

Praying God's Word back to Him pleases God and is powerfully effective. Moses shares with us a telling illustration of the power of such prayer. He was up on the mountain receiving the Law from God when Aaron and the people sinned by setting up a golden calf as the god who had brought them up out of Egypt. Animal sacrifices to this idol and celebrating through sexual orgy were all part of their great sin. God's anger was aroused to the point of severe judgment.

> "I have seen these people," the LORD said to Moses, "and they are a stiff-necked people. Now leave me alone, so that my anger may burn against them, and that I may destroy them. Then I will make you into a great nation" (Exodus 32:9,10).

Moses' response illustrates the kind of praying necessary to bring a revolutionary revival to our day:

> But Moses sought the favor of the LORD his God. "O LORD," he said, "why should your anger burn against your people, whom you brought out of Egypt with great power and a mighty hand? Why should the Egyptians say, 'It was with evil intent that he brought them out, to kill them in the mountains and to wipe them off the face of the earth'? Turn from your fierce anger; relent and do not bring disaster on your people. Remember your servants Abraham, Isaac and Israel, to whom you swore by your own self: 'I will make your descendants as numerous as the stars in the sky and I will give your descendants all this land I promised them, and it will be their inheritance forever.' " Then the LORD relented and did not bring on his people the disaster he had threatened (Exodus 32:11-14).

This is what I call "doctrinal praying." Moses pleaded the promises God had made to Abraham, Isaac and Jacob back to God. Though God was exceedingly displeased with Aaron and the people, Moses appropriated the valid ground that touched God's mercy and grace. That mercy and grace is not based upon our emotional desires or finite reasoning; rather, it flows from who God is and what He has revealed about Himself.

God never brings revival because we deserve it. God brings revival because we understand His promises, claim them, and persistently keep them before Him as we wait upon Him.

What unique promise from God will lead His intercessors to claim revival awakening in our day? I do not know. Since the conditions of the church today are so much like those of the Laodicean church described in Revelation 3, I think we might find the promise in verses 17-20. We have to confess our spiritual pride, our rich materialism and our self-satisfied complacency. We have to acknowledge truthfully that we are "wretched, pitiful, poor, blind and naked," and that we are powerless to do anything about it. In faith we need to buy from our Lord Jesus Christ His gold refined in the fire, His white clothes to cover our nakedness, and His eye salve to remove our spiritual blindness. We need to plead the truth of His knocking at the door of His church and of our personal lives. We need to claim His promise that when we open the door He will come in with a revolutionary revival of His presence.

"Oh, dear Lord Jesus Christ, do come to Your church in mighty revival awakening."

Prayer That Saves a Culture Enlarges in Expectancy

"O LORD, let your ear be attentive to the prayer of
this your servant and to the prayers of your servants who
delight in revering your name. Give your servant success
today by granting him favor in the presence of this man." I
was cupbearer to the king (Nehemiah 1:11).

As we pray, faith and expectancy build. For us, it might take longer than four months. For the expectancy of God's people to build to the level of boldness that Nehemiah displays, we need a period of time. Read Nehemiah 2:1-10 to see the magnitude of his expectations. Let this list of what Nehemiah was looking for encourage you to ask God to build faith in your own heart.

1. He expected God to sovereignly touch the Persian king, Artaxerxes Longimanus, so that despite the king's heathen outlook, he would look with favor upon Nehemiah's request (1:11).

2. Despite his lowly position as a cupbearer, Nehemiah trusted God to use his unconcealable grief and his despondency to prepare the king for a good decision (2:1,2).

3. He was bold enough to share with the king his broken-hearted concern for the conquered city of his forefathers (verse 3).

4. He expected the king to put him in charge of an expedition to return to Jerusalem to rebuild and fortify it (verses 4,5).

5. He expected God to motivate Artaxerxes to supply him with safe conduct letters, materials with which to build, and all the other things he would need for such a giant undertaking (verses 6-8).

6. He expected to be successful in rebuilding walls, rehanging gates and re-establishing a valid government, despite all the enemies and hazards that Satan could throw at him (verses 9,10).

To believe God for revolutionary revival in our nation is a challenge equal to the one Nehemiah met by showing his expectant faith. From a human perspective, there is much against revolutionary revival ever happening. Evil has put its foundations deep and is on a bold revival march of its own. The church, ridiculed and even ignored by most people, seems unable to rise to the challenge. This noble body looks insipid and weak to its critics. The "shakers and movers" of our day have given up on the church—and for good cause.

Media notoriety has made a mockery of some well-known Christian leaders. Prayer meetings in the churches flounder in attendance. Many mainline denominational churches are pulling back in certain areas of ministry. Attendance is dropping and funds are shrinking. Where will we find an expectant faith like that of Nehemiah? Where can we turn for hope and help?

Faith That Rests Upon Facts

Faith that is not established on the absolutes of God's Word is not faith at all. Some things we call biblical faith are merely emotional desire, presumption or pure conjecture. Some things wrongly called faith are superstition or even occultic manipulation.

Faith that God honors always rests solely on the correct application of the promises of His Word.

> Consequently, faith comes from hearing the message, and the message is heard through the word of Christ (Romans 10:17).
> Now faith is being sure of what we hope for and certain of what we do not see. This is what the ancients were commended for (Hebrews 11:1,2).

Each of the many illustrations of faith given in Hebrews 11 is directly traceable to the foundational promises that God has given.

Nehemiah's confidence in what God would do had biblical foundation as well. He didn't act on the basis of some sentimental desire to see his homeland restored, nor was he impressed in his mind that the king would fulfill his dream because of his and the king's close association. It was much deeper than any human conjecture. There was no probability at all from man's reason that his plans would ever succeed. His faith was in God's Word and in God's Word alone.

Faith must always rest upon our knowledge of God's purpose and will as revealed in His Word. Sometimes people feel they have gotten some special promise from God in an experience or through a "prophecy" or "word of knowledge." Such "special revelations" must be viewed with a critical eye. If the "promise" cannot be supported from God's written revelation, we'd best discard it quickly and put no faith in it.

Some seem to feel that if they believe hard enough, and if they maintain a positive viewpoint, they can manipulate God and make miraculous things happen. Faith is not a human exercise in striving to believe. Rather, it is based upon a surety that one is praying in harmony with God's will and plan.

A Faith That Doesn't Quit

Faith that rests on biblical fact doesn't back away when evidence and adversity says that what we're asking cannot happen. It digs in at such times and remains quietly confident and aggressively active. Peter spoke of this truth in these words:

> In this you greatly rejoice, though now for a little
> while you may have had to suffer grief in all kinds of trials.
> These have come so that your faith — of greater worth than
> gold, which perishes even though refined by fire — may be
> proved genuine and may result in praise, glory and honor
> when Jesus Christ is revealed (1 Peter 1:6,7).

This is such an important truth to remember as we pray for revolutionary revival. That for which we pray is such an affront to Satan that he will deluge us with obstacles, disappointments and difficulties of every kind. The obstacles will seem to say, "No revival for you. Things are only getting worse." We must know that faith has no root in the appearance of things. If revival is to come, it can only be because it's all of God, and it's all of grace.

God must remain in charge. Faith rests in knowing God and letting Him be God. It doesn't retreat and quit when nothing seems to be happening.

> His divine power has given us everything we need for
> life and godliness through our knowledge of him who

called us by his own glory and goodness. Through these he has given us his *very great and precious promises, so that through them you may participate* in the divine nature and escape the corruption in the world caused by evil desires (2 Peter 1:3,4, emphasis added).

With the psalmist we can say:

> Though an army beseige me,
>   my heart will not fear;
> though war break out against me,
>   even then will I be confident. . . .
> I am still confident of this:
>   I will see the goodness of the LORD
>   in the land of the living.
> Wait for the LORD;
>   be strong and take heart
>   and wait for the LORD (Psalm 27:3,13,14).

REVIVAL PRAYER PATTERN 2
FOCUS: REPENTANCE AND INTERCESSION

Loving Heavenly Father, I come again to worship You in the wonder of who You are. I approach You in the merit and worthiness of our Lord Jesus Christ. I open my whole being to the controlling work of Your Holy Spirit. I invite Him to express His interceding, His groaning through my prayers in the ways that He may choose. I yield to You, Heavenly Father, all of the faculties and capacities You have placed within me to be used for Your glory. I open my mind, will and emotions to You that You might share with me Your burden for the church and for the lost around me.

I rejoice that my Lord Jesus Christ could weep over the people of Jerusalem as they passed up His presence and His caring love for them. Cleanse me of the coldness and indifference that keeps me from shedding tears for the rebellious sin of today. Share with me His tears. Allow me to feel the mourning of Your Spirit's groaning for my broken world. Grant me Your divine intervention expressing in me a willingness to fast and to spend time in extended sessions of prayer. Help me see those times when I awaken in the night as opportunities to cry to You for a revolutionary revival to visit Your church. What I pray for myself I pray also for a large number of other believers whom You are calling to a deeper prayer burden.

I confess my sins to You, dear Heavenly Father. Wash me clean in my Savior's precious blood from all that offends You. I recognize within my person a fleshly nature that can be rebellious in Your sight. Thank You for informing me of this fact in Your Word. I affirm that in my union with Christ in His death I am dead to the rule of that fleshly nature. I desire the new nature You effected within me to be in charge through the power of my Savior's resurrection. Thank You for having made this new creation in righteousness and true holiness, so I can love You deeply and serve You fully. May Your Holy Spirit enable me to manifest before You and others the fruit of His full control. In the name of the Lord Jesus Christ, I bind Satan and his host from interjecting any interference in my prayer.

I bring to You, Heavenly Father, the sins of my family, the church, and the culture in which I live. What great wickedness takes place in our homes. Thank You that it's not hidden from You. I repent of it for my family, other Christian families and non-Christian families. You established the home, and it's very dear to You. Forgive us for the way we too often talk to each other in anger and unkindness. How broken You must be over the physical, verbal and sexual abuse that is too much a part of the families in our culture. I not only confess this wickedness but I ask You to intervene and change it by Your mighty power. Show us our sins and grant us the grace of repentance.

I recognize that the sins of our nation and culture are an abomination in Your eyes. I repent for our culture of the terrible abuse of our sexuality. The misuse of this God-given gift is a curse upon our times. I apologize to You, Heavenly Father, for the abomination of pornography and the wide audience that makes it profitable. Turn our hearts from this perversion. You intended that our sexual desires should glorify Your name within the bonds of marriage. May this take place in our culture.

I repent before You, loving God, for the violence against innocent people that has invaded our culture. My heart grieves as Yours surely does for those millions of unborn babies that have been destroyed by legalized abortions. I repent for our legislators and court judges, and for the people who let it go on. Forgive and change the violence displayed in the entertainment media, in the inner city, and in the drug scene. I apologize for the burgeoning market for drugs and other intoxicants. My heart grieves for the cursing and vile talk that streams forth from people's mouths.

I see spreading through our culture a plague of fascination with the spirit realm of darkness. It poisons our little children in the themes of their toys, games and cartoons. It permeates our entertainment media. It subtly is becoming a part of the business and educational world through various "New Age" themes. A growing host of people are so deceived that they are worshiping Satan with animal and even human sacrifices. How terribly this dishonors You, O Lord. I cry out against it in prayer and I repent for them of this awful wickedness. I ask You to bring a revival awakening so intense that these things will be crushed by Your omnipotent power.

Forgive us for all our wickedness, O God. The sin of our land is so great. Religious sins of unbelief, legalism and self-righteous pride abound. Greed, covetousness, gluttony, gossip and spiritual indifference are almost as common to believers as to the lost. We desperately need a holy revival from You to confront our sins and bring us to humble repentance and spiritual renewal.

My hope, Heavenly Father, is in the promises of Your Word. Thank You for Your compassion for us in our sinful ways. In our arrogant lifestyle, we say to you, "I am rich; I have acquired wealth and do not need a thing." I repent of that! I confess that, as believers, we show our wretched, pitiful, poor, blind and naked condition. I accept that analysis by my Lord Jesus Christ as applying to me and my fellow believers.

Thank You that our Lord Jesus Christ has invited us to come and buy from Him gold refined in His disciplining fires. I want that gold for me and for Your church. I ask for the white clothes that my Lord Jesus Christ promised would cover our nakedness. Anoint our eyes with the eye salve that enables us to see things as our Lord Jesus Christ sees them. I open the door of my life to my Lord Jesus Christ. I invite Him to come to me, to the church and to our day giving us a mighty sense of His holy presence. May His nearness break us over our sins until we flee to the cross for cleansing by His blood. May this revival for which I pray bring to saving faith multitudes who are not yet in our Savior's fold. Heavenly Father, move everything out of the way that hinders the coming of revival. Cause revival to affect churches, legislators, courts, business, education, government and all that is before You. Will You not revive us again?

I lay all of this before You, Heavenly Father, basing every request on the merit and worthiness of our Lord Jesus Christ alone, and His finished work. I ask that You build a faith within me and countless other believers that is growing and contagious, and that rests totally upon Your will and plan for us in this day and upon the foundation of Your Word and the finished work of our Lord Jesus Christ. Amen.

◇ PART III ◇

Defeating the Powers of Darkness

◇ 10 ◇

Making It Happen

Revivals usually begin with only a few people. In the two previous chapters, we saw the saving of Jerusalem begin with the prayers of Nehemiah and of the few who were burdened with him. They experienced revival in their own lives first, and the movement could have stopped there. But to be widely effective, revival movements must reach out.

The satanic revival sweeping through our culture is alarmingly pervasive. A resurgence of devil worship has exploded in virtually every region of our country. Small-town communities are as affected as the poverty-plagued, gang-active ghetto areas of our great cities. Occultic activity reaches into areas of society we might never suspect. A high-ranking former satanist states that the "traditional satanists" have targeted four major areas of society for infiltration: the judicial, the legislative, the entertainment media, and the educational systems. Today's occultists include medical doctors, court justices, schoolteachers, lawyers, business people, government officials, military people and even pastors.

This satanic revival is so widespread that a spiritual revival of mass dimensions will be necessary to turn it around. God's people must understand God's methods of breaking the bonds of satanic power. The initiators God uses to catch the vision must be joined by large groups of believers who become alerted and are drawn in to what God is doing.

One thing believers must realize in today's threatening crises is that even though a person has a deep burden for revival and divine intervention, he must be careful not to try to carry that burden alone. Satan's subtle assaults would soon cause him to crumble. There is a better way.

It is fascinating to note how the revolutionary revival movement of Nehemiah's day involved the people of the entire city. Excitement and commitment built until they were all participating.

In more recent years God has granted other revival awakenings in diverse places, keeping an example before His people of what revivals can do. They encourage us. They also bear testimony that we must have a broad base of those who enter into the burden in order for revolutionary revival to visit our whole culture.

The Holy Spirit can arouse people to involvement. His powerful force is able to speak individually to those who belong to Him and who must be awakened to join the cause. If the Lord's people in our nation unite to seek His intervention, God will visit us with the greatest revival the world has known. The very gates of hell are no obstacle when Christ wills to build His church! (Matthew 16:18)

Let's take a brief look at a revival that took place not too long ago at a college here in America, and then we will discuss how to bring revival to where you are.

The Asbury Revival

Revival awakening flowed through several college campuses in 1970, beginning at Asbury, a Christian liberal arts college and seminary of Methodist roots in Wilmore, Kentucky, a town near Lexington. A small group of students began getting up thirty minutes early each day to gather for Scripture reading and prayer in search of a new touch from God. God granted meaningful experiences to those involved in this new discipline, and word of it spread through the student body. Group meetings to pray for spiritual awakening became common for both faculty and students.

On February 3, about a thousand students made their way to the 10 A.M. chapel service. The casual chatter as the students entered was accompanied by an air of unusual expectancy. The dean of the college, scheduled to be the speaker at the chapel service, laid aside his planned message and began to share with the students some of his personal experiences with God. A holy hush settled upon the audience. When the dean invited the students to share what God was doing in their hearts, they responded instantly and extensively. Immediately, a number of them were on their feet, giving fervent testimonies that reflected God's inner heart searchings. Tears of concern and repentance began to flow. The typical clichés common to many testimony services were absent. Intense, contagious sincerity characterized humility and brokenness before the Lord. Robert Coleman reports, "Everyone sensed that something unusual was happening. God seemed very near."[1]

As the allotted time for chapel ended, one of the professors made his way to the platform. He invited any student who desired to pray to come to the altar. The student body began to sing "Just as I am, without one plea . . . " and the response was instant and massive. The presence of God became so real that all other interests seemed suddenly unimportant. The bell sounded for classes to begin, but no one left the chapel. Faculty and students alike realized God was at work. Students lined up to share testimonies. Confessions were made. Old hostilities between individuals melted away. God's presence and love immersed them all. At lunch time the dining hall remained empty. Spiritual hunger supplanted physical hunger.

Classes were suspended indefinitely. Prayer, testimonies, music and Bible readings became a continuing part of the spontaneous participation. Some left the marathon service at the dinner hour, but shortly the auditorium began to fill again. At times, its 1550 seating capacity was not suffi-cient. Word spread to the nearby seminary and to the townspeople concerning what was happening. People stood along the walls and crowded into the aisles and doorways. Everyone wanted to be a part of what God was doing.

The 450 seminary students were so challenged by God's visitation at the college that they entered into an all-night campus prayer meeting. The next morning the planned ser-vice of seminary chapel hymn-singing was changed. One stu-dent stood to relate how the college revival had affected him, and spontaneously, others began to move to the front and kneel at the altar in prayer. Students and faculty members formed in line at the pulpit, awaiting their turn to give tes-timony or relate spiritual needs.

The seminary and college merged into united meetings, and smaller group prayer meetings spilled over everywhere. Classrooms were often filled with intercessors and seekers. Local churches and townspeople were drawn in and began to participate. The chapel meeting was continuous. Even at 3 A.M. two or three hundred people would still be meeting for testimony, prayer, Scripture reading and singing. For an en-tire week, 185 continuous hours, the auditorium was wholly or partially filled with worshipers.

Numerous other colleges were touched as well. Henry C. James, the director of publicity at Asbury Theological Semi-nary, stated that at least 130 colleges, seminaries and Bible schools across the world were affected by what happened at Asbury. Colleges like Azusa Pacific College in California and Greenville College in Greenville, Illinois, had revival awaken-ings. Southwestern Baptist Theological Seminary in Fort Worth, Texas, experienced an awakening on their campus.

Those who participated in the overflow of the Asbury revival will never forget that unusual visit of God's grace.

Accounts of recent revival awakenings are encouraging. They provide a taste that motivates God's people to desire more. Yet, so *much* more is needed. Hunger for God's intervention must come to the Christian people of *every* community, town and city. When that happens, a continent-wide revival will be possible. But where do we start?

People Involvement in Awakenings

First, we must ask the question: How does a broad base of people involvement in revival awakening happen? Here are some of the answers.

1. God's sovereign intervention prepares people.

The enemy is using his broad base of "people power" to keep his revival of evil spreading at a phenomenal rate. His success is beyond human challenge. So what is our response?

"But God . . . " Those two words have sparked every revival that has ever happened. *God* initiates and authors His powerful intervention. His sovereign grace brings revival.

Nehemiah knew this truth before he left the Persian capital. "And because the gracious hand of my God was upon me, the king granted my requests" (Nehemiah 2:8*b*).

God had prepared Nehemiah's heart well. As he journeyed toward Jerusalem, he knew he faced an awesome task. Obstacles too great for any human solution faced him. He knew the remaining Jews were a demoralized people. He also knew his foes would never permit walls to be rebuilt, gates rehung or a Jewish government reintroduced to Jerusalem. As he viewed the enormity of his task, his dependence upon his God kept deepening. Prayer was constant in his life: "The king said to me, 'what is it you want?' Then I prayed to the God of heaven, and answered the king" (Nehemiah 2:4,5*a*).

After Nehemiah arrived in Jerusalem, his dependence upon the Lord increased. For three days he simply waited, observed, and doubtlessly prayed. Only God could move the people to believe with him that the city would be restored.

The core of students at Asbury who dedicated them-selves to prayer brought God's intervention to their campus and the surrounding community.

As I write, I wonder: Who will join me concerning revival awakening for our nation?

The people are there. Evangelical Christians are everywhere. Yet we seem demoralized, passive and almost in-different. Some wish revival would happen but the desire for personal involvement is missing. Disillusionment with Chris-tian movements abounds. Contentment with the status quo characterizes the average evangelical church. How will the church, the sleeping giant of spiritual power, awaken to the challenge for revolutionary revival? Sovereign, merciful grace from the hand of God will make it happen.

2. Testimony and timing bring people involvement.

> I set out during the night with a few men. I had
> not told anyone what God had put in my heart to do for
> Jerusalem. There were no mounts with me except the one
> I was riding (Nehemiah 2:12).

The right timing is necessary to inspire people involve-ment. One can imagine the curiosity that was aroused when this Jewish dignitary with royal credentials rode into the city. The priests, nobles and officials of the Jewish remnant were abuzz with speculation. Why had he come? What was he doing? For three days Nehemiah kept quiet. The seeds of curiosity were allowed to grow and permeate the culture while he waited upon God, observed everything, and listened attentively. He was creating a readiness for people to hear what he had to say.

At the end of the three days, under the cover of dark-ness, Nehemiah quietly slipped out of Jerusalem through the Valley Gate. A few trusted men joined him as he surveyed the ruins. He was intent on allowing the magnitude of the broken walls to fully impress these men. The rubble was so extensive he was forced to dismount and walk over the ruins.

Rebuilding could not be done without enlisting all the people. As Nehemiah retraced his steps, a burning awareness captured his heart. God must stir His people to action! God would do it!

In the meantime, curiosity had done its work. The officials didn't know where or why he'd gone but they knew he'd left the city. As their curiosity reached a fever pitch, Nehemiah called together all of those "who would be doing the work" (Nehemiah 2:16b). His timing was perfect. The people were ready to listen to God's plan. Nehemiah told of the miracle of his coming and God's provisions. "I also told them about the gracious hand of my God upon me and what the king had said to me" (Nehemiah 2:18a).

That must have been a great meeting. A quick, decisive response came from the people. "They replied, 'Let us start rebuilding.' So they began this good work" (Nehemiah 2:18b).

Such a gigantic undertaking demanded that planning, organization and administrative responsibility be worked out. It was a part of the beginning of "this good work." Nehemiah 3 unveils that the procedure was made possible because the people were behind it. The motivation through Nehemiah's testimony and the timing had captured the people. They were ready for the challenge. As God graciously moves us toward a revival awakening, I'm confident this same process of people involvement will emerge.

3. Personal interest keeps people involved.

Some reoccurring phrases in Nehemiah 3 reveal how people involvement was kept at such a high level. The chapter begins with, "Eliashib the high priest and his fellow priests went to work and rebuilt the Sheep Gate. They dedicated it and set its doors in place" (verse 1a). The Sheep Gate was the gate through which the sacrificial sheep were brought to the rebuilt temple. Not only did the priests administer the sacrificial system, but most of them would also live near the temple. Their personal interest gave them intensity of involvement.

Verse 10 states, "Jedaiah, son of Harumaph, made repairs *opposite his house*" (verse 10, emphasis added). A major consideration of where a person would work began to emerge. Similar statements occur at least ten times in the chapter. Phrases like "for his district" (verse 17), "in front of their house" (verse 23), "beside his house" (verse 23*b*), and "opposite his living quarters" (verse 30), all tell a vital story. Should fierce opposition rise up, weak-hearted dedication might quickly retreat. Yet, when the threat was close to home, love and devotion would demand that they stay.

This principle has special application to revival effort. Before believers will be motivated, they must be touched personally with the crying need for revival. As we look around, the awareness of that need comes closer and closer. We even see it in our homes: Drugs or alcohol are causing problems, we experience divorce or unwanted pregnancy, we are victims of rape or robbery, a child in our family has been abused, or a family member is drawn into pornography, or . . . you fill in the blank.

We can no longer say it's someone else's problem. The satanic revival is my problem! It's your problem! Awareness is building. Everywhere I go, I find more and more people are alarmed. I hope it means we are ready to get involved.

4. Encouragement keeps the involvement level high.

Saving a city, a nation or a culture never comes easy. Revival requires time, hard work, patience and an overflow of steady confidence. Nehemiah 4 tells us that some of the people grew fainthearted. The threats of the enemy got louder, the people were intimidated, and they spread alarm (verse 12). Nehemiah responded with tactful encouragement. He posted them "by families, with their swords, spears and bows" (verse 13*b*). He then walked among them saying:

Don't be afraid of them. Remember the LORD, who is great and awesome, and fight for your brothers, your sons and your daughters, your wives and your homes (verse 14).

The work is extensive and spread out, and we are widely separated from each other along the wall. Wherever you hear the sound of the trumpet, join us there. Our God will fight for us! (verses 19,20)

We must have no misgivings about our need for constant encouragement. As God's people rise up with the repentance necessary to bring revolutionary revival, the opposition will be fierce. As believers exercise faith to clear away the rubble of sin and rebuild walls of spiritual integrity, all hell will be threatened by what we do. The satanic revival will not take such a threat lying down.

We will have to be encouraged time and again to "remember the LORD, who is great and awesome," and to know that "Our God will fight for us!" We will need to remember that our brothers, sons, daughters, wives and homes are worth defending from such assault.

A Place to Begin

About now you may be asking, "How can I get involved to bring revolutionary revival?" A culture-wide, revolutionary revival necessitates extremely broad involvement of God's people, but that starts one person at a time. Some simple guidelines will help you.

1. Start close to home.

Involvement begins with you. Set aside at least a weekly time when, in the privacy of your own devotional life, you begin to pray for revolutionary revival to come to your heart, your family, your church, your city, your nation and your world. We will never believe God for revival on a large scale until we can believe Him in the smaller dimensions. Ask God to raise up more intercessors to pray for revival.

2. Be open to enlarging your circle.

Everyone interested in revival should desire and expect to find at least one other person with whom he can pray regularly. Schedule your prayer times with discipline. When your prayer group grows to three or four, start another. It's better to increase the number of groups than to grow too large. Distractions multiply as numbers grow.

3. Keep your format simple.

Read some Scripture and begin to pray. The seven suggested prayer patterns for revival presented in this book may help you. Those who can set aside a daily time can use a different one each day. Begin to pray them back to God with a planned dedication. Make them yours, or let them be a creative beginning for writing out your own prayer petitions.

The suggested prayers in this book can be particularly helpful in group prayer. Each person could pray a different prayer when you meet, adding your own intercessions as you pray. Alternating paragraphs between those praying helps you concentrate on the subject at hand. Learning to pray doctrinally honors God and focuses His power against evil.

4. Read good books on revival awakenings.

Intercessors are motivated by keeping the testimonies of past revivals constantly in focus. A suggested bibliography on revivals has been supplied by Richard Owen Roberts in his excellent book, *Revival*. His incisive comments on many of the books will help you determine your preference.

5. Seek a community-wide revival prayer focus.

Ask the Lord to enable you to be a part of an inter-denominational revival prayer focus for your area. It's important that this gathering not become just another planning group for a program, crusade or organized evangelistic effort. Revival requires God's people to humble themselves, seek

God's face and wait upon Him. God's timing and God's plan will always be made known to those who trust Him.

6. Wait and watch with expectancy.

Patience, perseverance and faithfulness are the most vital ingredients for those interceding for revival.

> Wait for the LORD;
>   be strong and take heart
>   and wait for the LORD (Psalm 27:14).

Believing God for revival requires an expectant, anticipating heart. Ask God to give you such expectancy and thank Him for the work He's about to do.

REVIVAL PRAYER PATTERN 3
FOCUS: REVIVAL PRAYER GROUPS

Loving Heavenly Father, I worship You as the God who loves people. You have declared in Your Word that You are patient with people, not wanting anyone to perish, and you have provided opportunity for everyone to come to repentance. Thank You for Your patience that brought me to saving faith in the Lord Jesus Christ. I praise You, Heavenly Father, for demonstrating Your love by having the Lord Jesus Christ die for ungodly people while we were still in our sins. It is wonderful to know that You have loved humanity with such outreaching sacrifice that provides forgiveness and eternal life for all who will believe. Thank You, Lord Jesus Christ, for praying for those who would believe in You. Thank You for the other sheep that You must bring to Yourself.

I pray with You, dear Savior, for those other sheep that You must bring. Multitudes are bound by sin and Satan, and I ask forgiveness for me and for other believers who have cared so little for those perishing people. I acknowledge that the same sinful culture that blinds and binds the lost has made my heart cold and apathetic. Please forgive

me. Grant me a burden for the lost around me. I pray for
(*name* persons you care for who are lost.) In the name of
the Lord Jesus Christ, I tear down the blindness Satan is
putting upon _____. I pray You will bring these dear
ones to saving faith in our Lord Jesus Christ.

Thank You, Father in heaven, for the revival awakenings of history. I praise You for giving revival blessings in
various places even in recent years. Thank You for opening
my eyes to see the need for a revolutionary revival from
Your omnipotent hands that will glorify You, startle the
world, and bring multitudes into saving faith. I ask You to
grant me a burden for such a revival. Help me to believe
that it can come to my city. I humbly offer myself as an intercessor for such an awakening. Lead me to at least one
other person with whom I can pray regularly for its coming. I ask You to raise up revival prayer groups in every
city, town, suburb and rural area of our nation. I ask You
to build a broad base of people nationwide who are expecting revival. Grant to each group a consuming burden for
You to bring revival. Make the involvement of people broad
enough so that when You sovereignly know we are ready,
You will visit us with Your holy presence. Your promise is
that, as we seek to draw near to You, You will draw near to
us. I pray this nearness will truly be revolutionary. Make it
humble us, break us, revive us and change the direction of
our disintegrating culture.

We desperately need a movement of Your mighty grace
that will transform the lives of multitudes of people. Move
our culture back to the absolutes of a Judeo-Christian
ethic. Grant to us a legal system with courts who fear God
and establish justice. Invade our penal system with such
regeneration and reform that our jails will gradually empty
until we wonder what to do with the unoccupied buildings.

I ask for such a transformation of our educational system that the humanistic, atheistic trends of our day will be
completely reversed. I pray this revival will touch every
political leader, every business enterprise, and every person
in the mass media and entertainment industry. May revival
clean up the music industry. I ask that the poverty,
drunkenness, drugs, immorality and violence so common to

our inner cities be overwhelmed by the transformed lives of regenerated people who live there. Bring the pornography industry to its knees through the repentance of the producers and consumers. Melt the divorce scandal away into nothingness because of the righteous, forgiving, encouraging lives of families made right with You.

The need for revolutionary revival in the churches, Lord Jesus Christ, is perhaps the greatest need of all. I invite You to walk among us who are believers and expose our sins as You see them. Grant to Your church a thoroughly repentant spirit where jealousies, suspicions and competiveness evaporate in the abundance of joy that revival brings. I ask that every denomination and church that honors You and proclaims Your Word will so overflow with people that petty differences will disappear and worship that honors You will be established in the land. Enable the people to enjoy their preference of worship style in the fullness of Your Spirit.

Loving Heavenly Father, we are people with needs far greater than we understand. Come in the fullness and power of Your Holy Spirit and minister to them all. I open my life to You. Take every part of me and do with me whatever You know needs to be done. I hold back nothing from You. I believe there is sufficient grace supplied in the person and work of Christ to do far more than I have even begun to ask. I acknowledge that the Holy Spirit is mighty enough to humble a whole world with conviction of sin and the exalting of righteousness. I acknowledge, Almighty God, that You can quickly bring a world to judgment, or to revival. In the name of my Lord Jesus Christ, I plead for revolutionary revival to sweep over us like a fire that cannot be quenched. Amen.

Protecting the Participants

> Our struggle is not against flesh and blood, but against the rulers, against the authorities, against the powers of this dark world and against the spiritual forces of evil in the heavenly realms (Ephesians 6:12).
>
> Be self-controlled and alert. Your enemy the devil prowls around like a roaring lion looking for someone to devour. Resist him, standing firm in the faith, because you know that your brothers throughout the world are undergoing the same kind of sufferings (1 Peter 5:8,9).

"Pastor Bubeck, I just had to call you. I've been a pastor here for seven years. Your counsel helped me about three years ago when I called about my own spiritual warfare problem. Practicing the warfare principles you taught me has freed me from the problem with pornography and immoral thoughts. I have victory over that, but now I'm facing something else that baffles me. In fact, my wife and I are both frightened. It's our 8-year-old boy!"

He paused in his effort to hold back the tears. Then he said, "He hears voices. Whenever he's around little girls or women these voices tell him to do immoral things. He's so tormented it's about to destroy him—and us. Can you help?"

The words the voices were using were vile, and the pastor said, "Our boy has lived a sheltered life. He couldn't think those things up himself."

This pastor called me just as I began writing this very chapter. Since writing my books on the believer's warfare, I have received frequent calls like this and an increasing number come from pastors. It's fresh evidence of the battle. They face family problems or church-related problems that point directly to Satan's work.

The Fierce Battle

Unseen "spiritual forces of evil in the heavenly realms" come at us in strong challenge. The fierce battle between light and darkness is heating up. The more bold the sin of our culture becomes, the more arrogant and bold is the enemy's intrusion.

The battle started in the Garden of Eden and has plagued humanity ever since. At certain times, though, it becomes more obvious and fierce. A sinful culture filled with immorality, occultism, violence and drug addiction arouses the Christians, and the battle intensifies because any move toward a spiritual revival threatens Satan's kingdom.

Nehemiah found the battle heating up as he proceeded with God's plans for rebuilding the walls, rehanging the gates and re-establishing a viable government in Jerusalem. We can be sure the kingdom of darkness was not pleased. The battle was brewing even before Nehemiah began to build.

The work of "the spiritual forces of evil in the heavenly realm" usually appears first through the lives and attitudes of people under Satan's control. That's his tactic. Those of us who work with demonized people have witnessed this innumerable times. As I began this writing effort, people who had been looking to me to help them get free from demonization began to feel intensified oppression. Also, the number of distressed phone calls during my first month of writing increased phenomenally.

It's important for revival intercessors to know their battle. As we engage in this ministry, we must wear our weapons and be ready to fight while at the same time remaining absolutely fearless. We must never shrink back in the face of this war. To do so leads to disaster.

Let's look at the nature of our struggle:

1. The battle will be insidious and subtle.

Satan's opposition is always subtle, sometimes so elusive we miss it completely. Paul warns of this in Ephesians 6:11:

> Put on the full armor of God so that you can take
> your stand against the devil's *schemes* (emphasis added).

The Greek word is *methodāas* and other translations communicate "wiles" and "craftiness." Paul is talking about an evil, clever trick designed to deceive. That's how Satan approached Eve in the garden temptation, and it's how he approaches us today. He lies, and he makes the deception so clever that we miss it.

That kind of opposition came to Nehemiah. Nehemiah 2:10 shows Sanballat and Tobiah disturbed and angry. It wasn't long before their subtle opposition became threatening: "They mocked and ridiculed us. 'What is this you are doing?' they asked. 'Are you rebelling against the king?' " (Nehemiah 2:19)

The subtle threats and innuendos of these powerful political leaders were lethal. People with less dedication than what God had built into Nehemiah might have succumbed quickly. Knowing the effect the threats might have on the less committed Jewish leaders, Nehemiah responded quickly and boldly:

> The God of heaven will give us success. We his ser-
> vants will start rebuilding, but as for you, you have no
> share in Jerusalem or any claim or historic right to it
> (Nehemiah 2:20).

When our own city-wide revival prayer focus first started, my friends and I sought a neutral meeting place.

One of the leading hotels offered to rent us a room overlooking the city for thirty dollars a week. We rented the room for several months, but the costs were difficult for our small number to meet.

Someone suggested we try to influence management to lower the costs in light of the noble purpose of our prayer for our city. The managers' response was almost sarcastic scorn. Obviously, revival prayer was not wanted there. God met our need by opening a door at a local hospital, at no cost, but the hotel's rejection of our preferred place was one of those subtle attacks.

We need to be watchful for the sneak attacks Satan makes on our lives. We'd be wise to memorize Nehemiah's appropriate response: "The God of heaven will give us success." Then when the subtle attack comes, we are armed and ready.

2. The battle will be fierce and intimidating.

When what we're doing threatens Satan's plan, the battle moves from subtle to heated. The stakes rise. Intensity builds. The more threatened the opposition feels, the more determined they become to do something about it.

> But, when Sanballat, Tobiah, the Arabs, the Ammonites and the men of Ashdod heard that the repairs to Jerusalem's walls had gone ahead and that the gaps were being closed, they were very angry. They plotted together to come and fight against Jerusalem and stir up trouble against it (Nehemiah 4:7,8).

The opposition threatens war, bloodshed and even death.

Wheaton College experienced a revival in 1950 much like the Asbury revival mentioned in the last chapter. My oldest brother shared a fascinating detail concerning the Wheaton revival. Two of the five missionaries who were martyred by Auca Indians in Ecuador in the early '50s were student leaders in that revival awakening. Though Satan's effort to keep the gospel from the Aucas was violent, it was also futile. These men had a heart for God that even death could not stop.

The results of their sacrifice are well known. God in His sovereignty used the shock of these men's deaths to move many others to volunteer for missionary service. The Aucas were reached. Some of those who committed the murders even became evangelists and leaders of the new church.

Perhaps I should warn you that the kingdom of darkness hates the United States with a violent, cruel hatred. Satan hates our history of Christ-exalting churches. He hates our freedom and prosperity which enables believers to support world evangelization and missionary outreach. He hates our technology that makes possible wide and diverse means of communicating the gospel. He hates the large numbers of evangelical Christians who pray, love and support the things of God. His hatred is so great he'd rather destroy us than fight us.

Even if he gets the nation's majority totally coming his way, Satan is still terribly threatened by believers. He knows the awesome potential of even a remnant of Bible-believing Christians. If we unite behind God's will and plan for world revival, mighty advancement for Christ will result. Even a *desire* for a revival awakening terrifies the kingdom of darkness. It's the one remedy that can intervene in our national, downward plunge toward total destruction.

Proper understanding and use of warfare principles and praying will provide secure protection. No believer need fear Satan's threats or intimidations. If a believer carefully uses his God-supplied protection, he's more than a match for Satan's schemes. Fearless courage in the face of enemy threats belongs to prepared believers. "The God of heaven will give us success. We his servants will start rebuilding" (Nehemiah 2:20).

When Nehemiah's enemies tried to get him to come and dialogue with them, his reply was fearlessly firm: "I am carrying on a great project and cannot go down. Why should the work stop while I leave it and go down to you?" (Nehemiah 6:3) If he had not been sure of his higher authority of protection, it would have been folly for him to face these murderous enemies with such courage. Many of the other Jews working with him, because they did not know the same surety that God had taught Nehemiah, nearly fell apart under such threat. (See 4:11,12.)

Fearless Warfare

Two important points need to be stressed.

First, it is utter folly to walk in a presumptuous manner into battle against evil supernaturalism. When believers arrogantly assume that Satan cannot cause harm, they are soon brought to disaster. The writer to the Hebrews speaks of the devil as the one "who holds the power of death" (Hebrews 2:14,15). He would kill believers if he could. Those who work with demonized people have frequently heard the kingdom of darkness spill out death-threatening hate. I've heard Satan's emissaries speak through demonized persons, threatening to kill my wife, my children, and my grandchildren. Satan is a killer on the loose. "He was a murderer from the beginning" (John 8:44b).

In our own strength, we are no match for Satan's destructive power.

Second, believers *can* launch a fearless warfare against the enemy. When believers are careful to put on their armor of God's protection and claim His sovereign presence between them and violent demons, Satan's murderous intent becomes an idle threat.

> The one who is in you is greater than the one who is in the world (1 John 4:4b).

Once we gain biblical understanding of our position in Christ and use our God-given authority protectively, our abiding, moment-by-moment appropriation of Christ's victory provides complete protection. The apostle Paul pictures the armor-clothed believer as one "able to stand your ground, and after you have done everything, to stand" (Ephesians 6:13b). It's important for you to know this when you get serious about praying for revolutionary revival.

You may be threatened by intimidations, taunts, even clouds of death, but you are invincible to do God's will in God's way.

Some pastors have shared with me that they refrain from speaking about the devil because of the flak they experience when they do. What a tragic defeat when we succumb to that!

The mother of the little boy mentioned at the beginning of this chapter called me later for some encouragement in their effort to protect their son. The battle was particularly fierce at that moment; the enemy seemed determined to rule that child. It was an attempt to strike a deadly blow against that pastor's ministry.

After sharing some of the resistance measures needed in such battle, I began warfare praying with the mother for the child. I was just getting into the intercession when I heard a click on the line and then a dial tone. That happens often — the enemy uses his devious tricks to interfere, and telephone communication seems particularly vulnerable to his tactics. Did that intimidate me or stop me? Not in the least. I hung up the phone and went right on praying the same focus of victory against the tormentor. Phone contact with the mother wasn't necessary for effective prayer. The parents called back later to tell of remarkable improvement. For a while, the battle abates.

3. The battle will be deceptive and full of lies.

Even when Satan tells the truth, he uses it to promote deception. He knows no other tactic. "There is no truth in him. When he lies, he speaks his native language, for he is a liar and the father of lies" (John 8:44c).

As the progress on the walls of Jerusalem went forth and the gaps were filled in, a consortium led by Sanballat tried a new tactic, one doubtlessly devised by Satan himself. They sent a conciliatory letter to Nehemiah, with the invitation: "Come, let us meet together in one of the villages on the plain of Ono" (Nehemiah 6:2). The letter seemed to say, "We see that you're determined and progressing well, so now let's try to live together. Let's talk it over in a friendly way."

Nehemiah wisely read the deception. He stated, "But they were scheming to harm me" (verse 2*b*). He responded to their conference invitation to Ono with, "Oh, no!" His work was too important for him to leave for any such negotiations. Four times the invitation came and four times the response was the same.

The fifth letter was a clever, devilish lie that could have produced great trouble for Nehemiah. The entire project could have been put in jeopardy. Here's what it said:

> It is reported among the nations—and Geshem says it is true—that you and the Jews are plotting to revolt, and therefore you are building the wall. Moreover, according to these reports you are about to become their king and have even appointed prophets to make this proclamation about you in Jerusalem: "There is a king in Judah!" Now this report will get back to the king: so come, let us confer together (verses 6,7).

Several factors reveal the insidious nature of this lie.

First, the letter expressed a possible unspoken longing of Nehemiah and probably every Jew in Jerusalem. They longed to be a viable nation again, and to have Nehemiah as their king could well have been a part of that longing. No doubt Satan already had planted the thoughts of the letter in Nehemiah's mind many times. Satan's forces can and do project thoughts into our minds that tempt us to act independently of the will of God. But Nehemiah was a man of integrity. He would not yield to such a temptation. Artaxerxes had trusted him to keep his word and to remain loyal, and Nehemiah would do so.

Second, this lie could have tempted the Jews to try for the very thing it suggested. Word would spread through the ranks, excitement could build on the rumors, and some of the people might well have become motivated to do what the letter inferred.

Third, this lie could have undermined Artaxerxes' confidence in Nehemiah. A written accusation of this nature from these leaders could have been due cause for the king to recall Nehemiah.

Nehemiah put his answer in writing: "Nothing like what you are saying is happening; you are just making it up out of your head" (verse 8). I'm sure he kept all the correspondence on file in case further documentation might be needed, and he probably sent copies of everything by courier with his regular reports to the king. Nehemiah had nothing to hide.

This incident reveals a strategic element of Satan's methods. Though he lies about our motives, he usually touches dangerously close to where our hearts are. For example, he might accuse those forming a prayer group for revival of wanting to have a place of prominence when revival comes. Or he might tempt them to desire praise for leading a revival prayer group. Who of us in leadership positions have not been tempted to reach for some glory?

Recently the Los Angeles Billy Graham Crusade celebrated its fortieth anniversary. Those Christians living at the time of that crusade will never forget it. It drew world attention to his ministry. I was a young man, just beginning my own ministry, and a report from the crusade spoke deeply to me. A college faculty member at Northwestern College where Billy Graham was president attempted to visit him in his hotel room. As he reached the door of the room, he heard the evangelist praying. Not wanting to interrupt, he turned and left, but he did overhear Dr. Graham walking and praying in his room: "Oh God! Help me to see that it's not my doing. Help me to see that it's not I. Give me grace to let You have all the glory."

We understand a prayer like that. We understand the temptation to elevate ourselves, and we understand feelings of guilt when we do. The accuser is always busy, and he tempts us where we're vulnerable. He projects the temptation into our minds—and then he taunts us with accusations about that very temptation. It's one of his most proficient tricks.

4. The battle can produce fear.

> Also our enemies said, "Before they know it or see us, we will be right there among them and will kill them and put an end to the work" (Nehemiah 4:11).

> They were trying to frighten us, thinking, "Their hands will get too weak for the work, and it will not be completed" (Nehemiah 6:9).

Fear is the complete antithesis of faith. The most direct attack upon faith is that which makes us afraid. Next to the lie, fear is the enemy's most effective tool.

In the African bush where lions roam freely, the stronger lions rarely roar. They prefer to stalk their target, relying upon a quick ambush to destroy them. The older lion, whose quickness and strength is failing, relies on his roar to paralyze his prey with fear. When fear is present, even a weakened enemy can capture and destroy the one targeted.

The roar of the devil who "prowls around like a roaring lion looking for someone to devour," is meant to make us afraid (see 1 Peter 5:8), but Satan is not a lion. He may roar like one, but it is just another attempt to be like Him who *is* the "Lion":

> Then one of the elders said to me, "Do not weep! See the Lion of the tribe of Judah, the Root of David, has triumphed" (Revelation 5:5; see also Hosea 11:10; 13:7,8; Jeremiah 49:19; 50:44).

Jesus Christ has weakened our foe. The best Satan can do is roar. His growls are not to be feared by the Christian; he has been defeated by the Lord Jesus Christ. Christ alone is worthy to be reverenced and feared by believers.

The Lord Jesus Christ instructs us not to be fearful of our enemies, including Satan himself:

> So do not be afraid of them. There is nothing concealed that will not be disclosed, or hidden that will not be made known. . . . Do not be afraid of those who kill the body but cannot kill the soul. Rather, be afraid of the one who can destroy both soul and body in hell (Matthew 10:26,28).

Fear must be recognized for what it is—the enemy's war club. The believer's greatest weapon against it is the Word of God. Used in doctrinal praying, as illustrated in the written prayers of this book, God's Word puts fear to flight.

5. The battle will induce religious leaders to speak for the enemy.

Historically some of the enemy's best spokesmen have been respected religious leaders. Eli's two priestly sons, Hophni and Phinehas, had to be judged with death because of their sinful example and wicked deeds (1 Samuel 2:22-36). The religious leaders of Jerusalem under the high priest, Caiaphas, were used to instigate our Lord's crucifixion. They later actively opposed the spread of the gospel (see Matthew 26:57-67; Acts 5:17-42).

Religious leaders in our day are often a part of the enemy's camp too. They promise "instant heaven" and superior rewards for those willing to be killed in their "holy wars." And one does not need to look outside the Christian faith to see religious leaders being used for the enemy's cause. Extravagant lifestyles, immoral living, and financial dishonesty of recognized Christian leaders repeatedly gain top billing in the media. Disgrace comes to the cause of Christ through those leaders who allow sin to rule them.

Religious leaders with notable scholastic credentials likewise can become cohorts of Satan's deceptions. Some of their scholastic pronouncements cast doubt on the authority of Scripture, on the deity of Christ, and on other major doctrines. This makes these leaders some of the enemy's most effective allies. They often oppose revival awakenings, especially in the early stages. They brand these efforts as a move toward emotionalism or fanaticism. They refer to those who speak of revivalism as "escapists," accusing them of wanting to evade the real world and their responsibility to meet the urgent issues of the day. I've had such words addressed to me.

After I preached a message on the need for revival, a fellow pastor confronted me about making revival a door of escape from my duty to act. He was very sincere. He believes the way to meet the sin challenge of our day is to confront it with organized opposition. He saw my emphasis on revival as an excuse to not be involved.

I have no quarrel with those who organize and oppose sin's advance. That has its place—but so much more is needed. The confrontational approach will never of itself be enough to turn the tide. The satanic revival has gained too much ground. While the good effort is being put forth to confront sin, the revival of evil keeps accelerating. Only revolutionary revival can bring the changes in people's hearts that will make the stand against evil effective. Confrontational challenge will be much more successful when regenerated legislators, born-anew judges and converted leaders of the executive branches of government have righteous interests.

The enemy uses many approaches to oppose God's work done in God's will. Subtle opposition will always be present. The battle may become fierce, even murderous. Half-truths and outright lies will be employed. Fear will lurk in the shadows. We may even see religious leaders joining the enemy's entourage to defeat revival effort. Satan and his kingdom will do all they can to turn us back from God's will and plan, but Nehemiah's example confirms that victory consists of faithfully using our weapons of warfare in fearless application.

REVIVAL PRAYER PATTERN 4
FOCUS: PROTECTION FROM THE ENEMY

Loving Heavenly Father, I worship You as the provider of my protection from the hurtful, murderous intent of my enemies. "See how my enemies have increased and how fiercely they hate me" (Psalm 25:19). I desire to not passively assume my safety but to step deliberately with faith and understanding into that victory You have provided. Teach me how to appropriate my victory. I am listening for wise insights from You even as I address You in prayer. Teach me deeper love and understanding of Yourself even as I open my whole person to You right now.

I plead that mighty name You have exalted above every name—Lord Jesus Christ—over my personal life and my walk with God; over my wife (husband), my children and all for whom I am responsible in my family; over the ministry You have given to me and all for whom I am responsible in ministry. I hold the name of my Lord Jesus Christ over Your church and all of Your will and plans for the bringing of revolutionary revival. I worship my Savior. I affirm that He is Lord—He is Jehovah God—the more we know of Him the more we know of You. He is Jesus, Savior. He is my Savior—there is no Savior but Him. I worship Jesus as the one who took away my sins. He is the Christ—the Anointed of God. He is the anointed Prophet who proclaimed the way and who is the way. He is the anointed Priest who offers a better sacrifice and is Himself that sacrifice for sin. He is the anointed King who now rules in His sovereign power and who will one day rule as King of kings and Lord of lords.

I seek to abide in my Lord Jesus Christ and to hide in the protection of His almightiness and my oneness with Him. I abide in His incarnation, His humanity. How wonderful that You planned that our Savior should be one of us. The mystery of that remains beyond my capacities for understanding.

I abide in the surety that He experienced all of life's temptations and never failed to meet sin's fullest challenge. He fulfilled all righteousness. He obeyed every particle of Your expectancy for us as expressed in Your Law. As one of us, He pleased You, His Heavenly Father, as a child, as a youth and as an adult in every aspect of His life.

Thank You that as one of us He completely overcame sin. In His humanity, He never yielded to sin's entice- ments, though He was made in "the likeness of sinful flesh." The world was never able to entice Him to accept its values or to press Him into its mold. Thank You that though Satan himself and all of his demons tried to cause Him to sin, in His humanity He willed not to sin. With joy I enter into His sinless, worthy human life and expect Your blessing because You have placed His worthiness upon me. There is safety and peace here and I abide in it.

By faith, I abide in the death and sufferings of my Lord Jesus Christ. I claim the shelter of His precious blood over myself and those for whom I am responsible. It was in the work of His sufferings and the cross that You have removed the guilt of my sins. Cleanse me through His blood from all sins of omission and commission that would hinder my fellowship with You.

I abide in the suffering and death of the Lord Jesus Christ who "destroyed him who had the power of death, that is the devil." I hold the victory of the cross against the devil and all of his kingdom. In the power of the sufferings and shed blood of my Savior, I resist all of Satan's efforts to harm me or those for whom I am responsible.

I affirm the mighty triumph of the Lord Jesus Christ in His resurrection from the dead. In the practical outliving of my life today, I desire to be clothed with that same mighty power that raised Jesus Christ from the dead. In His resur- rection power enable me to walk in newness of life. I ad- dress resurrection power directly against Satan and his kingdom in all his efforts to rule me and to hold back revival awakening from coming to Christ's church.

By faith, I enter into the ascension of my Lord Jesus Christ, where He is seated far above all principalities and powers. Thank You, Heavenly Father, for raising me up with Christ and seating me with Him in the heavenly realms. Teach me more perfectly how to rest in the safety of that lofty position and how to use that authority to pull down all of Satan's ruling tactics.

I abide in my Savior's glorification. I submit to Your lordship over my life, my family and Your church. I ask You to shepherd me in Your will and to hold me in the safety of your faithful protection. I ask You to shepherd Your church to revival awakening in this day of great darkness.

Heavenly Father, I reach out for Your Holy Spirit and the wonder of His work. I rejoice that He came in fulfillment of the promise of both the Father and the Son. I rejoice that He convicted me and brought me to Christ, opened my eyes to see and caused me to be born of the Spirit. Thank You that He came to live within me the moment I was saved. I invite the Holy Spirit to enable me to walk in Him, so that love, joy, peace, patience, gentleness, goodness, meekness, faithfulness and self-control may overflow from my life. May others see this, especially those close to me. May I see His fruit but most of all may His control be evident to You, O Lord.

I abide in His sealing, protecting work. I abide in His having made me a member of Christ's body. Help me to minister to the body of Christ today. I depend upon Him to breathe His quickening life and power into me. May the Holy Spirit pray through me and may He endue me with His power to witness of You before others. I pray the mighty work of the Holy Spirit as God's "holy finger" directly against Satan and his kingdom. May the mighty power of the Holy Spirit confront and defeat the devil in all of his hurtful designs for this day. I ask the Holy Spirit to increase His powerful work of convincing our world of sin, of righteousness and of judgment to come.

By faith I reach out for the wholeness of Your armor, Heavenly Father. I receive the girdle of truth and by faith I wear it. Help me not to deceive or be deceived in any way.

I wear the breastplate of righteousness. Having none of my own righteousness, I desire to walk in the adequate supply of Your righteousness.

Help me to walk in my shoes of peace. I claim my peace with God through justification, my peace of God through prayer and the Spirit's work and the near presence of the God of peace who makes even my enemies to be at peace with me.

Be my shield today, dear Lord. May Your presence hedge me in and quench all of Satan's flaming arrows.

Helmet my head with Your salvation. May the Savior cover my mind to protect me from Satan's intruding thoughts. May the Lord Jesus Christ think His thoughts in my mind today.

I receive the Word of God as the Spirit's sword. Teach me to use it proficiently in my protection and in my witness. Help me to memorize it and to know its power.

I thank You, Heavenly Father, that my victory in Christ is not merely protective. You have provided me safety, so that I might be bold to address my Lord's victory against everything that opposes Your will. In the name of my Lord Jesus Christ, I tear down all that Satan has strategized to hinder revival. I invite my living Lord Jesus Christ to sovereignly shepherd and lead His Church into all that is necessary to bring revival. I invite the Holy Spirit to sovereignly move to prepare the people whom You have chosen to be the leaders in each phase of revival preparation. I invite the Holy Spirit to prepare those special servants through whom the call for revival will come.

I give myself to You, loving God and Father of our Lord Jesus Christ. In the worthiness of my Lord, and in the enablement of Your Holy Spirit, I offer myself to You for any purpose You may have. Through Jesus Christ my Lord, I pray. Amen.

◇ 12 ◇

Assessing the Battle Strength

> For though we live in the world, we do not wage war as the world does. The weapons we fight with are not the weapons of the world. On the contrary, they have divine power to demolish strongholds (2 Corinthians 10:3,4).

He got up early and stepped out on the flat roof overlooking the town of Dothan. He and Elisha, the man he served, were guests in the home of Elisha's friend. Elisha had risen earlier and was quietly praying and reading the Holy Scriptures when his servant arrived. Things were very tense in Israel even though the war with the king of Aram (NIV; called Syria in the KJV) was going well. Every action the king of Aram attempted was thwarted—the king of Israel seemed to have advance warning about all of Aram's plans, and Israel was winning all the battles.

Elisha's servant felt uneasy. Word had circulated that Elisha was funneling information to Israel's king, and that meant trouble. The Aramean king would be filled with rage against Elisha. The servant felt relieved to see Elisha seated on the rooftop, so completely at ease. As the wings of the dawn spread their brightness over the city, Elisha's servant thought, *With Elisha so calm, all must be well.*

He stretched his arms and flexed his knees in his struggle to fully awaken. Suddenly he saw them. During the night, a great army had surrounded the city. Chariots and horses were everywhere. Enemy soldiers were quietly waiting, poised for attack. The Israeli troops stationed at Dothan were hopelessly outnumbered. Elisha's servant panicked. It was his responsibility to protect the prophet, but what could he do? Instinctively, he knew those troops were after Elisha.

Frantic desperation overtook him. He turned to Elisha, who was still calmly reading the Scriptures. "Oh, my Lord, what shall we do?" he cried. Many thoughts raced through his mind. *Why is Elisha so calm? Doesn't he see the danger? Doesn't he care that these troops are after him? Why isn't he hiding? Why doesn't he try to escape?*

The servant's response was typical of the way God's people react when they face spiritual battles. He saw only what his physical eyes beheld. Locked in to the natural perspective, he didn't consider the spiritual realm of truth. On the other hand, Elisha had more than physical sight—he had spiritual vision. Though Elisha couldn't physically see into that unseen spiritual realm where angels dwell and God's armies reside, he knew God was there. To him it was more real than the world he saw.

When he was Elijah's servant, Elisha had seen the evidence many times. Since being anointed as Elijah's successor, Elisha had grown in his awareness of the unseen world of the heavenly realm.

Elisha responded to his distraught servant with quiet calmness, "Don't be afraid! Those who are with us are more than those who are with them" (2 Kings 6:16).

The "More" Principle

What an important truth to know. Elisha's statement conveys to God's obedient people what we need to know in our hour of satanic revival. The forces of righteousness surpass the opposition in both numbers and power. No matter how large and threatening the opposition becomes, "Those who are with us are more than those who are with them."

That's an absolute for believers who prayerfully walk in the Lord's will.

This truth rests upon the foundation of God's omnipotent, omnipresent, omniscient, immutable and eternal attributes. He's always "more." Knowing and applying such an important truth is a must of spiritual warfare.

Elisha's response to the danger baffled his servant. An incredulous look betrayed the servant's inner thoughts. *There aren't enough Israeli soldiers within miles to come to our rescue. How can Elisha say such a thing?*

Seeing his servant's befuddlement, Elisha prayed, "Oh, LORD, open his eyes, so he may see." In answer to that prayer . . .

> the LORD opened the servant's eyes, and he looked
> and saw the hills full of horses and chariots of fire all
> around Elisha (2 Kings 6:17).

The servant probably experienced not only a severe shock but also a life-transforming enlargement of his faith. A mortal doesn't see supernatural, angelic scenes and remain the same.

Which kind of vision characterizes us? That's the heart of this chapter.

As the army of the king of Aram advanced to take Elisha captive and bring him back to their king, God's servant prayed again, saying, "Strike these people with blindness" (2 Kings 6:18).

It happened in an instant. The God who opened the eyes of Elisha's servant to the supernatural, now closed the eyes of the Syrian army to the natural. Blind and in a stunned stupor, the army was helpless. Elisha led the enemy troops into the very presence of the king of Israel at Samaria. At Elisha's suggestion, the king did not harm them. Their sight then returned and Israel's king treated them to a royal banquet instead of violent death. Afterward he sent them home to their nation and families. The king of Aram was so amazed by this whole turn of events that he stopped his war raids into Israel's territory. Peace prevailed.

What a beautiful story to give God's people a true vision of our victory. We need to know of our spiritual allies and their infinite superiority over all adversaries. We need to be able to say: "Those who are with us are more than those who are with them." We are immutably aligned with Him who is "more."

In recent years, God has sovereignly chosen to use some Christian novelists to help believers visualize this unseen war taking place in the heavenlies. I hope we don't have a flood of such novels now that wide popular interest has been aroused. That could lead to excessive unbiblical imaginations and fanciful extremes. We don't want to build any of our theology on such books, however they do illustrate that believers really are "more than conquerors through him who loved us" (Romans 8:37).

Revolutionary revival is not an impossible dream. God has provided adequate weapons of warfare to see it happen. The prayers, repentance and existing state of the church has a direct effect upon how the battle progresses. The faithful intercession of the saints has a direct relationship to whether the forces of darkness or the forces of righteousness prevail at a given time. That's remarkable but true. It's demonstrated all through the Bible. We mentioned before how Moses, Aaron and Hur praying on the mountainside affected Joshua's battle in the trenches. World evangelization in our day needs that kind of support and targeted prayer to continue in the face of Satan's strategy.

The Reality of Evil Supernaturalism

The Lausanne II Congress on evangelism convened during the summer of 1989 in Manila. The twenty-one affirmations of the convened delegates included a focus on spiritual warfare. Affirmation No. 11 stated: "We affirm that spiritual warfare demands spiritual weapons, and that we must both preach the Word in the power of the Spirit, and pray constantly that we may enter into Christ's victory over the principalities and powers of evil." [1]

God seems to be bringing back to His church a renewed perspective of what Dr. Ed Murphy has termed "evil supernaturalism."[2] God's Word extensively recognizes this battle, but westernized, evangelical Christianity appears to have suffered from a "secularized brainwashing."

The biblical view of believers being involved in close struggle with evil has been neglected. The concept of influencing nations and people has been generally dismissed as irrelevant. A believer's conflict with spirit beings has been relegated to the realm of superstition or ignorance. Evangelicals have preferred psychological answers for all problem areas. Evangelism and church planting have received the evangelical's total interest. All emphases have centered on helping nonbelievers to become Christians, and that, if a person does that, he need not be concerned about evil spirits. Though the supernatural has been given lip service by evangelicals, to teach and believe that Christians could be troubled by evil powers has been labeled "dangerous extremism."

In most evangelical circles, human struggles of an emotional nature are treated with Christian psychological counseling and proper medical care. In seminaries and Bible colleges, counseling courses have received a new "trendy" emphasis by both faculty and students. Believers' struggles with demonic powers are seldom, if ever, mentioned. Missionary leader Dr. Timothy Warner writes concerning these matters:

> This is a world view entirely foreign to that held by most of the cultures of the world and one that is foreign to that of our Lord as reflected in the Gospels. It is a world view in which spirits of any kind, and especially evil spirits, have little place. While we may give lip service to a belief in spirits both good and evil in our formal statements of theology, such spirits are not functional realities in

everyday life for most Christians—even for most theologians.[3]

One might add that a world view *de*-emphasizing evil supernaturalism was foreign to the apostles of Christ. A world view recognizing the believer's battle with evil spirits held center stage in epistles like Ephesians, Colossians and 1 and 2 Peter. God never intended that warfare with darkness should be relegated to a mental nod of friendly assent. Evil supernaturalism must be faced directly and boldly by using the spiritual weapons of warfare. The Epistles clearly set forth the believer's day-by-day battle with Satan's kingdom:

> Resist the devil, and he will flee from you (James 4:1).
>
> Resist him [the devil], standing firm in the faith (1 Peter 5:9).
>
> Dear friends, do not believe every spirit, but test the spirits to see whether they are from God (1 John 4:1).
>
> We know . . . that the whole world is under the control of the evil one (1 John 5:19).
>
> Put on the full armor of God so that you can take your stand against the devil's schemes. For our struggle is not against flesh and blood, but against the rulers, against the authorities, against the powers of this dark world and against the spiritual forces of evil in the heavenly realms (Ephesians 6:11,12).

This sampling of texts from the New Testament Epistles speaks plainly of the believer's authority and responsibility. One wonders how evangelicals could become so neglectful of resisting the enemy in our daily battle with evil supernaturalism—the biblical world view stresses it so strongly. Hope for world evangelization and revolutionary revival demands that believers recognize the truth of fierce opposition continuing to come from the world of darkness. Evil supernaturalism hates revival. If we ignore Satan's work, we will never overcome his schemes against a revival awakening. Our only hope is to aggressively apply Christ's victorious work over Satan. That's a truth we must not ignore.

Victory Through Christ's Authority

Paul's epistle to the Colossians establishes firm ground for confidence in our battle with Satan. Let's examine some major points.

First, Paul declares the full authority of the Lord Jesus Christ over darkness.

> [God] has rescued us from the dominion of darkness and brought us into the kingdom of the Son he loves (Colossians 1:13).

Then he declares our Savior's deity through His creation work and shows that this establishes His authority over Satan's kingdom:

> He is the image of the invisible God [His deity], the firstborn over all creation. For by him all things were created . . . whether thrones or powers or rulers or authorities; all things were created by him and for him (verses 15,16).

Christ created Satan and all of those angelic beings who serve Satan. He created them perfect, but rebellion caused their fall. Still, by right of the creator being greater than His creation, He retains full authority over them. This argument is stated even more forcefully in the next verse:

> He is before all things, and in him all things hold together (Colossians 1:17).

We have a striking picture here: Jesus Christ alone holds together that which He has created, including the entire kingdom of darkness. It would immediately disintegrate into nothingness without Christ holding it together! If it were not within God's sovereign purpose to allow it to continue for a season, Satanic thrones, powers, rulers and authorities would fly apart.

That's a dramatic revelation concerning our Lord Jesus Christ's total authority and total victory over Satan's kingdom.

Here's something even more dramatic: The Lord Jesus Christ chose to share this great victory and authority with His church! (verses 18-29)

In Colossians 2, the marvel of Christ's incarnation is lifted to its proper importance. We see there that the full authority of Christ's victory is brought to our level even more closely through Christ becoming a human being. In "the likeness of sinful flesh," He delivered the fatal blow to Satan's kingdom in our behalf. He is victor over Satan as the divine creator—but also as one of us. In His bodily human form, He won our victory, and His full authority over darkness and over Satan's kingdom is transmitted to us who believe.

> For in Christ all the fullness of the Deity lives in bodily form, and you have been given fullness in Christ, who is head over every power and authority . . . having been buried with him in baptism and raised with him through your faith in the power of God, who raised him from the dead (Colossians 2:9,10,12 emphasis added).

This victory came to us because Christ paid the penalty for our sins: His oneness with His Church transfers His victory to believers. His resurrection bestows upon us newness of life. In His ascension He lifts us into the heavenly realm and gives us authority over darkness in our oneness with Him.

Note how beautifully it is stated here:

> When you were dead in your sins and in the uncircumcision of your sinful nature, God made you alive with Christ. He forgave us *all* our sins, having canceled the written code, with its regulations, that was against us and that stood opposed to us; he took it away, nailing it to the cross. [Sin is gone, condemnation is removed; life and fullness have come.] And *having disarmed the power and authorities,* he made a public spectacle of them, triumphing over them by the cross (Colossians 2:13-15, emphasis added).

The Disarmed Enemy

Through the redemptive work Christ did in His humanity, the power of Satan and his kingdom over the lost no longer applies to believers (see Ephesians 2:1,2). Christ has disarmed our enemy.

When a believer knows and stands by faith in such promises, he has complete confidence of his authority and can apply his victory with courage.

In working with those suffering with demonization, I've never yet found (and I know I never will) any power of darkness manifesting itself that didn't have to admit that the believer has this full authority over all wicked spirits. Believers are "more than conquerors through him who loved us" (see Romans 8:37).

There may be even deeper ramifications to the believer's positional authority than most believers have been bold enough to practice. I refer to biblical statements such as these:

> How can anyone enter a strong man's house and carry off his possessions unless he first ties up the strong man? Then he can rob his house (Matthew 12:29).

> When a strong man, fully armed, guards his own house, his possessions are safe. But when someone stronger attacks and overpowers him, he takes away the armor in which the man trusted and divides up the spoils (Luke 11:21,22).

> In fact, no one can enter a strong man's house and carry off his possessions unless he first ties up the strong man. Then he can rob his house (Mark 3:27).

> And I tell you that you are Peter, and on this rock I will build my church, and the gates of Hades will not overcome it. I will give you the keys of the kingdom of heaven; whatever you bind on earth will be bound in heaven, and whatever you loose on earth will be loosed in heaven (Matthew 16:18,19).

I tell you the truth, whatever you bind on earth will be bound in heaven, and whatever you loose on earth will be loosed in heaven (Matthew 18:18).

I am sending you to them to open their eyes and turn them from darkness to light, and from the power of Satan to God, so that they may receive forgiveness of sins and a place among those who are sanctified by faith in me (Acts 26:17*b*,18).

Be self-controlled and alert. Your enemy the devil prowls around like a roaring lion looking for someone to devour. Resist him, standing firm in the faith, because you know that your brothers throughout the world are undergoing the same kind of sufferings (1 Peter 5:8,9).

Submit yourselves then to God. Resist the devil and he will flee from you. Come near to God and He will come near to you (James 4:7,8*a*).

Each of these texts has to do with the believer exercising his authority over Satan, the kingdom of darkness and the work that kingdom desires to do. The careful use of one's authority within the prescribed will of God is not only a privilege but a responsibility.

◇ 13 ◇

Using
Our Weapons

The Bible teaches that strongholds of darkness in Satan's kingdom are commissioned to carry forth his program in various geographic areas of the world and that his rule is powerful enough to cause spiritual blindness to unbelievers everywhere in the world:

> The god of this age has blinded the minds of unbelievers, so that they cannot see the light of the gospel of the glory of Christ (2 Corinthians 4:4).

God's Word also exposes an internal controlling work of Satan . . .

> the ruler of the kingdom of the air, the spirit who is now at work in those who are disobedient (Ephesians 2:2).

That extensive work seems to include every nonbeliever, no matter where he or she is located.

Satan's Organization

Since Satan is not omnipresent like God, how can he do such an extensive work, blinding unbelievers everywhere and cleverly working within them to keep them disobedient? He does it through the highly structured kingdom which he holds in his powerful rule.

Colossians and Ephesians give us limited insight into the organized structure of this evil kingdom. Satan is the commander-in-chief (Ephesians 6:11), and under him there seem to be at least six levels of authority overseeing his world-wide program. Colossians 1:16 identifies **thrones** (*thrónoi*) and **dominions** or lordships (*kouriótātes*) as the first two levels of authority under Satan. Both Colossians and Ephesians list the next two levels as **principalities** (*arkái*) and **authorities** (*exouséi*). Ephesians 6:12 carries the organized structure on to the two remaining levels of **world rulers of darkness** (*kosmokrátopas*) and **wicked spirits** (*ponarias, pneumatiká*). The structure appears like a human military chain of command with everything funneling to and from Satan. This means that, although Satan is not omnipresent, he does have a semblance of an omnipresent kingdom working to govern humanity and control their inner lives. That's a formidable network of darkness holding unbelievers in bondage.

This organized kingdom affects believers also. Passages like Ephesians 6:10-18 remind us that those in Satan's network are our formidable foes. They "wrestle" against us to hinder our walking in God's will and fulfilling God's plans.

Territorial Control

The Old Testament seems to verify the concept of satanic forces being assigned to carry out Satan's program in certain geographic areas. Daniel had a vision concerning a coming "great war." His understanding of the meaning of what he'd seen was limited, so he sought more enlightenment from God. Daniel 10 records his three-week fast and humbling before the Lord as he sought further insight. A heavenly messenger finally arrived with this word for Daniel:

> Do not be afraid, Daniel. Since the first day that you set your mind to gain understanding and to humble yourself before your God, your words were heard, and I have come in response to them. But the prince of the Persian kingdom resisted me twenty-one days. Then Michael,

one of the chief princes, came to help me because I was
detained there with the king of Persia (Daniel 10:12,13).

After delivering God's message to Daniel, the messenger
reveals more of this struggle between holy and evil angels:

> Soon I will return to fight against the prince of Per-
> sia, and when I go, the prince of Greece will come. . . . (No
> one supports me against them except Michael, your prince.
> And in the first year of Darius the Mede, I took my stand
> to support and protect him) (Daniel 10:20–11:1).

This pictures unseen forces of evil angels on the
"prince" level who exercise some territorial control over
Greece and Persia. These spirit beings battled against this
unnamed holy angel and Michael, "one of the chief princes,"
who is also called the archangel (see Jude 9). He seems to be
the holy angel with special assignment to protect Daniel and,
by implication, the nation of Israel.

Scriptures indicate that unseen demonic powers work
behind the scenes in every visible government, seeking to influence their philosophy, their policies, their course of direction and their political actions. This influence is particularly
evident in those governments that hinder the gospel, per-
secute Christians or terrorize people. Who could doubt that
the Nazi policy to destroy the Jews was of demonic origin?

Activity Assignments

The Scriptures imply that this large-scale, highly organized system of evil powers carries on an extensive warfare
against God's plan (see Matthew 12:25,26; John 12:31; 14:30).
The assignments given to these malevolent powers can influence virtually every facet of human life. The Word of God
speaks about numerous areas where the enemy is active:

1. They promote idolatry, witchcraft and sorcery, and
   all manner of false religious teachings and systems
   (1 Timothy 4:1-4; 1 John 4:1-4; Deuteronomy 32:17;
   Psalm 94:4,5; Revelation 13:4,15).

2. They cause or intensify physical ailments or hurts. They can cause seizures (Mark 9:20; Luke 9:39); physical crippling (Luke 13:11,16); blindness (Matthew 12:22); the inability to hear or speak (Mark 9:17-29; Matthew 9:21,33); and some physical injuries (Mark 5:5; 9:22; Luke 9:39).

3. They cause severe storms and sometimes control the elements in order to help Satan carry out his plans (Job 1:12,16,19; 2:7).

4. They promote sexual perversions and the vilest kind of human behavior (1 Corinthians 5:1-5; Ephesians 2:1-3; Romans 1:18-32; Revelation 18:2,3).

5. They influence God's people and cause them to dishonor the Lord Jesus Christ (Revelation 2:12-17, 20-26; 1 Timothy 4:1-4; Ephesians 6:10-18; Acts 5:1-6).

6. They cause severe emotional disorders and try to bring individuals to self-destruction (Luke 8:27-35; Mark 9:22).

7. They can conceal the truth of the gospel from unbelievers' spiritual seeing (2 Corinthians 4:3,4,13,15; 2 Thessalonians 3:1-3).

8. They masquerade as good spirits doing good things to lead people into deception and bondage (2 Corinthians 11:3-5,13,14,15).

When people are involved in these problems, it cannot always be directly attributed to Satan's work, but in many cases it can.

Using Our Victory Over the Enemy

How do we defeat this formidable force of evil that functions from the advantage of an unseen realm? It is highly structured, cooperative, organized, myriad in number, all conspiring together to defeat and destroy God's people and God's work—how can we cope with that?

Nehemiah gives us six vital guidelines for applying our predetermined victory over the enemy to defeat him:

1. Always understand our doctrinal authority.

> I answered them by saying, "The God of heaven will give us success. We his servants will start rebuilding, but as for you, you have no share in Jerusalem or any claim or historic right to it" (Nehemiah 2:20).

This marvelous text bases its bold authority on revealed truth. Understanding his God-given authority underlies every phase of Nehemiah's victory over his enemies. A solid doctrinal foundation is essential for the application of spiritual warfare victory. Nehemiah knew that his plan to rebuild the walls, rehang the gates and re-establish a viable government in Jerusalem was founded on God's promises. He had the promise to Abraham and the writings of prophets like Isaiah and Jeremiah to claim. The detractors under Satan's control had no God-given right or historic biblical claim to Jerusalem. Any victory over darkness must rest on the sure promises of God expressed in His Word.

2. Always depend utterly upon God and express it in prayer.

> Hear us, O our God, for we are despised. Turn their insults back on their own heads. Give them over as plunder in a land of captivity. Do not cover up their guilt or blot out their sins from your sight, for they have thrown insults in the face of the builders (Nehemiah 4:4,5).

Nehemiah's prayer life was aggressive in resisting the enemy and causing trouble for him. "Turn their insults back on their own heads" is the kind of praying that reverses the demonic curses of our enemies and creates pain of their own making among their ranks.

In the Loren Entz account in chapter 4 of *Abou and the sorceress, Makoura*, we see this dramatically illustrated:

Makoura got news that her evil spirit, which normally took on the form of a snake, had been sighted dead in the bush. On Makoura's arrival the snake's corpse accused her of giving it an assignment that was too difficult to do. Makoura lost control of herself. She was going mad and started confessing all the evil she had done, which was considerable. Her family quickly made arrangements for her to be removed, fearing she would reveal too many secrets.[1]

Her confession of her troubles not only led to her total confounding, but also to her eventual conversion. Through Abou's ministry, Makoura became a believer.

Nehemiah always resorted to prayer when the enemy pressed in. "But we prayed to the God of heaven" was his constant refrain as the enemies' threats increased.

3. Always be alert and willing to fight.

Prayer was backed up with great emphasis on watchfulness and readiness to do battle:

> But we prayed to our God and posted a guard day and night to meet this threat (Nehemiah 4:9).

> After I looked things over, I stood up and said to the nobles, the officials and the rest of the people, "Don't be afraid of them. Remember the Lord, who is great and awesome, and fight for your brothers, your sons and your daughters, your wives and your homes" (verse 14).

> Neither I nor my brothers nor my men nor the guards with me took off our clothes; each had his weapon, even when he went for water (verse 23).

Nehemiah and the people practiced what Ephesians 6 relates to believers about armor and alertness: "Be alert and always keep on praying" (Nehemiah 18b). Our enemy is no pushover. The battle is real, and it requires a high degree of attention to weaponry and alert guard duty as we utilize the weapons of our warfare.

4. Always be assured of the victory.

> When our enemies heard that we were aware of their plot and that God had frustrated it, we all returned to the wall, each to his own work (Nehemiah 4:15).
>
> So the wall was completed on the twenty-fifth of Elul, in fifty-two days (verse 15).

When God's people apply their biblical authority with prayerful dependence upon God, the ultimate victory is sure. We may not see it in "fifty-two days," or even in the time frame we desire, but God's promised victory always comes.

It's good to see how Nehemiah's enemies, who seemed such a strong threat to the whole project in the first six chapters, faded into insignificance. After the wall was completed, they are scarcely mentioned in the remaining seven chapters. A proper use of authority won the victory.

5. Always be courageous.

> But I said, "Should a man like me run away? Or should one like me go into the temple to save his life? I will not go!" (Nehemiah 6:11)

Someone has said, "When you're in trouble and your knees knock, kneel on them." That's the secret of the believer's fearless courage. Courage is not the absence of fear; it is the mastery of it. Nehemiah and his people mastered fear by biblical use of their resources.

When one enters into warfare against Satan's kingdom, the roar of threat will sometimes be very strong. Death may even be faced, but that is really no threat for a believer.

> Jesus said to her, "I am the resurrection and the life. He who believes in me will live, even though he dies; and whoever lives and believes in me will never die" (John 11:25,26).
>
> They overcame him by the blood of the Lamb and by the word of their testimony; they did not love their lives so much as to shrink from death (Revelation 12:11).

Courage in the face of death is a birthright for a believer in the Lord Jesus Christ. Our Savior entered death and came back out, victorious over the grave.

6. Always expect God's sovereign provision.

> When all our enemies heard about this, all the surrounding nations were afraid and lost their self-confidence, because they realized that this work had been done with the help of our God (Nehemiah 6:16).

In spiritual warfare, it's always God's divine provision that defeats the enemy and wins the victory. Second Corinthians 10:3-5 reminds us that believers' warfare weapons are sufficient to "demolish strongholds." Satan has organized his supernatural, unseen, powerful strongholds into thrones, dominions, principalities, authorities, powers of this dark world and spiritual forces of evil. Yet the psalmist reminds us: "The Lord is the stronghold of my life — of whom shall I be afraid?" (Psalm 27:1) and "The Lord is . . . a stronghold in times of trouble" (Psalm 9:9).

Nehemiah knew and lived that truth. The mighty are not really mighty when confronted by the almighty. All strongholds of Satan must yield to God who is our stronghold.

I challenge each reader to become confrontational and address the victory of Christ against Satan's hindrances to revival. The satanic revival demands a spiritual revival authored by God to send it into retreat.

REVIVAL PRAYER PATTERN 5
FOCUS: COMING AGAINST THE ENEMY

Loving Heavenly Father, You are the stronghold of my life; of whom shall I be afraid? I worship You and love You for being omnipotent, almighty and absolute in Your transcendent greatness and unequaled power. Thank You that, no matter how formidable and threatening the forces of darkness become, those who are with us are always "more" than those who are with them. I affirm that Your almightiness is unapproachable by any challenger and that Your power is full of glory.

I worship You, Heavenly Father, in the worthy merit of the Lord Jesus Christ. I affirm that He is Lord to the glory of God the Father. I hold all of His person and work directly upon my life as my protection during this time of prayer. I choose to abide in His incarnation, His cross, His resurrection, His ascension and His glorification.

I come in humble obedience to use the weapons of my warfare against the darkness that is seeking to rule the people of my city, country and world. I affirm that the weapons You have given to me to use are filled with divine power that is sufficient to demolish every stronghold Satan has built to hold back Your will and plan.

I confess the awful wickedness and sins that I, my family, my fellow believers and my culture have committed. Wash me afresh in the blood of my Lord Jesus Christ that there may be no hindrance to Your fellowship and blessing upon me. I apologize to You for the offense against You represented in the wicked sins characterizing our culture. I recognize that when people abandon themselves in such sinful rebellion, much ground is being given to Satan to rule in our culture. My only hope is knowing that the finished work of my Lord Jesus Christ is sufficient payment for even these. I ask You to bring about all that is necessary to grant us the gift of repentance and a broken humility before You. I invite You to draw near to the people of our day until we are humbled and broken before You in a revival awakening greater than any that has ever been.

In the mighty name of my Lord Jesus Christ, I use the weapons of my warfare to demolish and weaken every throne, dominion, princely ruler, authority, power of darkness and wicked spirit in the heavenly realm that is organized and strategized to hinder revival. I ask the Holy Spirit to hold the mighty power of the shed blood and finished work of my Lord Jesus Christ constantly against these strongholds to cause their destruction and defeat.

In the name of the Lord Jesus Christ and by the power of His blood, I pull down all levels of the stronghold of ___. [Choose items from the following list of areas of Satan's strongholds that you desire to pull down and smash. You may think of other things—the list is suggestive, not exhaustive.]

1. Pornography
2. Perverted sexual practices
3. Adultery and prostitution
4. Drug use and promotion
5. Drug suppliers' protection
6. Alcohol addiction
7. Abortion practices and promotion
8. Cursing and vile language
9. Unbelief and humanism
10. New Age teaching
11. Occult promotion and activity
12. Satan worship
13. Television and media distortions
14. Religious cults and isms (name those you know)
15. Liberal theology promotion and false doctrines
16. Divisive influences in the body of Christ
17. Violence and crime
18. Child abuse in all its forms
19. Divorce and family disunity
20. Materialism and greed
21. Peer pressure
22. Spiritual deafness and spiritual blindness
23. Blocking of people from sharing their faith
24. Blocking of people from receiving Christ
25. Lack of care for the homeless and hurting
26. Disunity and distrust in Christ's Body
27. Attacks on pastors, Christian workers and their families

28. Interest in spiritism and evil supernaturalism
29. Promotion of hate, rage and violent anger
30. Hindrance of the recruitment and funding of missionaries
31. Pride, spiritual haughtiness and indifference
32. Neglect of Bible study and prayer

I pull down these strongholds in the name of my Lord Jesus Christ and I pray their wicked work back upon themselves. I ask my loving Father in heaven to assign His holy angels to engage in direct combative defeat of these strongholds of evil. I bind the work of evil powers in each of these strongholds and I invite the Holy Spirit to unleash His mighty convicting power upon the people who are in bondage to them. I ask Him to exalt the ways of righteousness before the spiritual understanding of such people and to convict them deeply of their accountability to God in coming judgment. I ask the Holy Spirit to open their spiritual eyes to see their need for the saving grace of our Lord Jesus Christ. May this revival for which I pray bring multitudes into a saving relationship with Him.

I address my prayer against the strongholds assigned to keep God's people from believing You for revival awakening. Surely, there must be many that are working to make Your people lukewarm, satisfied with our materialism and blind to our spiritual needs. I pull down all such strongholds, named and unnamed, and I pray for a great moving of the Holy Spirit to bring to us a hungering and a thirsting after righteousness. May the Holy Spirit arouse in Christ's Body an insatiable appetite to memorize, study and know God's Holy Word. In the name of my Lord Jesus Christ I plead for a revolutionary revival to visit my heart, my family, my church and the whole body of Christ until it spills over upon the world around us and brings many souls into glory. Amen.

14

Body Unity Under Attack

As a prisoner for the Lord, then, I urge you to live a life worthy of the calling you have received. Be completely humble and gentle; be patient, bearing with one another in love. Make every effort to keep the unity of the Spirit through the bond of peace. There is one body and one Spirit—just as you were called to one hope when you were called—one Lord, one faith, one baptism; one God and Father of all, who is over all and through all and in all. But, to each of us grace has been given as Christ apportioned it (Ephesians 4:1-7).

Preacher Bubeck:

Why don't you just leave our church? You're causing so much trouble with your horrible, negative leadership. We always had a church of marvelous unity until you came as our pastor. Under our beloved Dr. Adams* we all got along so well together.

I understand some of our leaders asked you to leave quietly, and you've refused. Why do you have to do this to us? Remember, God is listening and expecting your resignation to insure the on-going of our great church according to His future plans for us. It is up to you to answer our request as soon as possible.

For the good of our church,

Sara Jones*
[*names changed]

Subtle Spiritual Pride

This is a portion of a longer letter that added to the burden I already felt. I never had faced anything like this before in my twenty-four years of pastoral ministry. The churches I had been privileged to pastor had been wonderfully united with a positive outlook upon ministry. My preaching had been commended for its expository, doctrinal style. Any threatened troubles had quickly vanished when handled with humility and prayer. My pastoral leadership had enjoyed strong support from the people.

It had been so good that I have to confess a subtle invasion of spiritual pride in my heart. I felt a spiritual superiority to other pastors who had allowed themselves to become the center of broiling conflict in their churches. I was convinced that, if these pastors had just been more patient, humble, prayerful and dependent upon God, they never would have gotten into such conflict. How subtle spiritual pride can be.

Now I faced the problem myself, and I had no solution. My accusers had made up their minds I was unworthy to serve any longer as their pastor and they were determined to have it their way. Though we held several "clear the air" forums where I answered any question anyone had submitted in writing, a minority group still was determined to force my resignation.

It all began two and a half years earlier when I had accepted a nearly unanimous call to become the senior pastor of this large, historic church in the heart of one of our great cities. Though those years had been hard in many ways, they'd also been rewarding. I had never witnessed so many people growing spiritually in such a short time. The majority of members seemed hungry for God's Word.

Ad-Hoc Committee

The major battle was in the spiritual realm. Frequently, I would get to church before any other staff members arrived, and walk and pray in the sanctuary. I will never forget the battles fought there. I also sensed great struggle when I preached; unseen forces seemed determined to resist me and the message. It was difficult not to be discouraged, even though I knew I was in the place of God's appointment.

The crisis came during the summer while I was away on vacation. A long-tenured staff person cast some negative aspersions against my pastoral leadership and resigned. When I returned, an ad-hoc committee of seven asked to have a private conference with me. I agreed, although I was not comfortable with such a meeting when our constituted church leadership was by-passed. At the meeting, the committee suggested my pastoral leadership was not meeting the expectations of a "large number" of influential congregation members. They had no desire to "dirty my name" by bringing the matter to a church vote—but if they had to, they would. They reminded me of a peculiar bylaws provision of that church: In case a vote of confidence was requested, the pastor would have to have a 75 percent supportive vote to stay. They assured me I would never receive that percentage.

Their request was completely unexpected and very confrontive, yet I sensed within myself a quiet, deep inner peace. I responded with, "I sensed a strong call from my Lord to come to this church, and I will have to sense just as strong a release from Him before I can resign. Unless He gives me such a sense of release, I will have to stay, regardless of any dirtying of my name that might result."

The Vote

Their determination and my response set in motion months of deep turmoil in the church. Some of the most painful experiences possible occur when believers quarrel with one another. Petitions calling for a vote of confidence were circulated. Both major boards expressed strong majority support for my continued pastoral leadership, but clouds of disunity were everywhere. The day for the confidence vote was set. Much prayer ascended, and most of the leaders and congregation expected a supportive vote.

However, an unexpected development altered the situation. A key issue had been whether I intended to lead the church out of the denominational convention with which it was affiliated. I'd stated clearly in the forums that I would not do that, but a week before the vote, one of my detractors received a solicited letter from a man in my former pastorate. This man's letter stated that I had never been a strong supporter of the convention and I probably would lead the church out. The letter was copied and circulated widely just before the vote. Though the man who authored the letter wrote a retraction later, it was too late. Some people assumed, "Where there's smoke, there's fire."

The vote was 69 percent supportive for me to stay on as pastor. My resignation became necessary. Some rejoiced, but the majority were crushed. Tears flowed freely. People were in a state of shock. Some were very angry, and they determined to reverse the decision.

They had private strategy meetings and later presented me with a number of alternatives. One was that we could appeal to the courts. State law prohibited a minority ruling over the majority in a recognized state corporation, and that particular bylaw of our church would be ruled out of order. The majority would still rule. I could not allow that in good conscience. I had known the provision was in the bylaws when I accepted the call. Besides, God could have sovereignly given me a 75-percent majority vote as well as 69 percent.

Other suggestions came. I should lead in the formation of a new church. Or I should just not resign and continue in this ministry, forcing the minority to take it to court.

Any of these suggestions, though well intentioned, would have violated my personal integrity. I felt I could do nothing but resign and allow the church to come back together under a new pastor. This might not be the Lord's direction in every similar situation, but I knew it was His plan for me. I did sense His release, so I resigned. The majority gave my wife and me a royal farewell, presented us with a phenomenal love gift, and continued my full-time salary for four months. They also changed the bylaws immediately, so that a minority could never again dismiss a pastor. The majority chose the pastoral search committee and led in the call of a new pastor. One of the pastoral staff, who happened to be my own son-in-law, continued as the interim pastor until the new pastor came.

I had hoped the new leader would be able to unite the body, but it did not happen. The minority group took him and the church to court several times, but without success. They ultimately left the church, and the church did eventually withdraw from the convention—the very thing I would not have allowed.

The sovereign workings of our Lord are indeed past finding out, and His disciplines are at times strangely ironic.

Internal Problems Exceed External Attack

That account from the journal of my life focuses on the greatest problem God's people ever face. The most threatening and painful area of attack upon any group of God's people is from *within,* not without. As we have seen, the external enemies of Nehemiah and his fellow builders were formidable. Yet, the problems within the Jewish community were even more threatening to his call to rebuild the walls. It's the same in Christ's church.

A number of years ago Dr. Bruce Shelley quoted a late medieval manuscript: "The church is something like Noah's Ark. If it weren't for the storm outside, you couldn't stand the smell inside."[1]

Such is the case in the church today. Our internal problems have devastated the witness of the church. Our internal sins have made Christian faith a mockery in the eyes of the questioning world. The news media gets caught up in the soap opera surrounding the trial of a prominent television evangelist. Recent news media accounts relish reports that other ministries are experiencing hardship due to a fall-off in support. Will the internal problems that hurt and disgrace the Christian witness ever cease?

Local churches feel this in-house problem most closely. Denominations feel it in battles over troubling issues. Parachurch organizations are torn by internal dispute. Yet in spite of all these expressions of internal dissension, God's sovereign ability to work out His will has enabled Christ's work to move forward. That's to the praise of His glory!

An admonition from the apostle Peter has an important message for believers who are hoping for revival:

> For it is time for judgment to begin with the family of God; and if it begins with us, what will the outcome be for those who do not obey the gospel of God? (1 Peter 4:17).

We believers need to clean up our act before the eyes of a holy God and the eyes of a scorning world. Our internal problems are terribly destructive.

The Internal Threat to Nehemiah

What Sanballat and Tobiah could not accomplish with their threats and henchmen, the internal dissenters could have done in a few days. The problems were so threatening that Nehemiah declared, "When I heard their outcry and these charges, I was very angry" (Nehemiah 5:6).

Although we are not given detailed accounts of these internal problems, we can synthesize the situation from biblical evidence. A serious famine broke out within Jerusalem. Several factors contributed to this problem. With Sanballat, Tobiah and the others opposing the people's efforts to rebuild, there was no flow of commerce between them and the builders. Also, at Nehemiah's request, most of the Jewish people were putting all their efforts toward rebuilding the walls, leaving them little time to grow food. Their large families created a constant demand for food, and, since they couldn't grow it, they had to buy it. When money ran out they had to borrow, and they put up their fields, vineyards and houses as surety. They also had to pay a real estate or "ground tax" to the king of Persia.

The common Jewish folk faced a dilemma. They had to borrow from their more wealthy Jewish brothers, and they were to pay the loans back with generous interest. Not earning any money, they could not repay their loans, so the creditors took advantage of the situation. They took the debtors' children into service, to work off the debt. This debt slavery (see Nehemiah 5:1-5) happened within the Jewish community and not with foreign lenders. These wealthy Jews were clustering around dire circumstances like vultures hovering over a wounded animal.

Nehemiah responded to this internal problem in several ways:

1. He became angry.

"When I heard their outcry and these charges, I was very angry" (Nehemiah 5:6). It's good for righteous people to be able to get angry over injustice. Dr. Donald K. Campbell of Dallas Seminary refers to columnist Louis Cassels who . . .

> has said that the hardest moral duty of our time is for men and women to keep on caring. We are exposed daily to so much human tragedy that we experience what someone has called "compassion fatigue." Having felt sorry for so many flood victims, earthquake victims, and war victims, we simply cannot muster the sympathy we know we ought to have for fresh casualties. But, even worse than compassion fatigue, said Cassels, is "indignation fatigue." Many of us seem to have lost the capacity to get mad—or at least, as mad as we ought to get—about lying, cheating, and stealing. . . . To be indifferent to wrongdoing, to shrug it off or laugh at it, is a symptom of advanced degradation of the moral sense. Someone seems to have administered a massive dose of novocaine to our national conscience.[2]

To Nehemiah, this was intolerable. Jewish people profiteering at the expense of their countrymen was a moral outrage. Taking family members of the debtors as slaves added to the offense. Though debt slavery under certain circumstances was allowed under Jewish law (see Exodus 21:1-11; Deuteronomy 15:12), this national crisis was no time for it. They all had their lives on the line, and they needed to sacrifice one for all and all for one with loving support.

2. Nehemiah took time to think things through carefully.

"I pondered them in my mind . . . " (verse 7a). When we feel what Nehemiah felt, we need to take time to measure our response carefully. This is no time to "shoot from the hip." Pastors, parents and Christian leaders, take careful note here. Hasty, angry responses to the wrongs of those for whom we are responsible can often be a form of self-righteous pride. Instead of correcting the situation, this response may only intensify it.

3. Nehemiah confronted the wrongdoers.

"I . . . then accused the nobles and officials. I told them, 'You are exacting usury from your own countrymen!' " (verse 7b). His approach was forthright, but it was also respectful and tactful. If confrontation is handled carefully, it can benefit the whole body as well as those confronted. Our text seems to indicate that Nehemiah first held a private conference with the offending wealthy people. In the spirit of Matthew 18:15, he went to the offenders and pointed out their wrong to them. Only after this approach apparently met with stony silence did Nehemiah take the next step.

4. Nehemiah assembled the larger body to solve the problem.

So I called together a large meeting to deal with them and said: "As far as possible, we have bought back our

Jewish brothers who were sold to the Gentiles. Now you
are selling your brothers, only for them to be sold back to
us!" They kept quiet, because they could find nothing to
say (verses 7c,8).

There are times when our guilt renders us silent. The
Law of Moses had forbidden the wealthier Israelites to
charge high interest to poorer people (see Exodus 22:25;
Leviticus 25:35-37; Deuteronomy 23:19-20).

Nehemiah let their silence hang for several moments,
letting every moment do its work. One can sense a change of
mood taking place. The combative confronter became the
correcting teacher:

> What you are doing is not right. Shouldn't you walk
> in the fear of our God to avoid the reproach of our Gentile
> enemies? (verse 9)

5. Nehemiah identified with the sins of his nobles.

> I and my brothers and my men are also lending the
> people money and grain. But, let the exacting amount of
> usury stop! (verse 10)

When we want to help those who are sinning greatly,
we'll do a better job if we can identify with them on a common ground. Nehemiah's investigations had revealed that
his own family was doing some of the same type of things
that made Nehemiah so angry. The Hebrew text indicates
that Nehemiah not only acknowledged the sins of his own
family members but he also assumed the responsibility for
what they were doing. It always adds weight to the correction process when the corrector admits his own guilt.
Nehemiah was a master at that (see Nehemiah 1:6,7).

6. Nehemiah stated the correction necessary, and he built in accountability safeguards.

> Give back to them immediately their fields, vine-
> yards, olive groves and houses, and also the usury you are

charging them — the hundredth part of the money, grain,
new wine and oil (Nehemiah 5:11).

When restitution is necessary, it's good to spell it out
clearly, leaving no room for misunderstanding.

"We will give it back," they said. "And we will not
demand anything more from them. We will do as you say"
(verse 12).

These wealthy people were on the spot. Their sins had
been exposed, and a pattern of correction made clear. To
their credit, they affirmed their willingness to correct the
wrong. The hardest thing we ever have to do is say, "I'm
sorry; I was wrong. I'll make it right. Please forgive me."

Nehemiah was glad to hear their confession, but knowing human nature, he also built accountability into their verbal agreement. He insisted that they formalize it with a
solemn oath before the priests. This was not merely a verbal
oath; it also carried a commitment. The priests in such instances were like a court of appeal. If a noble failed in his
oath, the sufferer could appeal to the priests for help.

Nehemiah then reminded the men that if they failed to
fulfill their agreement, God would deal with them:

I also shook out the folds of my robe and said, "In
this way may God shake out of his house and possessions
every man who does not keep this promise. So may such a
man be shaken out and emptied!" (verse 13*b*)

That's pretty strong. In essence, Nehemiah is asking
God to directly back up the accountability for correction.

Accountability of this nature provides motivation for
proper living within God's family. When we realize God holds
each of us accountable for righting our wrongs, we are
strongly motivated. That's a notable ingredient in revival.
It's also an absolute. No believer ever gets away with wrong-
ing his brother. If not made right, it either will be dealt with
in discipline now (see Hebrews 12:1-15) or be fully rectified at
the judgment seat of Christ (2 Corinthians 5:1-10).

15

Keeping Body Unity Functioning

External enemies can be destructive to any Christian movement. The large numbers of martyrs giving their lives for their faith even in our day tell us that external enemies are deadly. Yet what really robs the church of its spiritual power is internal warfare. When believers' hearts are not right with one another or not right with God, He holds back His power. The very heart of revival, therefore, needs to be a focus of believers getting their internal problems remedied.

In the previous chapter we looked at steps Nehemiah took to deal with the internal threat to God's call for the saving of a city. Now we'll examine seven important ingredients suggested by biblical passages for keeping the internal unity of the body functioning properly.

1. Be alert—the threat is always present.

> With this in mind, be alert and always keep on praying for all the saints (Ephesians 6:18b).

"We need to get back to the New Testament church!"

I heard that expression a lot during my pastoral training years. It implied that the New Testament church always did things the way they should be done. When I heard that, I often would respond with, "Which New Testament church?"

195

Not every church was worthy of following as an example. The church at Corinth, for instance, was filled with tragic internal problems, including: a four-way split brought on by carnal pride (1 Corinthians 1:11-17; 3:1-9); a believer living with his father's wife (chapter 5); use of godless secular courts to resolve disputes with each other (6:1-11); sexual immorality and marriage disharmony (6:12-20; chapter 7); eating food offered to idols without considering that others could connect that to worship of evil spirits (chapter 8); drunken, self-centered love feasts in connection with the Lord's supper (chapters 10, 11); and confusion concerning spiritual gifts, a lack of love among the people and a chaotic abuse of tongues (chapters 12, 13, 14). That is not the kind of church most of us would want to join. It was a spiritual mess.

Yet it was a correctable mess. That's why Paul wrote his letter. (A remarkable change occurred by the time he wrote his second epistle to the Corinthians.) In the beginning, the internal problems threatened the church constantly, and Paul's prayers and admonitions dealt with those internal needs. Pastors, elders, deacons and spiritually concerned believers need to be alert continually. We must maintain an attentive and prayerful watch for any internal threat to the body. When we fail to do that, we open ourselves to internal disaster.

2. Be doctrinal—the unity is already established.

On several occasions, churches with internal problems have called me to try to help them come together in unity. That's never easy for a church. When anger, resentment, hatred, jealousy, and defensive self-righteousness have festered internally, healing comes slowly. Careless words, vindictive actions, and choosing up sides allow little chance for internal harmony. That's what's behind most church splits—believers just agree to go their separate ways. Where do we begin to resolve such emotionally fired problems?

The essential starting place is for those involved to focus upon an important point of doctrinal truth that they may have neglected. Ephesians 4:3,4 states:

> Make every effort to *keep* the unity of the Spirit through the bond of peace. *There is one body* and one Spirit (emphasis added).

Believers are never called upon to create oneness in the body. We are called upon to *keep* what has been accomplished already by the redemptive work of Christ and the baptizing work of the Holy Spirit. "For we were all baptized by one Spirit into one body (1 Corinthians 12:13*a*). If we are true believers, we are already members of one another. We are already united with one another and with our Lord Jesus Christ who is the head of His body. That's an indisputable fact. Grace has already accomplished it.

It's difficult to hate a part of your own physical body. We usually treat even its parts that hurt with great love and tenderness. Only when a member of our physical body is hopelessly diseased or injured do we consent to removal. When that does happen, we may feel great pain over the loss.

The church body works the same way. When we understand how essential each member is, we treasure every one. We put up with a lot. We are patient and loving when we know the other believer is a part of us. Instead of amputation, we think of medication and tender loving care, and we seek to nurse the hurting part back to health. Focusing on the essential oneness of Christ's body not only helps to heal broken churches, but it also helps to keep healthy churches functioning in unity through maintaining supportive, understanding attitudes among the believers.

3. Be exemplary—the leadership is responsible.

According to Dr. Bill Yeager of the First Baptist Church of Modesto, California, speaking at an Institute on Church Leadership, three ingredients are essential to a healthy, thriving church. In order of importance they are: leadership,

leadership and leadership. An important biblical truth is that much responsibility for what happens in a local body of believers rests upon the leadership.

In Nehemiah 5:1-13, after relating the confrontation with the greedy moneylenders and the resulting corrective measures, Nehemiah declares his own personal philosophy of being an exemplary role-model leader in financial matters. He humbly catalogs what his practice had been during his governing rule. He had forgone the customary salary, avoided land speculation, provided food for more than 150 officials, and entertained and fed visiting dignitaries.

The point he made is important to leadership: As a leader, he felt responsible both to the people and to God.

Nehemiah's leadership reached beyond financial integrity. He set the model for frequent and fervent prayer; his faith was magnificently displayed; his courage was undaunted; and his capacity for moral indignation boiled over with corrective action. He confronted even the most influential dignitaries willingly. Social justice and compassion for the oppressed were his trademark, and his work focused upon the approval of God rather than man.

There is no substitute for exemplary spiritual leadership. We desperately need Nehemiah-style leaders who practice lifestyles that are beyond reproach and who challenge their people to spiritual and moral excellence.

> Obey your leaders and submit to their authority. They keep watch over you as men who must give an account. Obey them, so that their work will be a joy, not a burden, for that would be of no advantage to you. Pray for us. We are sure that we have a clear conscience and desire to live honorably in every way (Hebrews 13:17,18).

No leader can ever be completely faultless, but he can be careful to measure his progress toward exemplary leadership. Leaders need to be a healing part of the solution and not a contributing cause to the problem.

Leaders must also be exemplary in their willingness to say, "I'm sorry. I was wrong. Will you forgive me?" I recall one instance when the Lord called me to account for an unconscious resentment in my heart. One of our fine deacons had made a remark at a deacon's meeting that offended me. Rather than go to him I simply buried it and went on. I wasn't even conscious of holding the resentment—I treated him as lovingly as ever.

Several weeks passed. As I was taking a spiritual inventory before the Lord one day in prayer, He reminded me of my offense at the remarks of this deacon. I tried to brush it off, but the Lord would not permit me to avoid the responsibility. My conscience bothered me for several hours. Finally, I called the deacon on the phone and made an appointment to meet him. As we met, I related with carefully chosen words, and without any accusation toward him, how I had been offended and of my sin of not going to him as Matthew 18:15 admonishes. I asked his forgiveness. Though he'd not been aware of my offense at his remarks, his eyes filled with tears. He in turn asked my forgiveness for being hasty in what he had said. Love flowed between us with a new deepness, and I learned that being an exemplary leader sometimes means painful admission of failure; but it's worth it.

4. Be protecting—the enemy is active.

Whenever strife arises in a body of believers or even between two individual believers, you can be sure Satan's kingdom is participating. One of his chief functions is to accuse and find fault. He is always trying to cause us to think accusing, negative thoughts about fellow believers. His actions are described accurately in Revelation 12:10,11:

> Now have come the salvation and the power and the kingdom of our God, and the authority of his Christ. For the accuser of our brothers, who accuses them before our God day and night, has been hurled down. They overcame him by the blood of the Lamb and by the word of their tes-

timony; they did not love their lives so much as to shrink
from death.

Galatians 5:19-21 makes very clear that much trouble
and strife between believers can flow out of our fleshly nature. However, no sin more quickly aligns us with Satan's
work than allowing negative, accusing thoughts and words
toward others to dominate us. It opens the door to accusing
spirits of darkness and the power of evil supernaturalism will
begin to rule that area of our life. Anyone who has been a
part of a church quarrel knows the satanic ugliness of it all.
Satan's kingdom is quick to move in and superintend the increasing disaster.

What can believers do to combat this problem? The
practice of biblical spiritual warfare can turn the tide. Faithful use of the weapons of our warfare is vital.

Suppose you sense a hostile relationship building between you and another believer, for no apparent reason.
Here's a warfare prayer approach you can take, silently in
your mind, even while you continue your conversation:

> In the name of my Lord Jesus Christ and by the power
> of His blood I pull down all hurtful relationships
> between _____ and me that Satan and his kingdom are
> seeking to build. I will only accept relationships
> between _____ and me that are authored by the Holy
> Spirit in the will of God.

That little resistance prayer is a powerful tool for
regular use in all negative relationships. You can enlarge the
scope of the prayer to apply to quarreling relationships between other individuals or groups, like this:

> In the name of my Lord Jesus Christ and by the power
> of His blood, I come against all powers of darkness trying to
> promote accusations and negative attitudes among the
> believers of our church. I take full authority over them, and
> in the name of the Lord Jesus Christ, I bind them until
> they are inactive, and I command them to leave our
> presence and to go where the Lord Jesus Christ sends

them. I invite the Lord Jesus Christ and the Holy Spirit to sovereignly work to create relationships between us all that are in God's loving will and plan.

Persistent usage of such prayer is notably productive. I've witnessed many reversals of divisive problems by such prayer. This practice is in keeping with our authoritative responsibility to resist the devil steadfast in the faith, thus forcing him to cease his wicked work and flee.

5. Be forgiving—the guilt is inclusive.

We touched upon this earlier when noting that Nehemiah identified personally with the moneylenders he was rebuking. He included himself and accepted responsibility for those in his own household who'd been doing similar things (Nehemiah 5:10). We are never in greater spiritual trouble than when we see only the sins of others and not our own. The development of a forgiving heart necessitates close familiarity with our own sinful capacities.

This truth is revealed in the parable Jesus told in Matthew 18:21-35 about the unmerciful servant. Peter had wondered how many times he was responsible to forgive his brother. He thought seven times might be the perfect number. The Lord Jesus stretched it out to almost infinity when he said seventy times seven would be more appropriate (verse 22). Jesus then told of a servant who owed his master the equivalent of several million dollars. When called upon to pay, the servant pleaded for mercy. A marvelous, concise picture of our forgiveness received at salvation is drawn: "The servant's master took pity on him, canceled the debt and let him go" (verse 27). When God in mercy forgave us for Jesus' sake, He canceled our enormous debt of sin and let us go, free and totally cleansed from guilt.

This forgiven servant, however, didn't give what he just received. A man who owed him a very small debt by comparison also pleaded for mercy. Instead of forgiveness, the forgiven servant threw the man in prison.

This is what we as believers do when we fail to forgive those who sin against us. Their offenses are always small when compared to the whole spectrum of sins God has forgiven and removed from us. The Lord Jesus taught us to pray: "Forgive us our debts as we forgive our debtors." The greatly forgiven are responsible to forgive greatly. Failure to do so always spells disaster.

The parable continues with how the master dealt with his unforgiving servant: "In anger his master turned him over to the jailers to be tortured, until he would pay back all he owed" (verse 34). The jailers are probably demonic tormentors unleashed to discipline the offending servant. All he owed at this point was to develop a forgiving heart—his previous debt had all been canceled.

We see how this applies dramatically to us by what is stated next by our Lord Jesus Christ: "This is how my heavenly Father will treat each of you, unless you forgive your brother from your heart" (Matthew 18:35). I personally am convinced that believers never open their lives more tragically to invite demonic affliction than when we allow accusing, negative, unforgiving attitudes and actions in our dealings with others.

Forgiving is not the same as being soft on sin. Nehemiah was severe in his rebuke, although he identified himself with their sin, but he conveyed the message that correction was what he was after. Forgiveness waited in the wings even before it was sought. Holding and expressing such an attitude is essential for a church to function in unity.

6. Be patient—the timing is often adjustable.

It's better to err on the side of patience and tolerance than to rush into judgment only to hurt others by fierce censure. That is the whole tenor of Scripture. God deals with His people in patience. He is longsuffering and willing to wait. It's part of the strength of His grace. Patience is not a sign of weakness.

Nehemiah dealt swiftly with the offenses of the money lenders because it was urgent in that situation. Sometimes believers must be quick to act. The rebellious moral sin noted in 1 Corinthians 5 was also such a time.

Another practice that needs immediate correction is the teaching of wrong doctrine. Yet even in these cases, the spirit behind the action must be patient and understanding. Harsh, vindictive actions against other believers are always out of order. The focus must always be correction and healing.

Nehemiah's corrective, loving approach brought far-reaching spiritual results among the people. Not only was the money-lending problem rectified, but the people also dealt with a host of other spiritual problems. Nehemiah 10:29-39 catalogs these measures: Intermarriage with heathen families was stopped (verse 30); Sabbath violations were corrected (verse 31); canceling debts after seven years was reinstated (verse 31b); proper tithing responsibility was assumed (verses 32, 35-39); the sacrificial system was re-established (verses 32-34); honoring the priesthood was renewed (verses 34,38,39); and a whole new emphasis on worship and love for God's house arose (verses 37-39).

Nehemiah's patient, correcting, loving approach played a great part in moving the people toward this revival. This is an Old Testament picture of grace in action: Grace is never license for sin; grace is loving confrontation, expressed in patience; grace is faith that allows God's sovereignty to bring about heart changes others may need.

7. Be loving—the offender is always undeserving.

Agape love loves those who do not want or deserve love. That's the way God loved us as lost sinners:

> God demonstrates His own love for us in this: While we were still sinners, Christ died for us (Romans 5:8).

> You see, at just the right time, when we were still powerless, Christ died for the ungodly (Romans 5:6).

God's love remains the most amazing of all theological concepts. The greatest philosophical minds grope for an understanding of its extremity and power. God's love reached out to a man who persecuted Christ and took part in the brutal murder of Stephen. That love redeemed Saul of Tarsus, transformed him and used him as one of history's greatest defenders of the faith.

The capacity of God's love to save and change an undeserving sinner seems measureless. The only thing that can quench that power is persistent unbelief. This fact was dramatically illustrated by the experience of Ted Bundy, who was executed in January 1989 in Florida. Bundy was, by most accounts, one of history's most diabolical mass murderers. Just before his execution, Bundy requested an interview with Dr. James Dobson.

In the April '89 issue of *Focus on the Family* magazine, Rolf Zettersten writes:

> As Christians, we believe that God's love and grace are sufficient to redeem *every* sinner. But, would the Lord forgive a murderer?
>
> From a theological perspective, the response is an unequivocal "Yes." We are all familiar with biblical accounts of people like the apostle Paul and the thief of the cross who were saved in spite of treacherous pasts.
>
> From a human perspective, however, it is difficult for us to understand how God could forgive a murderer like Ted Bundy. He killed not just once, but at least 28 times. Among his victims were young, innocent girls who endured unspeakable tortures before he took their lives in cold blood. He had been. without question, one of the most depraved, wicked and violent criminals in our lifetime.
>
> So [we can understand] why some people may pause a moment before acknowledging that even a Ted Bundy could have entered into fellowship with Jesus Christ by repenting of his sins. Yet, to those who knew him in his final years, Ted Bundy's life was dramatically changed by his confession of faith. According to John Tanner, who led Bundy to the Lord and discipled him during 200 hours of

personal contact over several years, Bundy's conversion was real.[1]

Zettersten has stated well the amazing wonder of God's love that can save the vilest of sinners. Its power leaves us breathless. This same love of God invades the believer's life: "God has poured out his love into our hearts by the Holy Spirit, whom he has given us" (Romans 5:5*b*).

This love also can keep believers united, expressing the oneness God has created in them. Peter leaves with us a benediction of responsibility:

> The end of all things is near. Therefore be clear minded and self-controlled so that you can pray. Above all, love each other deeply, because love covers over a multitude of sins. Offer hospitality to one another without grumbling. Each one should use whatever gift he has received to serve others, faithfully administering God's grace in its various forms. If anyone speaks, he should do it as one speaking the very words of God. If anyone serves, he should do it with the strength God provides, so that in all things God may be praised through Jesus Christ. To him be the glory and the power for ever and ever. Amen (1 Peter 4:7-11).

It's not Satan, the world system, the last days or God's reluctance that hinders revival. From God's perspective it's still "My people, called by My name" who constitute the deciding factor for our land. Believers will personally answer for what we do with that fact at the judgment seat of Christ.

REVIVAL PRAYER PATTERN 6
FOCUS: UNITY IN THE BODY

Dear God and Father of our Lord Jesus Christ, I worship You in the wonder of Your triune oneness. I grope to understand the mystery of how three unique persons remain one God. I praise You for its truth and I bow before You in the wonder of such revelation of Yourself. By faith, I ask You to increase my capacity to appreciate and understand Your triune oneness that I might share new insights with others.

I also praise and worship You, Lord Jesus Christ, for the scope of Your finished work that unites me with You. I hold Your powerful name, Lord Jesus Christ, over my personal life, my family, my work and the whole body of Christ for benefit, protection and all that You have for us.

I rejoice that Your salvation has united me inseparably not only with Yourself but also with every other believer. Thank You, blessed Holy Spirit, for Your great work of baptizing me into this body of Christ. I rejoice to be a part of such perfect fellowship. Thank You, Lord Jesus Christ, for continuing Your mighty work of readying Your body to present her to Yourself as a radiant church, without stain, wrinkle or blemish of any kind. Thank You that this body will be holy and blameless in the mystery of Your finished work. I glory in the wonder of such truth.

I enter into repentance and confession before You to acknowledge how often I personally have violated the essential oneness of the body. Cleanse me of my wickedness of not honoring each part of the body as You do. I also confess the sins of my family and fellow church members in not living out the unity of the body which You have created. I confess the divisiveness existing in Your visible church as a violation of Your holy plan. I worship and praise You, dear Heavenly Father, for Your sovereign ability to use even our divisiveness to glorify Your name and finish Your work.

Yet I long and pray for the bringing together of Your born-again ones in a united movement for revival awakening. We have been so terribly wounded by those things that have divided us. Our capacity to bring about change in our world has been reduced to a feeble squeak. In humble embarrassment I repent over this fact, and ask Your Holy Spirit to move over Your body to cause change. Help us to come together under the oneness of the Holy Spirit's control. May His oneness of intercession wait before heaven's throne of grace in the hearts of millions of believers who ask God for revolutionary revival.

Thank You, Lord Jesus Christ, for planning for unity rather than uniformity. The diversity of Your body is part of its beauty and functional appeal to the lost. It adds to Your glory. Bless Your church in its wide diversity of expression in patterns of worship and songs of praise. Help us to love one another in our diversity.

Help me not to condemn my fellow member for what he is not. Grant me the wisdom to understand and the capacity to appreciate him for what he is. Above all, help me to love each part of the body. May that love express itself in patience and the capacity to hold my thoughts in check when I see the failures of another member of Your body. Forgive me for my quick practice to take comfort about my own failures when I see the sins of others.

Blessed Heavenly Father, I recognize that Satan and his kingdom are relentless in their efforts to keep believers divisive toward one another. As the accuser of the believers, he continually plants suspicions in believers' hearts. In the name of my Lord Jesus Christ, I pull down that work of darkness and bind our enemy that he might not succeed. I ask the Holy Spirit to supplant all divisive works with the unity of the Spirit actively working in believers.

Oh, Holy God, only Your sovereignty can move Your body into united action. May Your Holy Spirit brood over Your church and cause it to breathe out a united cry for revival awakening. I wait before You for this. Only You can work it out in a way that will startle the world and glorify Your name. Raise up the human leaders You can trust to touch not the glory that belongs only to You. I affirm again that what You have accomplished through the finished work of my Lord Jesus Christ is sufficient to do more than I ask. In Jesus' precious name I pray. Amen.

16

The Work of the Word

For the word of God is living and active. Sharper than any double-edged sword, it penetrates even to dividing soul and spirit, joints and marrow; it judges the thoughts and attitudes of the heart. Nothing in all creation is hidden from God's sight. Everything is uncovered and laid bare before the eyes of him to whom we must give account (Hebrews 4:12,13).

Quick Justice Is Possible

As my wife and sister-in-law returned from lunch, they saw a truck pulling my brother's trailer with his snow-mobiles out of the driveway. Someone was stealing them! The shock unnerved them, but they followed the thief to get his license number. There was no license plate on the rear of his vehicle, so they pulled ahead to see the tag on the front. The driver had it tucked in the windshield of his cab. When he realized their intent to see it, he quickly ditched the plate. Turning down a side street, he managed to lose them.

One of the investigating policemen said, "Snowmobiles are pretty valuable. What were they doing in your driveway?"

"I moved them there from summer storage so we could take them to the mountains," my brother explained.

The policeman said, "Well, we'll do all we can, but you'll probably never see your snowmobiles again. These guys are pretty smooth operators and they usually cover their tracks well enough that they avoid getting caught. It's pretty hopeless in a city the size of Denver."

My brother and his wife accepted the loss with Christian grace, but I felt very indignant. In my study for the writing of this book, I had spent considerable time on the accelerating decay of morality in our culture. This first-hand evidence of arrogant, lawless conduct angered me deeply. I prayed with righteous indignation, "Loving Heavenly Father, put Your holy finger on that thief. In the name of the Lord Jesus I ask You to bring him quickly to account for such bold sin against You. Bring confusion to him and cause him to make foolish mistakes that will expose him and reverse his apparent escape." I found myself frequently praying this way, and the other family members prayed too.

Returning from the Denver Seminary library the following Saturday afternoon, I was astonished to see the snowmobiles back in the driveway. I could scarcely wait to hear the story. The man had tried to dispose of them at a ridiculously low price at the local flea market. Suspicions arose, police computers were checked, the snowmobiles were impounded and returned to my brother, and the thief—now in great trouble—was made accountable. We all praised our Lord for such quick justice.

Accountability to God

That incident reminds me of how every person is accountable before a holy God, and He could just as quickly bring any of us to face that accountability through His Word, and to swift, sure justice. Yet His mercy and great love delay our answering to that justice:

> Because of the LORD's great love we are not consumed, for his compassions never fail (Lamentations 3:22).

The desire for revolutionary revival springs up in people who see their accountability to God. Such awareness breaks hearts concerning personal sin, and repentance quickly follows. Intimate fellowship with God is restored; the joy of that new relationship overflows and revival is in process. Witnessing to the lost through the power of God occurs. When people are won to Christ, a whole culture begins to change. Sinful people are transformed and they become God's people who desire holy living.

The Effect of God's Word

The real presence of revival begins when God's Word penetrates hearts and becomes intensely personal to every believer. When that happens, revival is on its way.

Good people, even Christian people, can easily become sinful in their lifestyle. Sin enters in so subtly that we fail to sense its presence. People conceal it from their own sight and from the sight of others. God's dealings with their sins are unrecognized, or they are excused with self-serving thoughts such as, "He'll forgive me"; or, "He understands my weaknesses"; or, "He knows what I have to live with."

David provides a biblical example of how good people can become wicked and sinful in their lifestyle without any apparent awareness. David excused himself from a whole catalog of sins as he was drawn into adultery and eventually murder. He knew God's Word, but God's plan for man to be morally clean and to have only one wife escaped his understanding. Multiple wives and concubines was the "right" of kings. Self-will spread through his inner soul and clouded his spiritual perceptions.

He compromised his loyalty to his fighting troops. The fact that Bathsheba was the daughter of one of David's "mighty men" and the wife of another didn't deter him in his lust. As he gave his sexual desire unbridled expression, he gave up his integrity, his identity with his men and his sacred trust in God. David's downfall was a continuum of excused weaknesses, and he was too blind to comprehend his condition.

David's experience illustrates how subtly Satan works. It also demonstrates how we believers show our need for revolutionary revival. When we become oblivious to our sinful ways, we lack motivation for corrective actions. Questionable spiritual conduct becomes so accepted that God's holy ways are overlooked. When such conditions prevail in a culture, pastors and Christian leaders fail to speak convincingly to the sin issues of the day. People's spiritual sensitivity becomes so dull they cannot recognize the obvious. We need to be warned that, since it happened to "a man after God's own heart," it can happen to us.

God eventually brought David to account, and the way He did it carries significant importance. God sent Nathan, a humble, lowly prophet, to speak to David. Through Nathan, David heard God say, "You're the man."

Revival begins to happen when believers hear God's Word speaking to their own hearts: "You're the one! This is what the Lord God says. It's your prayerlessness, your carnality, your indifference, your bitterness, your hardness, your unfaithfulness!" When revival awakening comes near, God's Word begins to speak personally to each individual. "You're the one!" begins to echo in the heart of each believer.

After hearing God's Word spoken through Nathan, David had his own personal revival. Though his repentance could not spare his little son's life, it did revive and refresh David's personal walk with God. The depth of David's worship is recorded in Psalm 51, which probably was written shortly after God's Word through Nathan had so deeply affected David.

God's Word and Revival Awakening

After the walls were rebuilt under Nehemiah's direction, a beautiful thing happened in Jerusalem. As a direct result of the reading of God's Word, revival came to the people. Nehemiah's inspiring leadership and Ezra's teaching ministry (see Ezra 7:10) created a hunger for God's Word in the people's hearts. They wanted to hear what He expected of them. They came by the thousands and gathered in the court area before the Water Gate. "Men and women and all who were able to understand" (Nehemiah 8:2) depicts the inclusiveness of the crowd—everyone except the youngest children.

It must have been a dramatic moment. To facilitate sight and hearing, Ezra and other officials stood on an elevated platform. With the scrolls of the Torah in his hands, Ezra began to praise and worship God. The people joined by raising their hands heavenward as they bowed down in worship. "Amen! Amen!" they cried. We are not told what Ezra read, only that the reading went on from daybreak until noon (verse 3). Long readings from Genesis, Exodus and Deuteronomy must have sounded forth. As the Levites, Nehemiah and others explained the Word of God, feedback from the people became a vital part of what was happening.

Quietly and intensely, a repentant brokenness for sin crept in and settled upon all those gathered. "For all the people had been weeping as they listened to the words of the Law" (Nehemiah 8:9b). The effects went deeper than mere feelings. The people's tears expressed a repentance that brought life changes, and revolutionary revival began to move through the culture. The Word of God remained the focus of all that was happening—at least six hours each day were devoted to its reading. The brokenness, tears and repentance moved the people to such emotional levels that Nehemiah and the Levites felt constrained to calm them and encourage them to rejoice (verses 9-11). Tears of repentance ultimately produce fountains of inner joy. It was in this revival setting that Nehemiah uttered these immortal words: "The joy of the Lord is your strength" (verse 10b).

The first stage lasted for seven days. The Israelites camped together, living in booths and tents, and they observed their spiritual festivals. As the revival matured, the people's rejoicing developed a stable consistency. "And their joy was very great" (Nehemiah 8:17*b*). That's what revolutionary spiritual revival brings to all who are touched by it.

The revival didn't end after this first week. On the 24th day of the month, another gathering took place. The revival spread. Hearing about this spiritual renewal, more people wanted to experience what God was doing. Awareness of sin once again motivated life changes:

> The Israelites gathered together, fasting and wearing sackcloth and having dust on their heads. Those of Israelite descent had separated themselves from all foreigners. They stood in their places and confessed their sins and the wickedness of their fathers. They stood where they were and read from the Book of the Law of the LORD their God for a quarter of the day, and spent another quarter in confession and in worshipping the LORD their God (Nehemiah 9:1-3).

The revival format in Nehemiah illustrates balance between instruction and expression. Six hours devoted to reading and exhortation from the Word of God were followed by six hours of testimony, confession and praise. The people vented their joy through music, psalm singing and other worship expressions. The rest of each day was for sleeping and family time. These are the ingredients common to most revival awakenings.

We are not told how long this revival expression lasted, but the resulting cultural changes were dramatic. The remaining five chapters of Nehemiah record these changes. Nehemiah's project of rebuilding Jerusalem would probably have failed without the revival—too much suspicion, scheming and greed had controlled the people—but the impact of the revival allowed completion of the project and led to lasting cultural reforms.

How God's Word Promotes Revival

An aged couple were living out their final days in a rest home. They couldn't talk much together because both were hard of hearing. With time on his hands the husband began to meditate and mentally review the wonderful life he had enjoyed with his wife. She'd been such a good wife to him and mother to their children. He reflected upon her hard work and how faithful she'd been. Overcome with love and emotion, he said to her, "I'm proud of you!"

"What did you say?" she asked.

"I'm proud of you!" he responded in a much louder voice.

"Say it again," she requested.

This time he fairly shouted out his words, "I'm proud of you!"

"Oh," she responded, "I'm sorry. I'm kind of tired of you too, but let's make the best of it."

We may smile at their loss of communication, but the story says something about the need of the evangelical church. Believers frequently suffer from spiritual hearing impairment—we don't hear what God is saying to us. As the glorified Christ addressed each of the seven churches in Revelation 2 and 3, He kept repeating, "He who has an ear, let him hear what the Spirit says to the churches" (see 2:7,11,17,29; 3:6,13,22).

Hearing God's Word holds promise of hope and spiritual healing: "Faith comes from hearing the message, and the message is heard through the Word of Christ" (Romans 10:16,17). Revival necessitates each believer hearing "the Word of Christ" in his inner heart.

We've seen that the Word of God was a vital element in renewing the hearts of the Jewish people in Nehemiah's time. Let's take a closer look at how that was done.

1. The Word was exalted in its public reading (Nehemiah 8:1—9:3).

In Nehemiah's revival, the Word of God was exalted to where the people gave it a deep, personal hearing.

To neglect the reading of the Word of God in our public or private worship is a calamitous error. Paul urged Timothy, "Until I come, devote yourself to the *public reading of Scripture,* to preaching and to teaching" (1 Timothy 4:13, emphasis added). We sense a lofty touch of infinite majesty when we read the Word of our eternal God.

> Ezra opened the book. All the people could see him because he was standing above them; and as he opened it, the people all stood up (Nehemiah 8:5).

We catch the note of dignity the people assigned to the reading of God's Word: They "stood up."

These people did not have our ready access to the sacred Scriptures. Reproductions had to be handwritten, and no one had his own copy. They were so starved for the Word that God's Spirit energized them to stand and listen to it being read for six hours at a time. Today we need God's people to get involved in reading and hearing the Word as enthusiastically as they did in Nehemiah's day. Innovative ways must be discovered to promote the reading of the Word. Here are a few ideas.

- Have believers commit to a one-on-one Bible reading plan with another believer. Accountability for Bible study and memorization would be the focus. Large sections of Scripture can be committed to memory by such steady accountability. Enhance motivation by meeting regularly and maintaining a disciplined procedure.

- To promote Bible reading among their members, some churches hand out schedules that take people through the entire Bible in a set time frame.

- One church has developed a three-year schedule that takes its people through the New Testament twice and the Old Testament once. In the weekly church worship service, a portion of that week's assignment is read and the pastor preaches from that text.

The plan for reading is not the important issue. Meaningful and increased reading of God's Word is—and His people will be blessed. Absorbing God's Word to the largest dimension possible is crucial to our hope for revolutionary revival.

2. The Word was exalted in repentance
(Nehemiah 8:9,11,12; 9:1,2).

Repentance is a beautiful grace from God. As the Word was read and the people heard it, their sins came into perspective. Intense sorrow for those sins was expressed in repentance. At first it was just tears, but as the Word continued to be read, the repentance deepened. They expressed it by "fasting and wearing sackcloth and having dust on their heads" (Nehemiah 9:1). They also stood up and openly confessed their wicked practices (verse 2). This repentance resulted from the reading of God's Word: "They stood where they were and read from the Book of the Law of the LORD their God for a quarter of the day" (verse 3a).

Repentance is not some kind of emotional frenzy. Emotions are involved, but biblical repentance involves the whole person—conduct and thoughts. It requires acknowledgment that we have violated the revealed will of God. It calls us to deliberately cease sinful thoughts and actions and supplant them with righteous thoughts and deeds. Only the constant ingesting of God's Word can keep that spiritual process in balance. As revival moves toward the transformation of a culture, hearing the Word of God must lead to repentance.

3. The Word was exalted in prayer (Nehemiah 9:5-37).

This passage records a long prayer that the people expressed as a body. We are left to conjecture as to how this was done, but from the textual evidence it appears the Levites led by an antiphony pattern. One group "called with loud voices to the LORD their God" (verse 4b). This group kept their prayer phrases short, enabling another group of Levites to lead the people in repeating each phrase. The second group of Levites instructed the people, "Stand up and praise the LORD your God, who is from everlasting to everlasting" (verse 5b). This got each person involved in the prayer. The participation was wonderful. The people spoke the prayer to God with their own lips. As this antiphony pattern progressed, each one's personal involvement deepened.

This type of prayer greatly honors God because it focuses upon praying His Word back to Him. What they'd heard as the sacred Scriptures were read was now verbalized in worshipful prayer. It illustrates the use of God's Word in doctrinal praying. It appropriates His Word in the application of His promises. The seven written prayers for revival included in this book are designed to develop this style of praying. The prayer in Nehemiah 9 deserves emulation by every believer.

4. The Word was exalted through corrected living (Nehemiah 10:29-39).

Nehemiah's cultural reforms rose from a solid basis. The people, with their leaders, pledged themselves . . .

> to follow the Law of God given through Moses the servant of God and to obey carefully all the commands, regulations and decrees of the LORD our Lord (Nehemiah 10:29b).

They followed the absolute standard of God's revealed will.

Nehemiah 10 records the living patterns instituted by the people. As they proceeded in their efforts, they frequently referenced what was written in the Law. Their changes were necessary for carrying out the commands of God.

There was a day when our own government and cultural system were undergirded by the absolute base of God's moral law. It was not lived out in total perfection, but it was there.

Today, it is remembered only as a part of our history. In fact, today the Supreme Court and our legislators studiously avoid making decisions based on biblical revelation. Separation of church and state is interpreted to mean separation from any reference to God or the Bible. Humanism and pluralism (giving equal honor to all religions and non-religions) have led our culture to the near annihilation of biblical absolutes.

Any society moves into chaos when human reason becomes the measuring tape for their moral living. When people choose that route, values become relative and society's standards of conduct lose stability.

Vested interests and warped prejudices of those with influence soon become the accepted standards, and these people sow the seeds of their own doom. Freedom cannot survive in chaos. Totalitarian rule soon arises to maintain order—the state becomes the absolute.

The satanic revival has been subtle but thorough. The humanistic die has been cast as the standard for the future function of our nation. Only revolutionary revival could make a difference now.

Encouragement comes to us from Nehemiah's experience. How quickly the chaotic disaster of that ruined culture was changed by revival. The change came because the people changed. They began to say, "We promise"; "We assume the responsibility"; and, "We will not neglect the house of our God" (see Nehemiah 10:30,32,39b). Any government "of the people, by the people and for the people" will function with biblical absolutes when its people become personally related with God.

5. The Word was exalted through the worship, praise and celebration of what God had done
(Nehemiah 12:27—13:1).

After such transformation, the people worshiped, praised and celebrated before the God of Israel. The dedication of the rebuilt walls of Jerusalem was a colossal event.

Two large choirs sang from the joining walls of the city. Cymbals, harps, lyres, trumpets and other musical instruments added to the crescendo of music and praise. The priests and Levites functioned again in the biblical pattern. The summation of this majestic event is expressed by Nehemiah's words:

> The choirs sang under the direction of Jezrahiah.
> And on that day they offered great sacrifices, rejoicing because God had given them great joy. The women and children also rejoiced. The sound of rejoicing in Jerusalem could be heard far away (12:42b,43).

When worship and praise flow from hearts made right with God through the understanding of His Word, the joy knows no bounds. It affects even the little children. The young people, the women and the men let their hearts overflow with gladness. Everyone got in on the joy of the Lord. One of the great delights of revival is its joy.

6. The Word was exalted by continuing reform, repentance and correction (Nehemiah 13).

A mighty revival like the one that came to Jerusalem under Nehemiah's leadership doesn't really have a conclusion. Chapter 13 reveals the deepening insights that enabled the people to continue to bring their cultural practices more perfectly into line with God's will. As new comprehension came to the people, more of their sinful ways of living were corrected.

Nehemiah expressed continuing concern that his own leadership would remain worthy of the Lord's favor and blessing. He repeatedly pleaded, "Remember me, O my God." This leader's relationship with His Lord was a growing process.

Many revivals last for years. Resultant blessings pour out indefinitely. Such was the case of the revival that began at Pentecost. The blessings of that revolutionary revival movement lasted for at least thirty years and overflowed into most of the Roman Empire. Fresh outbreaks happened in many great cities.

However, people are not fashioned to live constantly at such a high emotional pitch. The prayer time and the celebration at the dedication of the walls of Jerusalem required an abnormal elevation of emotion. As reviving and meaningful as these things were, their duration was limited. No revival movement can ever remain at such a high level of fervor. Such ecstasy may be a part of heaven's reward, but on this earth man needs a more subdued state. We are not equipped to sustain such levels on a long-term basis.

The emotional aspects of revivals fade quickly, and if that's all there is, the results will do little to change a culture. Emotionally charged revivals are like light from a shooting star: It's gone so quickly and then the darkness settles back in. Brief revivals are important to the spiritual life of any church, area or nation, but something much deeper is needed to change the course of an entire culture. The base must be extremely broad and deep, and, for revolutionary revival to defeat the satanic revival, it must have a long-range, staying application. The revival under Nehemiah continued to impact the people of Jerusalem because it was rooted deeply in God's Word. Our prayer is that God, in His mercy and grace, will bring a revival awakening to our day that will bear such long-range benefit. We cannot settle for anything less.

REVIVAL PRAYER PATTERN 7
FOCUS: THE WORD OF GOD

Loving Heavenly Father, I come to worship You in the wonder of what You have chosen to reveal in Your Word about Yourself. The majesty of Your creation displays Your awesome greatness. I see Your omnipotence when I look upon the vastness of the universe. I praise You that You are everywhere present in the extremities of the universe and that You are greater than Your creation.

I look upon the immensity of man's accumulated knowledge and remember Your omniscient possession of all knowledge. The steady march of time causes me to reflect upon the fact that You are eternal, without beginning or end. The lying, sinful ways of humanity evident everywhere cause me to long for the one who is Truth and who reigns in absolute justice.

I praise You, loving God and Father of our Lord Jesus Christ, for what You have revealed about Yourself in the written Word of God. I affirm that Your Holy Word is an inerrant revelation of Your holy Truth. I ask forgiveness for my neglect in reading, memorizing and meditating upon Your Word. What an ugly, sinful wrong it is for me, my family and my fellow believers to treat Your holy Word so lightly when it has been made so available to us. Wash away our guilt, and create within believers' hearts a longing to know and read Your Word.

Through Your Word, Heavenly Father, I came to know the Lord Jesus Christ as my Savior from sin. In Your Word He is revealed as the one who became God in human flesh and was victorious in Himself over the world, the flesh and the devil. In Your Word I learn that, though He was tempted in every way I am tempted, He never sinned. Your Word declares that, as one of us, He fulfilled all righteousness. Your Word declares that He was wounded for my transgressions and bruised for my iniquities. It declares that He became sin for me and that my sins and offenses against You were laid upon Him when He died in my place upon the cross.

It is in Your Word that the mighty truth of His triumph over death and the grave in resurrection power is established. Your Word declares with assuring detail the Lord Jesus Christ's ascension into heaven and His present glorified overseeing of His church. Because of the declarations of Your Word, I look for my Savior to come again with power and great glory. I love You, Heavenly Father, for having given me Your Word.

I praise You, loving God, that You have graced us with the coming of the Holy Spirit at Pentecost. Thank You for revealing Your Word to me in the wonder of His mighty work in this world and in believers. Thank You for declaring in Your Word that the Holy Spirit came to convict the world of its sinful guilt. I ask for the Holy Spirit to greatly intensify His work of convincing people of their sin against a holy God. May the Holy Spirit so open people to the spiritual seeing and hearing of Your Word that they again will cry out in repentance. Thank You, also, that the Holy Spirit exalts righteousness by revealing the righteous things of Your Word. I ask Him to do that with powerful persuasion.

I pray that the Holy Spirit will, by Your Word, reveal to human hearts the certainty of an approaching accountability to God. May that sobering fact settle upon people until they can find no rest apart from coming to our Lord Jesus Christ.

Blessed Holy Spirit, You are the one who breathed out God's Word in divine revelation through human instruments. I ask You now to use that Word to speak personally to believers. Grant new insights to God's appointed leaders to promote interest, reading, memorization and meditation upon God's Word among God's people. I ask You, Holy Spirit, to raise up anointed revivalists, evangelists and preachers who will be able to make the Bible known with compelling power to a lost world.

I pray the mighty power of God's holy Word against Satan and his kingdom. Confront and defeat Satan's lies with the truth of Your Word. May the comfort of Your Word relieve people from Satan's accusations, torments, and terror. I ask that the warnings of Your Word will alert people to Satan's tactics to bring them into bondage. Invade Satan's kingdom with salvation's message in Your Word and bring multitudes from the darkness of hell into the kingdom of light and eternal life.

I recognize, Heavenly Father, that revival will never come unless a deep, personalized hearing of God's Word comes to human hearts. In the name of my Lord Jesus Christ and by the power of His blood, I pull down Satan's power to dishonor and discredit God's holy Word. I bring in prayer the power of the Holy Spirit against all satanic strongholds assigned to hinder the Word of God from being heard and understood by the hearts of people. I invite the blessed Holy Spirit to exalt the Word of God and to reveal its mighty power in ways that will confound the enemies of truth. Cause people to hear Your Word with a new, profound depth, and move pastors and churches to proclaim and teach Your Word with a contagious freshness.

I affirm, Heavenly Father, that Your Word is alive and powerful. I rejoice that though heaven and earth will pass away, not one tiny word of Your holy truth will ever fail. Grant to Your Word great success in our day. Use Your holy Word to move our nation to revolutionary revival. I do love Your Word, O Lord, and I give myself to know it better and to live it more. I offer this prayer in the name of Him who is the Living Word, my Lord Jesus Christ. Amen.

17

The Time
Is Now

> You are going to have the light just a little while longer. Walk while you have the light, before darkness overtakes you. The man who walks in the dark does not know where he is going. Put your trust in the light, while you have it, so that you may become sons of light
> (John 12:35,36).

Has the dawn of revival vision broken over the horizon of your life?

There is an urgency to get involved. God has placed that which will bring revival awakening into the hands of believers who are ready.

Revival puts holy living back into the deep, inner desires of the heart. God's people don't do the sinful, or even questionable, things they once did, because a new light has come. An inner, holy fire has invaded them.

When the sun's rays lift above the horizon, they spread a pervasive light. It's quiet, but it's deliberate, relentless and inclusive. Only the most tightly closed places can shut it out. Revival is like that when it has the revolutionary dimension. Only the most obstinate efforts can avoid its penetrating light.

Signs of Revival Awakening

Are there signs that revival is near?

224

Unfortunately, we do not seem to see much evidence yet of a true revival awakening. Little outbursts happen here and there in the world, but in our Western culture where it is needed so much, things appear static.

There is cause for hope, however! Most of this hope rests upon the very desperateness of the times in which we live. James Burns wrote a book in 1960 on the subject, *Revivals—Their Laws and Leaders*. In 1978, Lewis A. Drummond used Burns's work as a reference point for his book, *The Awakening That Must Come*.

After discussing Burns's seven laws of revival, Drummond lists three awakening signs that precede revival.[1] These signs are evident in our day.

1. The sign of social, political and economic crises.

Crisis times have a way of shocking us out of our temporal, physical world. Trials bring us face to face with the eternal and spiritual dimensions of life. Part of our crisis flows from the natural chaos sinful living injects into everything it touches. However, possibility of sovereign divine intervention also must be recognized. After bringing revival awakening to Solomon and the people at the dedication of the temple, God spoke to Solomon about what He would do when the need for revival arose:

> When I shut up the heavens, so that there is no rain,
> or command locusts to devour the land, or send a plague
> among my people . . . (2 Chronicles 7:13).

Drought, pestilence and plagues. For any culture, these things spell crisis with a capital *C*. God does sovereignly use various types of crises to get people's attention, to awaken them to the urgency of the need.

Volumes could be (and have been) written about the many aspects of the *social crisis* of our times:

● The breakdown of family and home life

- Incest, child-abuse, drug addiction and the ever-increasing prominence of divorce.
- Welfare demands for AFDC payments and housing needs for the poor
- AIDS
- Increased Satan worship and satanic imagery throughout our culture

The educational needs of our children stand out. Despite our efforts, increasing numbers pass through the system but are still illiterate. Some statistics say up to 14 percent of adults in our nation cannot read, write or do simple math.

Good medical care is moving beyond the cost limits of many. Jails and prisons can't be built large enough or fast enough.

Social crisis is everywhere, and it's mounting. We see little hope of relief through human wisdom.

The *political crisis* looms. People in the highest elected offices are paraded before the world for ethics violations, immoral conduct, even illegal activities and criminal fraud. We can be thankful that our system can root out some of the political corruption, but that offers little comfort. Those who know tell us that we see only a small part of the corruption present in the political world.

The *economic crisis* ebbs and flows before our eyes. The explosive vibrations of the stock market crash of 1987 rocketed through the world's economic structure. People wonder when the next one will come. The savings and loan crisis requires a taxpayer's bail-out that may cost hundreds of billions of dollars. The national debt is out of control. Our negative trade balance keeps siphoning off our nation's wealth and it goes into the coffers of world trading partners. We have become a debtor nation of enlarging magnitude. The economic crisis appears destined to come home to every citizen's pocket.

The social, political and economic crises should get our attention. Hopefully, they are signs of a soon-coming revival. If we respond to the crises by revival praying, it will come.

2. The sign of the feelings of helplessness within the church.

As we look at the church today, these words of the psalmist seem most appropriate:

> They mounted up to the heavens and went down to
>   the depths;
>   in their peril their courage melted away.
> They reeled and staggered like drunken men;
>   they were at their wits' end (Psalm 107:26,27).

The image here is a ship on a tossing sea with little hope for survival. The church has indeed been staggered by the events of our day. The moral scandals surrounding religious leaders touch every denomination and every believer. How far it will go, no one knows. Guilt by association is widespread. A cloud of suspicion lurks near every religious group, and the watching public is wary. Unfortunately, sound Christian organizations suffer with the unworthy ones.

Organized religion is suspect to our youth. In increasing numbers, fifth- and sixth-grade children are following in the path of the youth culture; they want nothing to do with organized religion. Satanism seems to have more appeal. Cults and non-Christian religions capture youth from traditional Christianity by the multitudes. Secularism, humanism and New Age philosophy pick up many more. Our youth are in crisis. The church is in crisis—but it's not hopeless.

The psalmist continued the passage quoted above with these rescuing words of promise:

> Then they cried out to the LORD in their trouble,
>   and he brought them out of their distress.
> He stilled the storm to a whisper;
>   the waves of the sea were hushed.
> They were glad when it grew calm,

and he guided them to their desired haven
(Psalm 107:28-30).

The church always has a resource of hope: Rescue is available. Revival is a viable option—it offers hope. When we are overcome with feelings of helplessness, when we are unable to cope with the staggering demands, when we are overwhelmed, that's a good situation to be in. It's time then to believe God for revival. The answer begins with:

Then they cried out to the LORD in their trouble,
and he brought them out of their distress.

There is no problem beyond the solution of our Lord. He's waiting to respond to our cry with reviving intervention. The psalm closes with great hope:

He lifted the needy out of their affliction
and increased their families like flocks.
The upright see and rejoice,
but all the wicked shut their mouths.
Whoever is wise, let him heed these things
and consider the great love of the LORD
(Psalm 107:41-43).

That's a promise of revival blessings flowing out so strongly that "the wicked shut their mouths." Revival does that. It sends wickedness into retreat. It stops satanic revival.

3. The sign of concern for world evangelization and missions.

Not all signs of an impending revival awakening are dark—this is a bright one. The word *bright* in conjunction with this sign is appropriate because of Bill Bright and his leadership of Campus Crusade for Christ. For several decades now, Bill Bright has kept an aggressive approach to world evangelization before the Christian world. And by no means does he stand alone.

The Billy Graham Evangelistic Association has provided wonderful leadership in promoting world evangelization. The Lausanne Congress, Operation Mobilization, World Vision and other world relief agencies and denominational and missionary organizations are doing great work. More movements than we could ever name keep promoting world evangelization and missionary outreach. More than a thousand Asian missionaries from seven Asian countries are now a part of this expanding vision to evangelize the world. More seem destined to follow soon. The vision for world evangelization appears to burn brighter than it ever has.

Rapid travel, technological advances, communications networking and satellites are some of the new tools and methods being used to spread the gospel. These are exciting days for Christians. Never has the church had more concern or more capacity for the task of world evangelization.

The one ingredient desperately needed is the fuel that would flow from revolutionary revival.

- Revival would enlarge the needed manpower reserve in a short time. Revived people become eager missionary volunteers.

- Revival would energize God's people with spiritual power for prayer. United prayer pushes the enemy into hasty retreat.

- Revival leads to repentance and cleaned-up lives. God's power flows freely through a clean people.

- Revival would secure the needed funds to finance the evangelism projects. Revived people become joyful stewards.

- Revival would help create a political climate favorable to world evangelization. Changed people translate into changed political leaders who open doors for the gospel.

There is great encouragement for us. I personally believe that revival is not just a possibility but a probability.

My prayer is that an ever-increasing number of believers will envision that probability and enter into those activities that will help bring it to pass.

Activities and Attitudes That Promote Revival

Now it's time to give you some practical suggestions. Revival knowledge would have little significance if it only stimulated a surface interest in the subject.

Attitudes must become expectant.

Actions must head toward goals.

Motivation must produce fortitude.

Revival materials and tools need to be simple in format, applicable to every believer, and adaptable to each situation. In appendix D we have included some samples of printed materials that we hope will be helpful to you. These may be photocopied for your personal use.

Revival is not complicated. God gave the formula for it to Solomon in less than fifty words:

> If my people, who are called by my name, will
>   humble themselves and
>   pray and
>   seek my face and
>   turn from their wicked ways,
> then will I hear from heaven and will forgive their sin
> and will heal their land (2 Chronicles 7:14).

Specific Things You Can Do

1. Walk in personal victory over the world, the flesh and the devil.

> Therefore, I urge you, brothers, in view of God's mercy, to offer your bodies as living sacrifices, holy and pleasing to God—this is your spiritual act of worship. Do not conform any longer to the pattern of this world, but be transformed by the renewing of your mind. Then you will

be able to test and approve what God's will is—his good,
pleasing and perfect will (Romans 12:1,2),

God is pleased when people who are concerned for
revival commit themselves to godliness. Those He chooses to
use in a revival movement must know they are called to holiness. As we've seen, one of the first marks of revival awakening is when sin is seen as exceedingly sinful. Those burdened
for revival need to be on the cutting edge of a desire to live
above sin. Ask the Lord daily to reveal areas of compromise
or sinful indulgence that need to be removed from your life.
Be quick to confess such sins and appropriate God's cleansing.

An important factor in God's formula for bringing
revival is that the people who desire it would "turn from
their wicked ways." Through Christ's finished work, God has
given believers the power and grace to win the victory over
the world, the flesh and the devil. My books, *The Adversary*
and *Overcoming the Adversary*, give biblical insight into this
spiritual victory. Spiritual victory must be a factor in a
believer's life. There is so much at stake.

> Make every effort to live in peace with all men and
> to be holy; without holiness no one will see the Lord
> (Hebrews 12:14).

2. Commit to personal prayer for revival.

People who influence others are themselves deeply committed to their cause, so personal prayer for revival must
come first. Put private prayer at the top of your priority list
and develop it.

> When you pray, go into your room, close the door and
> pray to your Father, who is unseen. Then your Father,
> who sees what is done in secret, will reward you
> (Matthew 6:6).

There is no substitute for private, personal prayer. You
benefit greatly and you also honor God when you develop
your shut-away time with Him.

In doing this, determining a set time and place is important. Most people cannot work protracted prayer times into a daily schedule, but nearly everyone can do it several times a week. Some of those regular times should be devoted exclusively to a revival focus. If our very survival demands revival, then prayer for revival is not an option. It's a necessity!

You may develop your own style of intercessory prayer for revival, or you may wish to use the doctrinal approach prayer patterns suggested in this book. You will find them listed according to topic in the table of contents.

It's important to get moving and stay with it. Revival prayer should be sharply focused. Like Nehemiah's prayer, it needs to express worship, burden and repentance (Nehemiah 1:5-11). It should include biblical doctrine, and it should focus on God's revealed will. It should confront and resist Satan in all that he is doing to hinder revival. Remember that the basic ingredient of the broad-base revival is the personal prayer life of believers. Pray that God will give us a base of millions of Christians who are privately, personally praying for revival. "Then your Father, who sees what is done in secret, will reward you."

3. Become part of a revival prayer group.

Though revival is always intensely personal, it is also group centered.

In the Old Testament, the spiritual leaders often were "loners" who heard from God as individuals. Abraham, Moses, Elijah and Isaiah gave out their message to the people as singular heralds of God's truth.

In the New Testament, however, the emphasis is upon the body, the group, the composite church that heard from God and moved with God. To be sure, individual New Testament leaders like James, Paul and Peter were necessary, but they always functioned in harmony with the body. The forward movement of the church was group-centered from its inception—the Lord Jesus Christ had a group of twelve apostles. He also instructed the group of 120 faithful disciples to wait in Jerusalem for their enduing of power from heaven through the Holy Spirit:

> I am going to send you what my Father has promised; but stay in the city until you have been clothed with power from on high (Luke 24:49).
>
> Then they returned to Jerusalem from the hill called the Mount of Olives, a Sabbath day's walk from the city. When they arrived, they went upstairs to the room where they were staying. . . . They all joined together constantly in prayer, along with the women and Mary the mother of Jesus, and with his brothers (Acts 1:12,13a,14).

Men, women and children prayed together. Revival began with this group.

The place to begin a group prayer gathering for revival should be in one's local church, God's chosen entity to evangelize the world and to edify the body. God assigns the local church great importance.

Sadly, in this day in most local churches, prayer meetings seem to be at an all-time low, and some churches have even ceased to have them. This is just one more indication of the desperate need for revival in our time.

Innovative plans promoting church prayer are needed. Most of these meetings have a scattered focus: physical illnesses, family problems, job changes, employment needs, the programs of the church and the missionaries. These all deserve prayer support, but it's difficult to include much revival prayer in addition to those needs. Some groups should meet just to pray for revival. Revival praying requires more attention than it's currently getting.

Believers who sense God's burden for revival need to confer with their pastor for his blessing and support. The revival-focused prayer sessions should be listed in the weekly church announcements. The time and place should be chosen in the best interests of the participants—early mornings serve many people well; noon hours sometimes work; some groups schedule meetings from 9 to 10 P.M., after the children are in bed. It is advisable to have a time limit, and people should be free to come and go as their schedules permit. Revival prayer groups in local churches are a must.

Interdenominational group prayer times for revival are also needed. These may flow out of existing interdenominational fellowships, such as Christian businessmen's committees, women's ministry groups, and interchurch Bible studies. It is vital that interdenominational groups see the urgent need for revival to visit all churches. When revival comes, all churches will be filled. Praying together for revival is an important foundation of preparation.

4. Be persistent in waiting upon the Lord for revival.

God can move quickly to bring revival awakening. The 120 people gathered in the upper room at Jerusalem had to wait only ten days. The sound of a blowing wind and the sight of a burning fire announced its beginning. Once that happened, thousands responded almost immediately. Yes, God can move quickly, but . . .

The groundwork for that revival had taken much longer. Its foundations reached back into the three years the Lord Jesus Christ spent fulfilling His earthly ministry. Without those years, there would have been no revival. Even the revival of Pentecost required a protracted time of preparation. God's great, "sudden" movings have deep roots.

God is responsible for the times—believers are responsible for persistent intercession. Those who "stay by the stuff" will surely see the refreshing come.

As Ronald Dunn so aptly states in *Don't Just Stand There, Pray Something:*

> In the recorded history of the church there has never been a mighty outpouring of the Spirit in revival that did not begin in the persistent, prevailing prayers of desperate people. Revival has never come because men placed it on

the calendar. It has come because God placed it in their hearts.[2]

5. Protect the results of revival.

Revivals have had a wide variance of duration. Martin Luther felt the outer limits to be about thirty years, and he thought the church needed a new awakening at least that often.

Some revivals have had a much shorter duration. The Welsh revival of 1904 ended rather quickly. The chief leader in that revival, Evan Roberts, and author Jessie Penn-Lewis both felt it ended prematurely. Their book, *War on the Saints,* first published in 1912 after the results of the 1904 revival had largely abated, deals with the subtle ways Satan can hinder what God desires to do through believers. The authors presented Satan's deceptions and the believers' passive attitudes about spiritual warfare as the chief causes for spiritual defeats. They felt that aggressive spiritual warfare could have greatly extended that revival's influence.

Prayer for revival awakening needs to include petitions for its protection. The heavenly Father alone is able to protect revival awakening from the devious ways Satan will use to try to stop it.

The awakening changes hearts, reverses downward trends, establishes new direction and greatly strengthens the Christian faith in the culture where it happens. Once this new direction has been established, the church continues to function at a much higher level of spiritual fervor. Everything enjoys the blessings of renewed spiritual life even though the emotional intensity and elevated activity of revolutionary revival begins to tone down. The revived people settle into an enjoyment of long-term worship, evangelism, steady teaching and missionary outreach.

We should pray for the revival duration just as fervently as we pray for it to come. What a complex religious world a revival would meet today! How quickly it could be weakened by man's capacities to "quench the Spirit," to say nothing of Satan's work. Tangents of extremism could quickly divert its influence. Balance between sound doctrinal teaching and evangelistic outreach to the lost must remain the focus and the ongoing message of true revival. World evangelization is the major outflow from revival awakening. God doesn't bring revolutionary revival just to bring us joy and to make things better for His people. God loves the lost world and He longs to reach every person in it. Watchful, protective prayer to that end is an indispensable part of revival praying. Pray that our heavenly Father will sovereignly superintend both the doctrinal soundness and the duration of revolutionary revival.

Preserving the Revival

Even before revival comes, the American mind is tempted to design programs to promote, protect and continue its long-term freshness. Much is needed to provide structure and balance to revival awakening, such as:

- Bible study nurture groups for new believers
- Action brigades carrying Christ's love to the homeless and needy
- Alert support teams assisting new converts exiting from satanism
- Evangelism training promoting varied outreaches to the lost
- Mobilization for world evangelization and missionary recruitment
- Structures of support details to rescue and redirect hurting people
- Seminars providing biblical balance in spiritual warfare training
- Prayer ministries to undergird and protect the revival movement

- Individual and cell-group discipling strategies
- Christ-exalting fellowship festivals and creative worship/praise celebrations

Long-distance walking requires strong legs, and revolutionary revival needs the strong legs of organized structure and skillful leadership to keep it going. I was tempted to address this obvious need, but I've been constrained not to do so, for two major reasons:

1. An abundance of evangelical Christian programs and organizational structures are already in place.

- Half-empty church buildings housing struggling congregations abound.
- Fast-moving parachurch organizations with defined ministries are bumping into each other.
- The best in media communication is already promoting world-wide evangelism.
- Evangelism training programs are in place to meet everyone's style preference.
- Discipleship programs of proven performance are widely available.
- Outstanding seminaries, Christian colleges and Bible institutes are ready for more students.
- Denominational and faith missionary boards are equipped to funnel new volunteers to the fields.
- World hunger organizations and inner city ministries are presently doing much great work.

These structures would need Holy-Spirit-led fine tuning to handle the rush created by revolutionary revival, but they are there, ready and waiting. More program-centered plans are not needed. God's sovereignty has provided.

2. Revolutionary revival fuels its own continuance.

As I stood watching the exploding kernels rapidly filling my popcorn popper, I saw an illustration of revolutionary revival. The fires of revival regenerate and transform multitudes of people. Hardened kernels of sinful human lives are suddenly transformed into regenerated, useful members of Christ's body.

That story unfolds in the Book of Acts. As the revival flowing from Pentecost got under way, "a sound like the blowing of a violent wind came from heaven." This sound of wind filled the whole house, and the people gathered there "saw what seemed to be tongues of fire that separated and came to rest on each of them" (Acts 2:1,2).

In the world of nature, the mixture of wind and fire unleashes the most powerful elements of creation. The 1989 fires that roared through Yellowstone National Park displayed the unstoppable power of wind and fire. In that combustible environment, wind and fire created their own explosive fuel, defying massive control efforts.

God planned only one Pentecost, and it demonstrated important lessons we need to learn. The Holy Spirit's coming in the symbols of wind and fire illustrate far more than any of us fully understand. In part, I believe these volatile symbols communicate the unstoppable strength of Christ's Spirit-controlled church. When heaven-sent wind and holy fire combine in multiplied numbers of yielded believers, the results are explosively powerful.

When the Holy Spirit was poured out, the resulting revolutionary revival fueled its own continuance. The life, death, resurrection and ascension of God's Son set in place all that was needed for the Holy Spirit's work. The long term results were phenomenal:

- Program-centered disciples became power-filled apostles (Acts 2).

- Church-elected "table servers" shone as stars of faith who laid down their lives, following the forgiving example of their Lord (Acts 6,7).

- Hate-filled persecutors were transformed into giant defenders of the faith (Acts 9).
- Scattered, persecuted believers became missionary church planters (Acts 8).
- Racial, religious and ethnic barriers melted away (Acts 8:26-40; 10,11).
- Religious traditions and deep disagreements were resolved (Acts 15).
- World-wide evangelism moved through the known world (Acts 13-29).
- Satan's opposition was neutralized and rebuked (Acts 13:6-12; 16:16-21).
- Cruel, evil people became ardent believers (Acts 16:22-34).
- Entire cities and cultures were dramatically changed (Acts 19).
- The Roman Empire was invaded by the gospel's power (Acts 23-29).

God-authored revolutionary revival fuels its own continuance. The satanic revival has come upon us with alarming power and determined goals, and only a God-authored revival can meet Satan's challenge. God's people are called to see it happen. The tools are in our hands.

Wait for the Lord; be strong and take heart and wait for the Lord (Psalm 27:14).

Revival Concepts and the Role of the Holy Spirit

A demonized culture can be saved and brought back from ruin only by a powerful movement of a Holy-Spirit-authored revival. In this appendix, I want to focus upon what such a revival means. Believers can never hope to turn the tide of the present cultural, moral and spiritual rebellion by human efforts. Boycotting the products of sponsors of unwholesome television is good, but it won't be enough. Right-to-life marches and sit-ins at abortion clinics will have some effect, but they will not resolve this moral travesty. Stronger medicine is needed. Revival must come.

Definitions of Revival

Let's consider some definitions of revival by worthy students of the subject.

J. Edwin Orr, internationally respected historian and student of revival awakenings, has probably traveled farther and collected more first-hand material on the subject than any other author. Most of his books that record the historic details of what he calls "Evangelical Awakenings" around the world share a common introduction. The opening paragraph of that introduction gives his understanding of revival:

> An Evangelical Awakening is a *movement of the Holy Spirit* bringing about a revival of New Testament Christianity in the Church of Christ and its related community. Such an awakening may change in a significant way an individual only; or it may affect a larger group of believers; or it may move a congregation, or the churches of a city or district, or the whole body of believers throughout a country or a continent; or indeed the larger body of believers throughout the world. The outpouring of the Spirit effects the reviving of the Church, the awakening of the masses, and the movement of uninstructed peoples toward the Christian faith; the revived Church, by many or by few, is moved to engage in evangelism, in teaching, and in social action.[1]

In *Heart-Cry For Revival,* written in the early '60s, Stephen F. Olford seeks to synthesize the definitions of revival advanced by some of God's renowned servants of the past and present such as

William B. Sprague, Charles G. Finney, G. J. Morgan, Arthur Wallis, J. Edwin Orr, and Joseph Kemp. He pulls their contributions together into this abbreviated definition:

> Revival is that strange and *sovereign work of God* in which He visits His own people, restoring, reanimating and releasing them into the fullness of His blessing. Such a divine intervention will issue in evangelism, though, in the first instance, it is a work of God in the church and amongst individual believers.[2]

Richard Owen Roberts keeps his definition short and to the point:

> In using the term *revival,* I am speaking of *an extraordinary movement of the Holy Spirit producing extraordinary results.*[3]

Roberts has made a lifetime study of revival, providing us with a valuable bibliography of more than 150 titles on the subject. His concise definition says much by what it leaves unsaid. He recognizes that it is difficult to harness revival with restrictive definitions. The nature of its being an "extraordinary movement of the Holy Spirit" leaves most of what happens in revival to the sovereignty of the heavenly Father—God effects His will and plan and carries it forth by the Holy Spirit's working in each revival situation.

Revivals are emotional events. As such, they are often experience-centered in their outworking. The results, however, go much deeper than emotions and feelings in genuine revival awakening. People's lives, attitudes, and actions are dramatically changed. Whole cultures are changed.

Broadcaster David Mains, director of *The Chapel of the Air,* is one of America's strongest contemporary advocates of revival. We owe much to him and his broadcast ministry as a stimulating, motivating force for revival in our nation. Mains defines revival as "an extraordinary sense of *the nearness and presence of the Lord Jesus Christ* among his people." Such a definition again focuses upon the experiential. It's similar to J. Edwin Orr's statement in the *Second Evangelical Awakening in Britain:*

> The best definition of revival is the phrase, "Times of refreshing . . . from the *presence* of the Lord."[4]

Like Mains, Orr indicates the mystical note of revival as being an unusual sense of the near presence of the Lord—and that near presence brings great refreshing and new life.

Biblical Meanings of the Word Revival

The Hebrew word for "revive" (*chaya, khaw-yaw*) is used twelve times in the Old Testament. The Hebrew lexicon says the word means to "keep (leave, or make) alive." Other descriptive words and phrases from the Hebrew dictionary are "to give life, to suffer to live, to nourish up, to preserve, quicken, recover, repair, and restore life. To save alive and to make to become whole." Those words describe well what revolutionary, spiritual revival can do.

Sometimes in the Old Testament the word simply means the restoring of physical life and breath as in the case of Elijah raising the son of the widow of Zaraphath:

> The LORD heard Elijah's cry, and the boy's life returned to him [he revived], and he lived (1 Kings 17:22).

The dead boy came to life.

At other times, the word speaks of the lifting of physical weariness or emotional stress. As Jacob viewed the special carts that Joseph had sent to bring his family to Egypt, "The spirit of their father Jacob revived" (Genesis 45:27). Because of the good news about his long-lost son, emotional renewal surged through Jacob's being.

Samson, following his great victory over the Philistines at Ramath Lehi, was supplied water miraculously by God. The Scripture records that "when Samson drank, his strength returned and he revived" (Judges 15:19). Physical renewal flowed into Samson. Water supplied Samson with energy-giving life and he revived.

However, the larger number of biblical usages of this Hebrew word for revive refer to spiritual renewal in people and cultures. "Will you not *revive* us again, that your people may rejoice in you?" (Psalm 85:6, emphasis added). The psalmist's cry is for spiritual renewal (see also Isaiah 57:15; Habakkuk 1:5-11; 3:2,18,19).

Old Testament Concept of Revival

Psalm 85 establishes three major assumptions that make up the Old Testament concept of revival:

1. Need for revival assumes past spiritual excellence. The very word *revive* conveys the thought of a life that previously exceeded what it now is. Psalm 85:1-3 speaks of such prior spiritual elevation:

> You showed favor to your land, O LORD;
>   You restored the fortunes of Jacob.
> You forgave the iniquity of your people
>   and covered all their sins.
> You set aside all your wrath
>   and turned from your fierce anger.

A time of past spiritual excellence is acknowledged by the psalmist. An earlier restoration of the nation is recognized with praise. Forgiveness of the people's sins and the covering of those sins by God had brought wonderful hope for a bright future. God is praised for setting aside His wrath and anger against His people. The restoration has effected great rejoicing and precious memory in the psalmist's heart.

Our need for revival always looks back to a prior state of spiritual excellence to establish a measuring standard and a basis for hope.

2. Need for revival assumes a state of present spiritual declension. A period of spiritual declension had followed the success of that initial return of the Babylonian exiles. Some twelve to fifteen years had elapsed since Ezra's initial reforms when Nehemiah learned of the state of his beloved Jerusalem. His brother returned from a visit to Jerusalem and brought a shocking report to Nehemiah. The people living there were in terrible need (Nehemiah 1:3). Nehemiah's cry for Jerusalem, recorded in Nehemiah 1, and Psalm 85:4-7 are remarkably similar in tone and content. One could envision Nehemiah praying with the psalmist:

> Restore us again, O God our Savior,
>   and put away your displeasure toward us.
> Will you be angry with us forever?
>   Will you prolong your anger through all generations?
> Will you not revive us again,
>   that your people may rejoice in you?
> Show us your unfailing love, O LORD,
>   and grant us your salvation (Psalm 85:4-7).

Nehemiah's prayer is a bit more detailed, but it is remarkably similar in desire to the psalmist's:

> O LORD, God of heaven, the great and awesome God, who keeps his covenant of love with those who love him and obey his commands, let your ear be attentive and your eyes open to hear the prayer your servant is praying before you day and night for your servants, the people of Israel. I confess the sins we Is-

raelites, including myself and my father's house, have committed against you. We have acted very wickedly toward you. We have not obeyed the commands, decrees and laws you gave your servant Moses.

Remember the instruction you gave your servant Moses, saying, "If you are unfaithful, I will scatter you among the nations, but if you return to me and obey my commands, then even if your exiled people are at the farthest horizon, I will gather them from there and bring them to the place I have chosen as a dwelling for my Name" (Nehemiah 1:5-9).

Nehemiah's learning of broken-down walls, burned-up gates and a people under great oppression made him see the terrible spiritual losses the people had experienced. His cry, like the psalmist's, is for God to enable the people to regain what they previously had enjoyed from His hand.

Recognition of the need for revival begins with the realization that we have fallen into spiritual decline.

3. Need for revival assumes anticipated spiritual renewal. Recognition of former spiritual excellence and acknowledgment of present spiritual decline, important as they are, do not automatically bring revival. If we stopped there, we could only lament and despair. We must also pray expectantly for spiritual renewal. That's how the psalmist prayed:

> I will listen to what God the LORD will say;
>   he promises peace to his people, his saints—
>   but let them not return to folly.
> Surely his salvation is near those who fear him
>   that his glory may dwell in our land.
> Love and faithfulness meet together;
>   righteousness and peace kiss each other.
> Faithfulness springs forth from the earth,
>   and righteousness looks down from heaven.
> The LORD will indeed give what is good,
>   and our land will yield its harvest.
> Righteousness goes before him
>   and prepares the way for his steps (Psalm 85:8-13).

The Old Testament concept of revival recognized former spiritual excellence, acknowledged present spiritual decline, and anticipated spiritual restoration from God's hand.

New Testament Standard for Revival

Although the New Testament concept of revival is similar, there is a much higher expectation. This concept has a *beginning standard of spiritual excellence* in this day of grace that far exceeds anything known in Old Testament times. The word *revival* is not used in the New Testament, but when the spiritual tone of the church dips below the standard, renewal is not only in order, but it is also demanded by our Lord Jesus Christ (see Revelation 2 and 3).

What is this New Testament standard of spiritual excellence?

The Holy Spirit and Revival

I believe the New Testament standard of revival focuses upon the work of the Holy Spirit in His coming:

- His coming at Pentecost fulfilled the promise of both the Father and the Son.
- His coming lifted believers to the highest state of human spiritual excellence ever known.
- His coming confronted the world with the most powerful, direct challenge it had ever known.
- His coming gave to believers both an inner spiritual dynamic and a new, explosive evangelistic power.

John 14, 15 and 16 reveal what the coming of the Holy Spirit will do in the world of humanity.

Benefits to Believers

What the Holy Spirit's coming did for the disciples of the Lord Jesus Christ is legendary. Shrinking cowards became strikingly courageous. Impotent, defeated men became strong proclaimers and fearless confronters. The transformation in believers' lives reached a zenith never before known in the world.

When believers are living at a level below what the Holy Spirit brought to us, we need revival. When His impact upon the world in which we live is less than what He is able to do, we need revival.

Here is a partial list of the good things the Holy Spirit has promised believers:

1. He will be with each believer forever (John 14:16).

2. He is the Spirit of truth, and will guide believers into all truth (John 16:13); He will not deceive us (John 14:1).

3. He dwells with and in every believer (John 14:17).

4. His presence internalizes the presence of Jesus Christ and God the Father (John 14:18,23).

5. He enables us to spiritually see and know the Lord Jesus Christ (John 14:19).

6. He will carry out resurrection life in us (John 14:19b; Romans 8:11).

7. He brings to reality and understanding the oneness we have with each other, and with the Father and the Son (John 14:20,21b).

8. He enables us to show our love for God by our walk of obedience to Him (John 14:21a,23,24).

9. He teaches us the Word of Christ (John 14:26; cf. 1 Corinthians 2:10-12).

10. He brings an inner peace that frees us from troubled hearts and debilitating fear (John 14:27).

11. He is the secret of a believer's abiding in Christ and producing the fruit of the Spirit (cf. John 15:1-17 and Galatians 5:22-26).

12. He is the comforter and counseling paraclete who comes alongside both internally and externally to help (John 14:16,26; 16:7).

13. He is sent by both the Father and the Son (John 16:7; 14:1b,26).

14. His presence is more crucial to us in this age of grace than is the physical presence of Jesus Christ (John 16:7).

15. He speaks only what comes from the Father and the Son (John 16:13b).

16. He gives prophetic insight in accord with God's will and plan (John 16:13).

17. He glorifies the Lord Jesus Christ (John 16:14,15).

18. He greatly empowers believers to witness of the saving power of Jesus Christ to a lost world (Luke 24:49, Acts 1:4,5,8).

Benefits to Non-believers

When revival comes, the believers are the first to experience the Holy Spirit's powerful work, but when believers walk in and benefit from the empowering of the Holy Spirit, even the world gets in on the blessings.

When believers are rightly related to Him, they manifest those benefits listed above. Yet the real test of whether believers are walking in the fullness of the Spirit is what He is doing with non-Christians who live among the believers. When the Holy Spirit has full control of believers' lives, the evangelistic results are explosive in nonbelievers' lives. A demonized culture will be affected dramatically by a Holy-Spirit-authored revival.

> When he [the Counselor] comes, he will *convict* the world of guilt in regard to *sin* and *righteousness* and *judgment:* in regard to *sin,* because men do not believe in me; in regard to *righteousness,* because I am going to the Father, where you can see me no longer, and in regard to *judgment,* because the prince of this world now stands condemned (John 16:5-11, emphasis added).

When believers get revived and rightly related to the person and work of the Holy Spirit, when He is empowering their lives, He is then able to deal deeply with nonbelievers, convicting them of their guilt. The Greek word, *elenkō* ("convict" or "reprove"), means to pronounce a judicial verdict at the bar of justice, defining and fixing guilt. It denotes an inescapable sense of conviction that forces the offender to realize his shame and defenselessness before a holy God.

The Holy Spirit focuses His conviction work in three areas:

The **first** is that *sin becomes sinful* to the nonbeliever. When nonbelievers practice sin with little conscience in the presence of believers, it shows how much the believers need revival. When the Holy Spirit is free to work through obedient, Spirit-filled believers, He intensely convicts the nonbelievers near them of their own sin, particularly the sin of unbelief concerning the Lord Jesus Christ.

Second, *righteousness becomes desirable.* The earthly presence of the righteous Christ convicted sinners of their unrighteousness, and the Holy Spirit's presence and power works on them in an even more intense and personal way. Righteousness becomes a desirable grace to a convicted person.

Third, *nonbelievers begin to sense the coming judgment.* Conviction confronts nonbelievers as the Holy Spirit reveals to their hearts that Satan, the prince of this world, stands condemned. The Greek word is *kekriti*, "the condemnation is a settled state, an absolute." Satan's judgment is fixed and permanent and so is the judgment of those who follow him and are under his control.

A sinner suddenly has all of his false securities stripped away. He begins to feel painful guilt over his sins. He cannot brush them aside. A personal, powerful Holy Spirit bears that truth home to the deepest recesses of his being. The guilt intensifies as righteousness, goodness and holiness begin to rebuke the sinful contrast of his wicked life. The final nail is driven home when the awful awareness of judgment to come settles upon the heart of the nonbeliever.

When you have Holy Spirit conviction like this, a crisis of personal need confronts the sinner. An urgent decision concerning Christ is demanded of him. He must find an answer to his pain of conviction.

The greatest evidence of how far we've fallen from the state of spiritual excellence that believers are meant to have is measured right here.

When sinners around us go on arrogantly sinning, when righteousness is eroding and despised by the world, when sinners with whom we live and work exhibit little or no fear of coming judgment, the Holy Spirit is hindered from doing His work, and believers need revival.

When the Lord of Glory draws near to His people, they stop. If not physically, at least spiritually and emotionally, they stop. They are on their faces on the ground. There is brokenness, repentance, a sense of unworthiness, and many tears of sorrow mingled with tears of joy. Both go with revolutionary revival. I believe it was like that in that upper room in Jerusalem when the Holy Spirit came near in His mighty rushing sound and His fire.

When the Holy Spirit is free to move through believers in His mighty power, sinners begin to get saved. In cultures like our own where there has been a strong history of a Christianized culture, true revival will bring them by the thousands.

Revolutionary revival is our Lord Jesus Christ drawing near to His people by the power of His Holy Spirit. Everything else that happens—the transformed lives, the changed culture, the renewed fervency—everything else flows out of His drawing near. It's His glory that precipitates revolutionary revival, and when that happens, He receives all of the glory! God can motivate us to believe Him for such a greatly needed move of His grace. Nothing else will effect the change we need at this late hour. The satanic revival is moving on like a steam roller, but when our holy God chooses to draw near, no people will remain standing. Every knee shall bow to Him. Even Satan's program will be halted.

A Revival Cry

Gracious, merciful Heavenly Father. Hear the cry of my heart. I sometimes feel such a need for personal revival. At times my heart seems cold as ice and hard as stone. Have mercy upon me. I affirm that the work of our Lord Jesus Christ was sufficient to enable You in mercy and grace to draw near to us. I affirm that the mighty person and power of the Holy Spirit are sufficient to convict the lost of sin, of righteousness and of the judgment to come, and can bring those lost to You. Our day, our lives, our world, and Your church desperately need revolutionary revival. I invite Your Holy Spirit to begin His work in me. I invite Him to work in Your church. I invite Him to work in all of Your created people in this awful day of engulfing evil. Open the eyes of the lost to see their need of Christ. The overwhelming sense of Your power and presence through the Holy Spirit can bring us all to revolutionary revival. May it be so in Jesus' name. Amen.

Have You Made
the Wonderful Discovery
of the Spirit-Filled Life?

EVERY DAY CAN BE AN EXCITING ADVENTURE FOR THE CHRISTIAN who knows the reality of being filled with the Holy Spirit and who lives constantly, moment by moment, under His gracious direction.

The Bible tells us that there are three kinds of people:

1. NATURAL MAN

(One who has not received Christ)

"But a natural man does not accept the things of the Spirit of God; for they are foolishness to him, and he cannot understand them, because they are spiritually appraised" (1 Corinthians 2:14).

SELF-DIRECTED LIFE

S -Ego or finite self is on the throne
† -Christ is outside the life
● -Interests are directed by self, often resulting in discord and frustration

2. SPIRITUAL MAN

(One who is directed and empowered by the Holy Spirit)

"But he who is spiritual appraises all things . . ." (1 Corinthians 2:15).

CHRIST-DIRECTED LIFE

† -Christ is in the life and on the throne
S -Self is yielding to Christ
● -Interests are directed by Christ, resulting in harmony with God's plan

3. CARNAL MAN

(One who has received Christ, but who lives in defeat because he trusts in his own efforts to live the Christian life)

"And I, brethren, could not speak to you as to spiritual men, but as to carnal men, as to babes in Christ. I gave you milk to drink, not solid food; for you were not yet able to receive it. Indeed, even now you are not yet able, for you are still carnal. For since there is jealousy and strife among you, are you not fleshly, and are you not walking like mere men?" (1 Corinthians 3:1-3)

SELF-DIRECTED LIFE

S -Self is on the throne
† -Christ dethroned and not allowed to direct the life
● -Interests are directed by self, often resulting in discord and frustration

1 GOD HAS PROVIDED FOR US AN ABUNDANT AND FRUITFUL CHRISTIAN LIFE.

Jesus said, "I came that they might have life, and might have it abundantly" (John 10:10).

"I am the vine, you are the branches; he who abides in Me, and I in him, he bears much fruit; for apart from Me you can do nothing" (John 15:5).

"But the fruit of the Spirit is love, joy, peace, patience, kindness, goodness,

251

faithfulness, gentleness, self-control; against such things there is no law" (Galatians 5:22,23).

"But you shall receive power when the Holy Spirit has come upon you; and you shall be My witnesses both in Jerusalem, and in all Judea and Samaria, and even to the remotest part of the earth" (Acts 1:8).

THE SPIRITUAL MAN—Some personal traits which result from trusting God:

Christ-centered
Empowered by the Holy Spirit
Introduces others to Christ
Effective prayer life
Understands God's Word
Trusts God
Obeys God
Love
Joy
Peace
Patience
Kindness
Faithfulness
Goodness

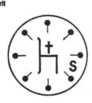

The degree to which these traits are manifested in the life depends upon the extent to which the Christian trusts the Lord with every detail of his life, and upon his maturity in Christ. One who is only beginning to understand the ministry of the Holy Spirit should not be discouraged if he is not as fruitful as more mature Christians who have known and experienced this truth for a longer period.

Why is it that most Christians are not experiencing the abundant life?

2 CARNAL CHRISTIANS CANNOT EXPERIENCE THE ABUNDANT AND FRUITFUL CHRISTIAN LIFE.

The carnal man trusts in his own efforts to live the Christian life:

A. He is either uninformed about, or has forgotten, God's love, forgiveness and power (Romans 5:8-10; Hebrews 10:1-25; 1 John 1; 2:1-3; 2 Peter 1:9; Acts 1:8).

B. He has an up-and-down spiritual experience.

C. He cannot understand himself—he wants to do what is right, but cannot.

D. He fails to draw upon the power of the Holy Spirit to live the Christian life (1 Corinthians 3:1-3; Romans 7:15-24; 8:7; Galatians 5:16-18).

THE CARNAL MAN—Some or all of the following traits may characterize the Christian who does not fully trust God:

Ignorance of his spiritual heritage
Unbelief
Disobedience
Loss of love for God and for others
Poor prayer life
No desire for Bible study
Legalistic attitude
Impure thoughts
Jealousy
Guilt
Worry
Discouragement
Critical spirit
Frustration
Aimlessness

(The individual who professes to be a Christian but who continues to practice sin should realize that he may not be a Christian at all, according to 1 John 2:3; 3:6,9; Ephesians 5:5.)

The third truth gives us the only solution to this problem . . .

3 JESUS PROMISED THE ABUNDANT AND FRUITFUL LIFE AS THE RESULT OF BEING FILLED (DIRECTED AND EMPOWERED) BY THE HOLY SPIRIT.

The Spirit-filled life is the Christ-directed life by which Christ lives His life in and through us in the power of the Holy Spirit (John 15).

A. One becomes a Christian through the ministry of the Holy Spirit, according to John 3:1-8. From the moment of spiritual birth, the Christian is indwelt by the Holy Spirit at all times (John 1:12; Colossians 2:9,10; John 14:16,17).

Though all Christians are indwelt by the Holy Spirit, not all Christians are filled (directed and empowered) by the Holy Spirit on an ongoing basis.

B. The Holy Spirit is the source of the overflowing life (John 7:37-39).

C. The Holy Spirit came to glorify Christ (John 16:1-15). When one is filled with the Holy Spirit, he is a true disciple of Christ.

D. In His last command before His ascension, Christ promised the power of the Holy Spirit to enable us to be witnesses for Him (Acts 1:1-9).

How, then, can one be filled with the Holy Spirit?

4 WE ARE FILLED (DIRECTED AND EMPOWERED) BY THE HOLY SPIRIT BY FAITH; THEN WE CAN EXPERIENCE THE ABUNDANT AND FRUITFUL LIFE WHICH CHRIST PROMISED TO EACH CHRISTIAN.

You can appropriate the filling of the Holy Spirit **right now** if you:

A. Sincerely desire to be directed and empowered by the Holy Spirit (Matthew 5:6; John 7:37-39).

B. Confess your sins. By **faith** thank God that He **has** forgiven all of your sins—past, present and future—because Christ died for you (Colossians 2:13-15; 1 John 1; 2:1-3; Hebrews 10:1-17).

C. Present every area of your life to God (Romans 12:1,2).

D. By **faith** claim the fullness of the Holy Spirit, according to:

1. HIS COMMAND—Be filled with the Spirit. "And do not get drunk with wine, for that is dissipation, but be filled with the Spirit" (Ephesians 5:18).

2. HIS PROMISE—He will always answer when we pray according to His will. "And this is the confidence which we have before Him, that, if we ask any-thing according to His will, He hears us. And if we know that He hears us in whatever we ask, we know that we have the requests which we have asked from Him" (1 John 5:14,15).

Faith can be expressed through prayer . . .

How to Pray in Faith to be Filled With the Holy Spirit

We are filled with the Holy Spirit by **faith** alone. However, true prayer is one way of expressing your faith. The following is a suggested prayer:

> "Dear Father, I need You. I acknowledge that I have been directing my own life and that, as a result, I have sinned against You. I thank You that You have forgiven my sins through Christ's death on the cross for me. I now invite Christ to again take His place on the throne of my life. Fill me with the Holy Spirit as You **commanded** me to be filled, and as You **promised** in Your Word that You would do if I asked in faith. I pray this in the name of Jesus. As an expression of my faith, I now thank You for directing my life and for filling me with the Holy Spirit."

Does this prayer express the desire of your heart? If so, bow in prayer and trust God to fill you with the Holy Spirit **right now.**

How to Know That You Are Filled (Directed and Empowered) by the Holy Spirit

Did you ask God to fill you with the Holy Spirit? Do you know that you are now filled with the Holy Spirit? On what authority? (On the trustworthiness of God Himself and His Word: Hebrews 11:6; Romans 14:22,23.)

Do not depend upon feelings. The promise of God's Word, not our feelings, is our authority. The Christian lives by faith (trust) in the trustworthiness of God Himself and His Word.

This train diagram illustrates the relationship between **fact** (God and His Word), **faith** (our trust in God and His Word), and **feeling** (the result of our faith and obedience) (John 14:21).

The train will run with or without the caboose. However, it would be futile to attempt to pull the train by the caboose. In the same way, we, as Christians, do not depend upon feelings or emotions, but we place our faith (trust) in the trustworthiness of God and the promises of His Word.

How to Walk in the Spirit

Faith (trust in God and in His promises) is the only means by which a Christian can live the Spirit-directed life. As you continue to trust Christ moment by moment:

A. Your life will demonstrate more and more of the fruit of the Spirit (Galatians 5:22,23) and will be more and more conformed to the image of Christ (Romans 12:2; 2 Corinthians 3:18).

B. Your prayer life and study of God's Word will become more meaningful.

C. You will experience His power in witnessing (Acts 1:8).

D. You will be prepared for spiritual conflict against the world (1 John 2:15-17); against the flesh (Galatians 5:16,17); and against Satan (1 Peter 5:7-9; Ephesians 6:10-13).

E. You will experience His power to resist temptation and sin (1 Corinthians 10:13; Philippians 4:13; Ephesians 1:19-23; 6:10; 2 Timothy 1:7; Romans 6:1-16).

Spiritual Breathing

By faith you can continue to experience God's love and forgiveness.

If you become aware of an area of your life (an attitude or an action) that is displeasing to the Lord, even though you are walking with Him and sincerely desiring to serve Him, simply thank God that He has forgiven your sins—past, present and future—on the basis of Christ's death on the cross. Claim His love and forgiveness by faith and continue to have fellowship with Him.

If you retake the throne of your life through sin—a definite act of disobedience—breathe spiritually.

Spiritual Breathing (exhaling the impure and inhaling the pure) is an exercise in faith and enables you to continue to experience God's love and forgiveness.

1. **Exhale**—confess your sin—agree with God concerning your sin and thank Him for His forgiveness of it, according to 1 John 1:9 and Hebrews 10:1-25. Confession involves repentance—a change in attitude and action.

2. **Inhale**—surrender the control of your life to Christ, and appropriate (receive) the fullness of the Holy Spirit by faith. Trust that He now directs and empowers you, according to the **command** of Ephesians 5:18 and the **promise** of 1 John 5:14,15.

* * * * *

> *To help you make the most of your relationship with God, you may wish to obtain THE SECRET: HOW TO LIVE WITH PURPOSE AND POWER by Bill Bright. This book is available in Christian bookstores everywhere, or you can call 1-800-950-4457 to order from the publisher.*

(© Campus Crusade for Christ, Inc. 1966. All rights reserved.)

Quick Reference Guide
to Revival Praying

I want to share a list of the noticeable features of revolutionary revivals. While some of history's revivals have had much larger geographic impact than others, they all share a commonality of fruits. Each feature listed is paired with a meaningful prayer petition. My earnest hope is that God will bring our united prayers for revival into a concert of intercession.

Features of Revolutionary Revival	Prayer Focus for Revival Praying
A. Features of the prelude to revival	**A. Prelude praying**
1. A cultural acceleration and absorption with what the Bible calls sin and gross wickedness.	1. Express repentance and apology to God by naming the prominent cultural sins in ongoing intercession.
2. Apathy, carnality and a program-centered emphasis on church ministry.	2. Ask God to grant spiritual sight to the eyes of His church leaders.
3. Indifference toward spiritual matters by the church young people.	3. Pull down spiritual blindness and worldliness that Satan promotes to our youth.
4. The beginning of a burden for revival awakening on the part of individuals and groups.	4. Ask God to raise up intercessors who will spend the time and pay the price required in revival praying.
5. The presence of a crisis atmosphere throughout the culture.	5. Ask God to precipitate whatever He knows will awaken a spiritual hunger in human hearts
6. A drawing together of hungering people across denominational lines to pray and seek God.	6. Ask God to raise up inter-denominational prayer groups that will persevere until revival comes.

B. Features of the revival awakening

1. The coming of an awareness of the nearness of God to individuals, communities and cultures.

2. God's sovereign choice of special leaders whom He desires to anoint for the awakening.

3. The "outbreak" of revival, in a sovereignly chosen place, and subsequent spreading from that point to others.

4. A deep, personal conviction of sin, painful to saint and sinner alike, which leads to spiritual renewal or new birth; transformed lives which begin to transform the culture.

5. A spiritual concern for people which results in increasing Christian service and ministry.

6. Large numbers of people coming to know Christ as Savior. Evangelistic efforts reaping a large harvest of believers who need to be brought into the church.

7. Opposition attacks on the work of God's revolutionary revival awakenings.

8. God sending supernatural happenings (e.g., trancelike states, healing, etc.) as He moves in revolutionary revival awakenings (may or may *not* happen).

B. Supportive prayer for revival awakenings

1. Pray with Isaiah: "Oh, that you would rend the heavens and come down, that the mountains would tremble before you" (Isaiah 64:1).

2. Pray for God to prepare the hearts and minds of those whom He has chosen to lead in revival awakening.

3. Ask the Lord to prepare His chosen place for the revolutionary revival to begin.

4. Ask the Holy Spirit to intensify His ministry of convicting the world of guilt in regard to sin, righteousness and judgment; ask God to make sin exceedingly sinful to His people.

5. Pray that the Lord of the harvest will stir His people for local and worldwide evangelization.

6. Ask the Lord to bring in multitudes who are not yet in His fold; pray that the churches will bring the newly converted into full body life.

7. Ask God to grant wisdom, boldness and humility to revival leaders to handle opposition; pray for opposers to be convicted, converted and enfolded.

8. Pray that people will allow God to be God in His dealings and that He will protect the revival from those seeking or promoting supernatural occurrences.

9. Joyful music, worship and praise expressed spontaneously and frequently; people compelled to share what God means to them and what He is doing.

9. Ask God to prepare leaders to aid people in expressing their worship and praise, and for protection from showmanship or celebrity-centered leadership.

10. Satan's hatred of revival manifested in subtle attempts to discredit or neutralize the movement.

10. Ask God for intercessors who understand spiritual warfare and who will continually protect the revival awakening in prayer.

11. Extended meetings, conviction of sin, prayer burden for souls, etc., robbing people of sleep and rest; some people may overextend themselves, leading to physical exhaustion.

11. Ask God not only to quicken people in such times but also to help them balance their capacities and priorities.

12. Outbreaks of extremism, often coming from well-meaning people but discrediting the movement and quenching the Holy Spirit.

12. Pray for God's protection from extremism and that He will quench any such action before it can gain a following.

13. Churches beginning to overflow with seekers and worshipers, to the point where they cannot handle them all.

13. Ask God to grant wisdom and innovative ideas to the church leaders so they can handle crowds without expensive building programs.

14. Mushrooming of volunteers for Christian service.

14. Pray that spiritually qualified colleges, Bible schools, seminaries and training centers will be ready to train the influx.

15. Media attention becoming alert to what God is doing and beginning to give the movement favorable publicity. (This may not happen, but it often does.)

15. Ask God to prepare leadership in every area of the media in order to facilitate the spread of the revival message.

Some Helpful Tools

SAMPLE LETTER OF INVITATION FOR BEGINNING
A COMMUNITY-WIDE PRAYER FELLOWSHIP

Dear Brother in Christ,

Greetings in our Savior's name.

Most of us have repeatedly read Luke's account of the triumphal entry of the Lord Jesus Christ into Jerusalem. Luke tells us that as Jesus approached Jerusalem, He saw the city, wept over it, and spoke to it in prayerful love. With fresh concern, some of us are feeling the spiritual need for our city, but these needs are too large for any of us to bear alone. It seems time for pastors and laymen, those who feel the burden and see the needs, to come together for united prayer. We ask you to join us.

We have found a convenient, neutral setting at   (place)   Beginning on ____(date)____, we invite you to meet with us there at 6:30 A.M. each ____(day)____ morning for an hour of prayer for our area. We want to see our city as our Lord Jesus Christ sees it. Perhaps we may feel God's burden deeply enough that we can weep for the city and, through our prayers, begin to speak to its great needs.

We suggest the following guidelines as a basis for our united prayer:

1. Each week we will share in reading two chapters from God's Word, without editorial comment. Each person will be free to participate by reading five verses. We will cover the first two chapters of John at our first meeting.

2. Immediately following the Scripture reading, we will pray together in small group settings of three or four people. (Conversational style of praying would be in order, but the praying will not be limited to that mode.)

3. Prayer requests will be in order, but our prayer will focus on the great needs of our community. Areas of focus might include churches, youth, economic conditions, crime, prostitution, pornography, drugs, alcohol, violence, pulling down strongholds that hinder revival, repentance, and a united

258

laying hold of God's grace and mercy to touch our city in a fresh visit.

4. To make sure that all who attend will be comfortable in the prayer setting, we ask that our praying be limited to the English language.

5. Though we may pray for ministries and spiritual outreaches in the city, this prayer group will avoid the sponsoring or planning of any such programs.

6. The prayer times are open to all who feel a common spiritual concern. Participants may come and go according to their own schedule.

7. The prayer times will begin promptly at 6:30 A.M. and conclude promptly at 7:30 A.M.

8. Formal organization will be avoided, and the group will not make any "pronouncements" on issues facing the city. Our motive is to pray.

9. These meetings will continue as long as the interest remains at a level to so warrant.

10. We will attempt to keep the place of meeting at a denominationally neutral setting.

Sincerely,

(Signed by six pastors and
Christian lay businessmen)

P.S. Please spread the word.

**SAMPLE RESOLUTION FOR TAKING FURTHER
REVIVAL ACTION STEPS**

Eventually, some may feel they would like to explore a united evangelistic effort on a larger scale. After an extended time of prayer meetings for revival has elapsed, some may sense that God is leading toward action. This needs to be explored. Following is a suggested resolution to bring the interested churches together for further revival steps. It would be wise to keep such moves separate from the prayer focus for revival.

WHEREAS, there is an abundant need for spiritual renewal in our city as evidenced by such things as:

1. the increasing problems of gang activity, violence, drug addiction, sexual promiscuity and alcohol consumption among our children and youth;

2. the appeal and proliferation of various expressions of satanic cultism that is afflicting our local culture;

3. decreasing attendance of younger people in worship at most of our mainline denominational churches;

4. unbiblical and unwholesome pervasiveness of perverted sexual materials and practices which often lead to incest and sexual abuse;

5. the questionable emphasis upon gambling as being suitable recreation for our citizens and tax revenue for our government;

6. the morality breakdown characterized by cursing and degrading speech in the work place, frequent hostility between labor and management, general indifference toward the needs of the poor and suffering, and the widespread problem of family disintegration; and

WHEREAS, the Christian faith and the gospel message of our Lord Jesus Christ is capable of confronting human needs and transforming the culture through changed human lives; and

WHEREAS, we believe that the Lord Jesus Christ is God the Son who came in human flesh, was crucified for our sins, and rose again from the dead for our justification; and

WHEREAS, Jesus Christ declared that the Holy Spirit has come into our world to "convict the world of guilt in regard to sin and righteousness and judgment to come" (John 16:9); and

WHEREAS, we desire to reach out to our loving heavenly Father that He might grace us with a refreshing breath of spiritual renewal in our city;

THEREFORE, BE IT RESOLVED that we unite our hearts and efforts together to seek such spiritual renewal in these several ways:

1. We will commit ourselves to regular corporate and private prayer to God for His sovereign intervention to bring to our city the spiritual renewal it needs.

2. We call together the spiritual leadership of the churches and denominations of our city to share our concerns and to unite our efforts to see spiritual renewal visit our city.

3. We are open to establishing an interdenominational task force of spiritually-minded Christian leaders as a planning and coordinating group to promote renewal in our area.

A PRAYER GUIDE FOR CONCERNED CHRISTIANS
WHEN PRAYING FOR NON-CHRISTIANS

1. Pray that God draws them to Himself (John 6:44).

2. Pray that they seek to know God (Acts 17:27; Deuteronomy 4:29).

3. Pray that they believe the Scriptures (1 Thessalonians 2:13; Romans 10:17).

4. Pray that Satan be bound from blinding them to the truth (Matthew 13:19; 2 Corinthians 4:4).

5. Pray that the Holy Spirit works in them (John 16:8-13).

6. Pray that God sends someone to lead them to Christ (Matthew 9:37,38).

7. Pray that they believe in Christ as Savior (John 1:12; 5:24).

8. Pray that they turn from sin (Acts 17:30,31; 3:19).

9. Pray that they confess Christ as Lord (Romans 10:9,10).

10. Pray that they yield all to follow Christ (2 Corinthians 5:15; Philippians 3:7,8).

11. Pray that they take root and grow in Christ (Colossians 2:6,7).

(Reprinted from *Discipleship Journal,* Issue 34, 1986, by the Navigators. Used by permission. These tools may be photocopied for your personal use.)

NOTES

Chapter 1

1. Available from Michael-Paul and Associates, P. O. Box 151, Crockett, TX 75835.
2. Larry W. Poland, *How to Prepare for the Coming Persecution* (San Bernardino, CA: Here's Life Publishers, 1990), p. 140.
3. Poland, p. 140.
4. Tal Brooke, *When the World Will Be as One* (Eugene, OR: Harvest House Publishers, 1989), p. 67.

Chapter 4

1. See also *Spiritual Warfare* by Timothy M. Warner (Westchester, DE: Crossway Books, 1991).
2. Timothy M. Warner, "Teaching Power Encounter," *Evangelical Missions Quarterly* (January 1986), p. 67.
3. Gerald E. Otis, "Power Encounter—The Way to Muslim Breakthrough," *Evangelical Missions Quarterly* (October 1980), p. 217.
4. Otis, p. 218.
5. Loren Entz, "Challenges to Abou's Jesus," *Evangelical Missions Quarterly* (January 1986), p. 48.
6. Entz, p. 49.
7. James G. Friesen, *Uncovering the Mystery of MPD* (San Bernardino, CA: Here's Life Publishers, 1991).

Chapter 5

1. *Newsweek* (January 8, 1990), p. 16.
2. See Pacepa, Ion Mihai, *Red Horizons* (Washington, D.C: Regnery Gateway). The story of the Ceausescu crimes from one of his trusted lieutenant generals.

Chapter 6

1. Anne Ortland, *Up With Worship* (Ventura, CA: Regal Books Division, Gospel Light Publications, 1975), p. 3.
2. Shelley, Bruce L., *Church History in Plain Language* (Waco, TX: Word Book Publishers), p. 50.
3. Gerhard Kittel, ed., *Theological Dictionary of the New Testament,* vol. III (Grand Rapids, MI: Eerdmans), p. 798.

Chapter 7

1. Ronald Dunn, *Don't Just Stand There, Pray Something* (San Bernardino, CA: Here's Life Publishers, 1991), pp. 19-20.
2. *Sioux City Journal* (August 10, 1989).
3. Dunn, pp. 53-54.

Chapter 8

1. Arthur Wallis, *God's Chosen Fast* (Fort Washing, PA: Christian Literature Crusade). For an excellent discussion of the role of fasting in the Christian life, see chapter 14, "Fasting: a Biblical Survey," in Ron Dunn's book, *Don't Just*

Stand There, Pray Something (San Bernardino, CA: Here's Life Publishers, 1991).

2. If you are dealing with traumatic sins committed against you by a family member, the editors recommend *A Door of Hope* by Jan Frank (San Bernardino, CA: Here's Life Publishers, 1987). This book offers ten steps for the healing of emotional wounds.

Chapter 10

1. Robert E. Coleman, ed., *One Divine Moment* (Old Tappan, NJ: Fleming H. Revell), p. 18.

Chapter 12

1. From the *The Manila Manifesto*, published at the July 1989 Manila International Congress on World Evangelization.

2. Ed Murphy, *Spiritual Warfare Series*, 16 tapes, 112-page syllabus (Milpitas, CA: Overseas Crusades).

2. Timothy M. Warner, "An Evangelical Position on Bondage and Exorcism," *Evangelical Missions Quarterly* (January 1986), p. 77.

Chapter 13

1. Loren Entz, "Challenges to Abou's Jesus," *Evangelical Missions Quarterly* (January 1986), p. 49.

Chapter 14

1. Robert McAffee Brown, *The Significance of the Church* (Philadelphia, PA: The Westminster Press, n.d.), p. 17.

2. Donald K. Campbell, *Nehemiah: Man in Charge* (Wheaton, IL: Victor Books, n.d.), pp. 47,48. From *The Dallas Morning News* (September 27, 1972).

Chapter 15

1. Rolf Zettersten, "Part II of the Ted Bundy Interview," *Focus on the Family* (April 1989), p. 15.

Chapter 17

1. See Burns on Laws of Revival as by Drummond, Lewis A. *The Awakening That Must Come,* (Nashville, TN: Broadman, 1978), pp. 109*ff.*

2. Ronald Dunn, *Don't Just Stand There, Pray Something* (San Bernardino, CA: Here's Life Publishers, 1991).

Appendix A

1. Edwin J. Orr, *The Fervent Prayer* (Chicago, IL: Moody Press, n.d.), p. vii.

2. Stephen F. Olford, *Heart-Cry for Revival* (Old Tappan, NJ: Fleming H. Revell Company, 1962), p. 17.

3. Richard Owen Roberts, *Revival* (Wheaton, IL: Tyndale House Publishers, 1982), p. 17.

4. Olford, p. 17.

Quality reading
to counter the satanic revival . . .

Don't Just Stand There,
PRAY Something
by Ronald Dunn

In one of the most helpful books on prayer ever written, Ronald Dunn teaches you how to pray more effectively for your personal needs, for the needs of others, and for national revival. Includes free bonus section, "How to Start an Intercessory Prayer Ministry in Your Church." $7.95

Uncovering the Mystery of MPD
by James G. Friesen, Ph.D.

The startling role of satanic/ritualistic abuse in today's tidal wave of multiple personality disorder. "One of the first books that combines sound mental health treatment with spiritual deliverance ministry. Both are needed." —H. Newton Malony, Ph.D., Professor of Psychology, Fuller Theological Seminary. $10.95

How to Prepare for the Coming Persecution
by Larry W. Poland, Ph.D.

A fast-paced look at how today's events are converging as never before to fulfill biblical prophecy. Persecution of Christians is on the rise in America as the prophetic clock ticks down to zero hour. Will you and your loved ones be ready for what lies ahead? $8.95

Witnessing Without Fear
by Bill Bright

Winner of the prestigious Gold Medallion Award for excellence, this step-by-step guide shows you how to overcome fear and share your faith with confidence. Learn how to handle questions and objections and help others receive Christ as Savior and Lord. $8.95

At Christian bookstores everywhere. Or call

Here's Life Publishers
1-800-950-4457
(Visa and Mastercard accepted.)